REASON FOR BEING

Reason for Being

—— *A Meditation on Ecclesiastes*

JACQUES ELLUL

Translated by Joyce Main Hanks

WILLIAM B. EERDMANS PUBLISHING COMPANY
GRAND RAPIDS, MICHIGAN

Library of Congress Cataloging-in-Publication Data

Ellul, Jacques.
    [Raison d'être. English]
    The reason for being: a meditation on Ecclesiastes/Jacques Ellul;
  translated by Joyce Main Hanks.
      p.   cm.
    Translation of: La raison d'être.
    Includes bibliographical references and index.
    ISBN 0-8028-0405-5 (pbk.)
    1. Bible. O.T. Ecclesiastes—Criticism, interpretation, etc. 2. Bible
  O.T. Ecclesiastes—Meditations.   I. Title.
BS1475.2E4613   1990
223'.806—dc20   90-41598
                                            CIP

I dedicate these final words
to the one who all my life
has been
the imperative
and the hope
of the Reason for being:
my wife

Contents

I   Preliminary, Polemical, Nondefinitive Postscript   1

My Purpose in This Book   1

The Ultimate Paradox: Another Book on Ecclesiastes   4

Presuppositions in Studies of Ecclesiastes   6

Critical Agreement and Pseudonymity in Ecclesiastes   16

Wisdom and Poetry   22

Philosophy, Truth, and Reality in Qohelet   26

Qohelet as Ritual Incantation   31

Structure in Qohelet   33

Contradiction as an Essential Principle of Qohelet   39

Qohelet and the Feast of Sukkot   42

**II   Themes of Vanity: Vapor, Smoke,
Unsubstantiality, Fragility, and Evanescence   49**

The First Word   49

The Myth of Progress   60

Meditation   69

Power   75

Money   86

Work   93

	Happiness	106
	The Good	112
	Human Answers	115
	Conclusion	126
III	**Wisdom and Philosophy**	**128**
	Wisdom: What Is It?	133
	Irony	141
	Fragility and Impossibility	146
	Science	151
	The Wisdom of Small Things	158
	Finiteness and the Future	160
	Finiteness and Death	171
	Tests for Wisdom: Applications and Examples	185
	The Word	186
	Possessions	190
	Women and Men	195
	Conclusion	204
	Epilogue	207
IV	**God**	**213**
	Elohim	214
	Contradiction	231
	The God Who Gives	249
	God's Gifts: Quest and Desire for Eternity	253
	God's Gift of Enjoyment	255
	God as Judge	263
	Approaching God	271
	Qohelet's Crowning Words	278
	Bibliography	**304**

CHAPTER I

Preliminary, Polemical, Nondefinitive Postscript

1. My Purpose in This Book

Another book on Ecclesiastes? A person would need uncommon vanity or exceptional rashness to write still another one these days! The Ecclesiastes bibliography goes on for countless pages, with dozens of commentaries,[1] one more erudite than the other. I am no scholar or exegete, neither interpreter nor theologian. My only qualification is that I have read, meditated on, and prayed over Ecclesiastes for more than fifty years. I have probably explored it more than any other book in the Bible. It has perhaps given me more, spoken to me more, than any other. We could say that I am now committing this dialogue to writing. I need to alert my reader to the way I have written this book, since it is the reverse of the academic method (which I have so often followed elsewhere).

In the academic method, you begin by compiling a bibliography of your subject. You read everything you can get your hands on. You make notes, then establish an outline. You write on the basis of what others have written, either building on their research or

---

1. Aarre Lauha, *Kohelet,* Biblischer Kommentar: Altes Testament (Neukirchen-Vluyn: Neukirchener, 1978), notes about two hundred (pp. 24-28).

pointing out their errors. I have done just the opposite in this book. I chose to read nothing at the outset. I wanted to continue confronting Ecclesiastes on a one-to-one basis. I slogged through the Hebrew text. Nine different translations helped, and kept me in check.

Then I wrote what you are about to read. Naturally, I cannot claim it is free from any outside influence at all! *I* wrote it—not some abstraction. So it involves my cultural background and my knowledge. Over the years I have read some books and articles on Ecclesiastes, including those by W. Vischer, J. Pedersen, W. Lüthi, and G. von Rad.[2] As I will explain later, my intention to write on Ecclesiastes dates from over fifty years ago. Thirty years ago, I summarized F. Delitzsch on Ecclesiastes.[3]

I am well aware, then, that I am not starting from scratch, that I cannot claim to be neutral. But as the moment to write this book approached, I carefully avoided reading anything on Ecclesiastes. After I had finished writing, I began to read everything I could find. E. Podechard, J. Steinmann, A. Barucq, and A. Lauha left me rather cold.[4] But two authors nearly made me throw over my whole project, because each seemed so perfect, although they are quite different: D. Lys and A. Maillot.[5] Lys stands as a model of scien-

2. Wilhelm Vischer, "L'Ecclésiaste au miroir de Michel de Montaigne" (trans. Albert Finet), *Foi et Vie* 38/95-96, new series 4 (1937) 379-407; Johannes Pedersen, "Scepticisme israélite," *Revue d'Histoire et de Philosophie Religieuses* 10/4-5 (July-Oct. 1930) 317-70 (also published as a book [Paris: Félix Alcan, 1931]; hereafter references will be to the former); Walter Lüthi, *L'Ecclésiaste a vécu la vie: Un commentaire pour la communauté chrétienne,* trans. Daniel Hatt (Geneva: Labor et Fides, 1952); Gerhard von Rad, *Wisdom in Israel,* trans. James D. Martin (Nashville: Abingdon, 1972; Ger. ed. 1970).

3. Franz Delitzsch, *Commentary on the Song of Songs and Ecclesiastes,* trans. M. G. Easton (Grand Rapids: Eerdmans, repr. 1980).

4. E. Podechard, *L'Ecclésiaste,* Etudes bibliques (Paris: Gabalda, 1912); Jean Steinmann, *Ainsi parlait Qohelet,* Lire la Bible (Paris: Cerf, 1974); André Barucq, *L'Ecclésiaste: Qoheleth, traduction et commentaire,* Verbum Salutis 3 (Paris: Beauchesne, 1968); A. Lauha, *Kohelet.*

5. Daniel Lys, *L'Ecclésiaste ou Que vaut la vie? Traduction; Introduction générale; Commentaire de 1/1 à 4/3* (Paris: Letouzey et Ané, 1977); Alphonse Maillot, *La Contestation: Commentaire de l'Ecclésiaste* (Lyon: Cahiers de Réveil, 1971).

tific, rigorous exegesis, of completeness and solidity. After examining all the different hypotheses in his ample introduction, he establishes the text word by word, giving us an erudite avalanche of everything that could possibly be said about each term. Maillot adds a certain touch of flashing prophetic insight, showing us how deep one's understanding of this book can go.

Faced with these two works, so different, yet complementing each other so perfectly, I had the feeling I had nothing left to say. In spite of this, I stuck with what I had written. In the end, my reading of a dozen commentaries gave me no reason to change a single line of what I had said. This approach seemed to me to be consistent with Ecclesiastes: once you have acquired a certain knowledge and experience, you must walk alone, without repeating what others have said.

When the pages that follow allude to the opinion of "historians and exegetes," this usually refers to commonplaces, accepted ideas to be found everywhere. But I have also added many footnotes, in which I express my opinion concerning what I found in the scholarly literature after writing my manuscript.

For this reason, I have called this introduction a "postscript," when it should have been a preamble! I have called it a "polemical" postscript, since in it I have already stated my criticism of certain authors, a posteriori. But I also want to indicate at this point the limitations of this book: I make no claims to offer a new "commentary," or a new "key" for understanding Ecclesiastes, or a religious exhortation that could be drawn from it.

What, then, is the meaning of what I have done here? Some forty years ago, I envisioned a modern meditation on Ecclesiastes that could serve as an adequate conclusion to the lifework I was beginning to foresee. I felt, however, that it could come only at the end of my intellectual and physical life. The book of Ecclesiastes is a conclusion, not a possible point of departure. This seems to me to be consistent with the text itself: all its affirmations and questionings come after the accumulation of experience, like a last word. This "last word" amounts more to a conclusion than an outcome, for I believe little of consequence can be said on the basis of Ecclesiastes, or following it.

In other words, whereas *The Presence of the Kingdom*[6] formed the general introduction to all of what I wanted to write, Ecclesiastes will be the last word. Indeed, I do not believe I will be able to write much more. I certainly cannot finish the plan of works I set out for myself. If God grants me the time, I may be able to write one or two more books, but they will merely complement what I have already written.[7]

2. The Ultimate Paradox: Another Book on Ecclesiastes

Again, I find myself faced with the paradox: undertaking to write a reflection, in the form of a book, about a book that warns against writing books. I must begin at this point, however. "The words of the wise are like goads, and authors of collections resemble driven nails; they are given by a single shepherd. As for doing anything more, my child, beware of it: making books in great number would have no end, and much study is weariness for the flesh" (Eccl. 12:11-12).[8] There it is. I had to say it here at the beginning. I take

6. Jacques Ellul, *The Presence of the Kingdom,* 3rd ed., trans. Olive Wyon (Colorado Springs, CO: Helmers & Howard, 1989; 1st ed. Philadelphia: Westminster, 1951). Originally published as *Présence au monde moderne: Problèmes de la civilisation post-chrétienne* (Geneva: Roulet, 1948; 2nd ed., Lausanne: Presses Bibliques Universitaires, 1988).

7. So far, Ellul has published several books since the present volume: *Ce que je crois* (Paris: Grasset & Fasquelle, 1987); Eng. trans., *What I Believe,* trans. Geoffrey W. Bromiley (Grand Rapids: Eerdmans, 1989); *La Genèse aujourd'hui,* with François Tosquelles (n.p.: Editions de l'AREFPPI, 1987; available from Dr. Marc Leclerc, Domaine de Clermont, Le Cellier, 44850 Ligné, France); *Anarchie et christianisme* (Lyon: Atelier de Création Libertaire, 1988; Eng. trans. forthcoming); and *Le Bluff technologique* (Paris: Hachette, 1988); Eng. trans., *The Technological Bluff,* trans. Geoffrey W. Bromiley (Grand Rapids: Eerdmans, 1990).—Trans.

8. Ellul generally follows the translation of Ecclesiastes by Antoine Guillaumont in *La Bible: L'Ancien Testament,* vol. II, ed. Edouard Dhorme, Bibliothèque de la Pléiade (Paris: Gallimard, 1959), which was included at the end of the French edition. Biblical passages translated directly from Ellul's text, when

this statement as the fitting conclusion to what I could call "my work."

The above statement highlights the opposition between the existential and the intellectual. The sayings of the wise are a goad: the goad enters the hide of the ox and makes it advance; the word of the wise makes us advance, and does not merely stir up vain and brilliant ideas. As the prophets demonstrate, no complicated explanations are required to produce this "organic" response.

At the same time, we have pegs or nails that have been hammered into something. They represent that other aspect of life's path: nails of certainty from which we must stretch our cords. Nails as reference points that allow us to make out our direction; nails that anchor, bringing life rudely to a halt in order to hold it to a certain truth. Surely we have no need of great speeches or intellectual demonstrations to give us such a revelation. Finally, Ecclesiastes is right to warn us against the temptation to intellectualize: "beware of doing anything more" (12:12).

Nevertheless, this is exactly what I am undertaking, all the while realizing that this last book, like all my others—I knew this from the beginning—falls under the judgment: "All is vanity." Going beyond expressing the very heart of the "message" of revelation is vanity. Jesus wrote nothing, and his words were few in number. One can remember everything he said. Each saying is a goad and a nail. It would be wise not to try to add anything. But I am not a wise person. As I said, since the beginning I placed my entire "work" under the judgment of Ecclesiastes. I know well that "making books in great number would have no end" (12:12).

Furthermore, it is astonishing that such a judgment was expressed in the time of Ecclesiastes, when books were rare. Once again, however, we see how the biblical message turns out to be

---

there is no apparent source, are labeled "JE." For other biblical references, various English versions have been used: the New Jerusalem Bible (NJB), the Revised Standard Version (RSV), the King James Version (KJV), the New American Standard Bible (NASB), and the New International Version (NIV). Finally, the reader should note that where the Masoretic (Hebrew) text differs from the English (i.e., 4:17–5:19 in Hebrew is 5:1-20 in most English versions—though not NJB), the English versification has been followed.—TRANS.

true after two thousand years of silence. It applies to our time, as if it had been written only yesterday, and just for us.[9] It is vanity to publish a book amidst the present Niagara of paper, not to mention ten thousand times more "information" coming from ten other media. What could be the point of still another book? "It would have no end," Ecclesiastes declared, and he was right, 2,500 years ago. He had seen that this "information-communication-dissertation-documentation-interpretation" craze has no end, and that people involved in it take infinite pains, all for absolutely nothing.

Faced with this warning, why do I do it? Why persist in writing still more pages destined for drowning in the jumbled magma of our media? Why yield to this vanity? Why write a last work, knowing full well that it is vanity? I have no explanation or justification. That is just the way it is. I do have available the exhortation of another part of Ecclesiastes: "All your hand finds to do with the strength you have, do it" (9:10, JE). But, the author would add, "understand that it is subject to the judgment of vanity." I know. I prepare this book accordingly, without aspiring any higher, but also not despising what I am doing. I am utterly aware of the irony of my situation—it assailed me half a century ago. I realize the paradox of indulging in this "weariness for the flesh," to no purpose. The only reason I do it is that today I have the strong feeling—but it is only a feeling—that I must do it, and that God might possibly preserve one page, among so many.

3. Presuppositions in Studies of Ecclesiastes

After all, why not begin a meditation on Ecclesiastes with a little polemic? Doesn't the text itself invite us to do this, since it is

---

9. In *The Meaning of the City,* trans. Dennis Pardee (Grand Rapids: Eerdmans, 1970), I showed, convincingly, I believe, that the Bible offers us a consistent revelation concerning the city, but this revelation becomes fully justified only in our day, with modern cities. The biblical writers had no such model to work from. We must not exaggerate the size of Nineveh or Babylon!

polemical with respect to everything people believed to be serious, important, and useful (and I mean to show this applies to everything we believe today to be serious, important, and useful!)?[10] In certain scholarly studies of Ecclesiastes, I believe I have observed tendencies that are fundamentally erroneous. Incidentally, this observation raises (in a more acute manner than for many other texts) a general question: When the unacknowledged presupposition is false, can a rigorous, erudite, scientific method (impeccably and rationally applied) lead to conclusions we can consider scientifically as correct?[11] In *almost* all (not all!) the exegetes who write on Ecclesiastes, I believe I detect three presuppositions:

(1) The necessity of formal, logical coherence in a text,[12] which is just another aspect of the principle of noncontradiction. According to this presupposition, an author cannot possibly write a precept and its opposite at the same time; he cannot attribute value to a given reality and then deny it, maintain that "A" is "non-A." Based on this

10. André Neher, in *Notes sur Qohélét (L'Ecclésiaste)* (Paris: Minuit, 1951), pp. 41-67, gives a good description of various readings, all intended to sweeten Qohelet so readers will find him acceptable! Eclecticism, relativism, aestheticism, etc., all try to outdo each other in their effort to co-opt this text. It would be pointless to repeat the details of Neher's presentation here.

11. I will not engage at this point in a debate on methods of biblical interpretation. They are numerous, and recent decades have seen them multiply. See Daniel Lys, *Comprends-tu ce que tu lis? Initiation au sens de l'Ancien Testament* (Paris: Cerf, 1972; hereafter, all references to Lys's name only will be to his previously cited *Ecclésiaste* rather than to *Comprends-tu ce que tu lis?*). As a curiosity, let me mention a very ancient Jewish text, quoted by Gershom Scholem in *Le Nom et les symboles de Dieu dans la mystique juive,* trans. Maurice R. Hayoun and Georges Vadja (Paris: Cerf, 1983), p. 121 (see also pp. 117-20). This text from the Zohar tells us there are four kinds of interpretation: a literal meaning, an allegorical meaning, a homiletical meaning (up to this point we are not surprised, since this division is well-known), and then "the seed of life, from which new mysteries of meaning continually spring up." This last meaning involves the truth of the text in which this seed of life has been deposited. I believe "our" Qohelet to be a living text from which new mysteries of meaning spring up, with or without new scientific methods.

12. For example, Barucq finds the "illogical thought" of Ecclesiastes shocking (p. 15)! Such exegetes find the use of paradox unacceptable, calling it a "stylistic device."

conviction of logical coherence and identity of a thing with itself, the exegete proceeds to judge the text.

At this point a small detour will serve us well, I believe. The exegete judges the text! In that we are dealing with texts considered holy, bearers of revelation, we cannot exactly treat them with the benevolent neutrality appropriate for an ordinary literary text. "These statements claimed to give us God's truth? Is that so? What is left of them when they have been dealt with scientifically?" I have felt this instinct in almost all exegetes of Ecclesiastes: the deliberate intention to prove that this text is like any other. By this I do not mean that these scholars work with a will to negate or destroy. But beginning with the idea that every biblical text is a literary text that can be treated like any other, a kind of aggressive attitude toward the text develops.

We can readily understand this stance: the scholar deals with books believed for thousands of years to be sacred and religious. They have a sort of aura about them. They have acquired certain prerogatives, and before one can examine the text simply, he must destroy this aura, this privileged position. This sense of duty explains the pugnacity we notice in exegetes and historians. Unfortunately, their combativeness takes them too far! It invades their relationship with the text from the outset, so that their exegetical science quickly becomes a weapon for combat. They seek (unconsciously, of course!) to prove that the text is not *really* inspired. The scientific approach thus becomes distorted. Such exegetes foster a kind of prejudice against the text, and thus belittle and rationalize it.

Seeing that I recognize an unconscious impulse is at work, how can I maintain this criticism? By comparing the studies in exegesis of Roman law I used over many years with these studies of Ecclesiastes. Works of exegesis in Roman law have a kind of serenity about them, an objectivity, a congeniality with the text and submission to it that I find very rarely in studies of Ecclesiastes. In the latter, often cold analysis suddenly becomes polemics. At the crucial point of a sentence, the reader senses something like: "So we see clearly that a text put together in this way cannot come from God!" This criterion of formal, logical coherence serves us well if we seek to desacralize the text. But such a criterion proves utterly inadequate if we want to *understand* the text. The Hebrew intellect did not follow that sort of logic.

This criterion of formal logic has produced some extremely radical conclusions. I will mention two. The first is that Ecclesiastes clearly contains formal contradictions. We will see many of these as we work through the book. Here, I give just one example: on the one hand, Ecclesiastes says boldly that wisdom is like the wind. On the other hand, we find many texts in which the author praises wisdom, in which he maintains the importance of the wise person, of the quest for wisdom, etc. A reasonable reader in our day concludes that the same person cannot have written two such contradictory things. They are so opposed that even the dialectical process cannot resolve their contradiction. It is impossible to "think" both ideas at the same time. Therefore, two authors must be behind Ecclesiastes, and this seems confirmed by differences in style, vocabulary, etc. This argument leads critics to divide the text into coherent portions, based on the principle of noncontradiction.[13] But, in so doing, these critics fail to take into account or raise certain questions.

For example, even if we agree for the sake of argument that the same person cannot write such contradictory things, how do we explain that a single person (the final redactor) inserted such utterly opposed fragments, mixing the text in this manner? We would have to recognize in this redactor the same lack of logic and mental coherence we refused to accept in a possible original writer. Worse yet, the redactor has produced this hodgepodge by shattering the unity of the texts he had at hand. He sewed them together so

---

13. In keeping with a rationalistic, positivistic framework, the introduction to the Centenary Bible [a translation published by the Bible Society of Paris in 1928 to commemorate the four hundredth anniversary of the first translation of the Bible into French—TRANS.], following Podechard, establishes four distinct authors for Ecclesiastes: an original radical, pessimistic writer; a disciple or epilogue writer, a great admirer of his teacher, who praises him (12:9-11); a "wise" person who defends wisdom; and finally a "pious" individual (obviously, the wise and the pious person could not possibly be the same!), who produced all the texts defending the justice of God, etc.

clumsily that contradictions loom like mountains. This rabbi really must have been preposterous. Still worse, a text doctored in such a manner was considered by God's chosen people as divinely inspired, and thus included in the canon. Somehow they chose this text rather than a purer, more authentic one. What a strange idea!

In addition, the critics fail to ask themselves if it is not possible, in a meditation on such fundamental issues, for a writer in a state of great anguish to affirm contradictory things. Can't we line up contradictory texts from Pascal, Kierkegaard, and Nietzsche, and conclude that it would be impossible for the same person to have written, for example, *Diary of a Seducer* and *Training in Christianity*?

A second radical conclusion produced by this principle of noncontradiction concerns the apparent distortion in the text caused by the tension between two kinds of passages. Some sections express quite openly the skeptical, disillusioned attitude of a person trapped inside an absurd world. But other sections affirm something about God. On a first reading of Ecclesiastes, one is certainly struck by the opposition between these two kinds of passages. The prayers to God appear as breaks in the book's flow, as parentheses containing something that seems superfluous. Especially since most of the book is so vivid and gripping, all the "religious" passages may appear insipid! And what shall we say about the conclusion, which appears to be an addition so that the book will end well?

The common explanation is that the original nucleus of Ecclesiastes was purely humanistic: a skeptical, nihilistic text with no reference to God. Commentators like Podechard consider it impossible that one who wrote "all is vanity" could also speak of God. There is a contradiction in terms as well as in thought. The author denies the traditional faith of Israel, and necessarily rejects any reference to God. Consequently, all texts referring to God have been inserted.[14] Someone else, a rather clumsy, pious editor or commen-

---

14. This same kind of "coherent logic" leads some scholars to write that it is impossible to consider Solomon the author of Ecclesiastes because it contains a harsh criticism of royal power. How could a king criticize royal power? they ask. Obviously impossible! These scholars betray their profound ignorance of the many historical writings of those who exercised power and yet attacked it energetically.

tator, added invocations to God here and there.[15] At the same time, this redactor sweetened the text. He toned down its bitterness, its rigor, by mixing in pious reflections that are completely out of keeping with the flavor of the original text. But this religious tint was essential for the book to be accepted into the canon.

Now I am really perplexed! Why was it necessary to have this book accepted into the canon?[16] Why was anyone impelled to see a word of God to his people in such a text? If this book was truly scandalous, skeptical, etc., the solution was obvious: leave it out of the canon; do not even consider it, rather than trying to make it into a religious text! No one deals with this problem. It seems obvious to scholars that since the book had to be included in the canon, it was necessary to make it religious. We must note how false this idea is. Take the Song of Songs, for instance: a "neutral" reading will detect absolutely nothing religious in it. No prayer or reference to God has been inserted into this text, which can seem rather shocking, just like Ecclesiastes, although for different reasons. This being true, no such insertion was necessary in Ecclesiastes, either.

(2) We can add two other equally debatable presuppositions to

15. This is Lauha's hypothesis, for example (see pp. 6-7, 68).

16. Concerning canonization, Robert Laurin gives a fine explanation in "Tradition and Canon," in Douglas A. Knight, ed., *Tradition and Theology in the Old Testament* (Philadelphia: Fortress, 1977), pp. 261-74. We must distinguish dynamic canonization (based on faith in the activity of the Spirit) from static canonization (a closing of tradition stemming from a need for security and for defense against threats). Laurin says, "What was important for canon was not *content,* but the community conviction of the authority for that moment of certain works" (p. 272, emphasis added). This was no affair of specialists, of scribes or priests, but rather the conviction of an entire community. Each generation of God's people must let the Spirit persuade them that the word of God is addressed to them, *hic et nunc.* Qohelet probably would have been received, then, not through a watering down of the text, but because in this precise situation (the confrontation with Greek thought, for example) the community of believers recognized revealed truth in the text. Furthermore, Qohelet seems to have encountered no opposition originally (Lauha, p. 21); objections surface in later Judaism. In any case, Qohelet was accepted in Christian groups from the beginning (Lauha gives a very impressive list of the parallels between passages in Ecclesiastes and New Testament texts, p. 21).

the principle of noncontradiction. First, in line with what we have already said, commentators limit themselves to a naive reading of the text. They understand the text in its most obvious sense, and then stop. This is a strange approach for exegetes. On the one hand, they refuse, a priori, to consider that the text might be original; they have suspicions about it and refuse to read it as is. They hunt for strata, they carve it up, etc. But all this is limited to the formal aspects of the text. On the other hand, they remain on the surface when it comes to meaning. They fail to realize that this book might have a more basic dimension that should be determinative in their research, even when they are dealing with forms and structures. Treating a text as they do, there is no limit to what they could make it say, even if Descartes had written it!

What shall we say about all the writers who use the well-known rhetorical tactic of presenting the opinion of their adversaries as their own, in order to let the reader gradually discover how impossible that opinion is? Such a text requires a reading on a second level. The historian and the exegete never venture out onto this shifting ground! But I believe all of Ecclesiastes requires just such a second-level interpretation. The thing that most surprised me in the majority of Ecclesiastes commentators was their extraordinary knowledge of Hebrew, coupled with the superficiality of their thought. Some of them know Hebrew better than the author of Ecclesiastes himself; they know other ancient languages, Babylonian and Egyptian culture, and offer us an impressive bibliography. But their thinking is inconsistent and their theology empty. In brief, their utter lack of comprehension of the text stems from a total lack of interest and research in this area.

(3) The third presupposition of commentators has to do with their certainty that Ecclesiastes is not based on authentic Hebrew thought, but rather derives from one of the surrounding cultures. When scholars make this hypothesis the center of their research, presupposing a foreign origin for the book, they plunge into very dubious waters.

The diversity of theories is amazing. Limiting ourselves to the matter of formal textual analysis, we find all sorts of hypotheses: for H. L. Ginsberg, Ecclesiastes is an Aramaic book; for M. Dahood, it is Phoenician; A. F. Rainey believes it was written in the language of the Mesopotamian commercial traditions of the Achaemenian period, before Alexander the Great.[17] Typically, we find as many different possibilities for source analysis as we have scholars.

If we move to the study of content analysis, we find two main hypotheses and one secondary hypothesis: that Ecclesiastes is of Greek origin (the classical, traditional interpretation), Egyptian origin (the prevailing modern theory), or, for a few scholars, of Babylonian origin.

As far as Greek origin and influence are concerned, the evidence seems readily accessible: many texts in Ecclesiastes suggest recollections of Greek thought. We must remember that it was written in an area where Greek cultural influence dated from the fourth century B.C. at the latest. And much earlier, "Asian Greece" was nearby! Without denying other possible influences, we may consider it likely, then, that Ecclesiastes was written in a Greek cultural atmosphere. So many different cultural influences intersected in Palestine! But this consideration does not justify the conclusion that Ecclesiastes basically expresses any particular Greek, cynic, or sophistic trend of thought.[18] Our book may echo

17. H. L. Ginsberg, *Studies in Koheleth* (New York: Jewish Theological Seminary of America, 1950), pp. 16-39; Mitchell Dahood, "Canaanite-Phoenician Influence in Qoheleth," *Biblica* 33 (1952) 30-52, 191-221; idem, "Qoheleth and Recent Discoveries," *Biblica* 39 (1958) 302-18; idem, "Qoheleth and Northwest Semitic Philology," *Biblica* 43 (1962) 349-65; idem, "Canaanite Words in Qoheleth 10:20," *Biblica* 46 (1965) 210-12; idem, "The Phoenician Background of Qoheleth," *Biblica* 47 (1966) 264-82; H. Lusseau, "L'Ecclésiaste (Qôhelet)," in Henri Cazelles, ed., *Introduction critique à l'Ancien Testament,* vol. 2 of Roger Lapointe, et al., *Introduction à la Bible,* new ed. (Paris: Desclée, 1973), p. 629 n. 1, attributes this view to Rainey, citing Rainey's "A Study of Ecclesiastes," *Concordia Theological Monthly* 35/3 (March 1964) 148-57; see especially pp. 149-53. Cf. the English trans. from the 2nd French ed., which fails to mention Rainey: A. Robert and A. Feuillet, eds., *Introduction to the Old Testament,* trans. Patrick W. Skehan, et al., repr. in 2 vols. (New York: Doubleday, 1970), 2:145-54. Hereafter references to Lusseau will be to this English edition.

18. According to Pedersen, the Greek influence was utterly negative: Greek philosophy tended to disintegrate Hebrew thought. But the author of

Heraclitus's (6th-5th century B.C.) *panta rhei,* but the influence
could be in the opposite direction. In any case, I do not believe we
need to hunt for direct influence on Ecclesiastes from any writer or
school of thought.

Scholars have given special prominence to Theognis of Megara
(a fifth-century B.C. poet whose complete works date from the 4th
century). H. Duesberg considers that this writer (whose work was
widely read and used in schools to teach Greek youth) could have
been known in Israel before the invasion of Alexander (322 B.C.).[19]
True, Theognis's verse resembles rather closely what we find in
Ecclesiastes. But Duesberg emphasizes that, on the one hand,
Theognis never rises to universal ideas. He limits himself to his own
personal experience. On the other hand, he expresses no "theology": he quarrels with the gods and complains about destiny. I
find this point significant, since the author of Ecclesiastes shows
his capacity precisely in this area! He may well make use of
Theognis, but our writer shows how this despair and anger are
transformed when incorporated within the faith of Israel.

Moreover, Greek thought certainly had penetrated Palestine
well before any military contact occurred. Isn't Ecclesiastes, therefore, rather a model of the way in which Jewish thought understood
and absorbed a given source of human wisdom, by integrating it
within a different context (the revelation given at Sinai)? Doesn't
this insertion effect a *radical* (affecting the *roots*) change in that
wisdom's meaning and value? In this case, rather than constituting
a feeble reflection of the finest Greek philosophy, wouldn't Ecclesiastes represent the fundamental reversal and redirection of that
philosophy? The author demonstrates its fundamental emptiness—
accomplishing for "wisdom" what the Elohist [the supposed author
of one of the four main sources of the Pentateuch] and the prophets
had done for "religion."

Presently, as I have indicated, specialists tend to favor an

Ecclesiastes made no use of Greek thought, although he knew it, since his book
is imbued with an "international spirit" (pp. 362-63, 365-66).

19. Hilaire Duesberg, *Les Valeurs chrétiennes de l'Ancien Testament*
(Paris: Casterman, 1960).

Egyptian origin. But the motivations are not the same as in the case of the theory of a Greek origin. In the case of Egypt, we have not so much a general "atmosphere" as comparisons with specific Egyptian texts that resemble Ecclesiastes, or comparisons of certain seminal ideas that mold society. Scholars believe that the author of Ecclesiastes may have reflected distinctly Egyptian concepts (such as the cycle of time, death as a remedy, and the use of the word "God" with the definite article).[20] Specialists have identified customs, poems, and maxims that seem related.

I remain rather skeptical of these parallels. I have read some of the texts that scholars consider related (the *Laments of Ipuwer* [also called *Admonitions of an Egyptian Sage*], the *Song of the Harper*), and in them I find primarily commonplaces one can find in China or among the Aztecs. These commonplaces occur in Ecclesiastes, but they are not sufficient to demonstrate its origin. As for the seminal ideas Ecclesiastes supposedly has in common with Egyptian concepts, I fear scholars have misconstrued what Ecclesiastes says. Thus I remain very reticent about this Egyptian influence.

But we must also take into account Lauha's opinion (pp. 11-14), which sees the main influence as oriental and Babylonian:

20. In *Recherches sur les sources égyptiennes de la littérature sapientiale d'Israël*, Mémoires de l'Université de Neuchâtel 7 (Neuchâtel: University of Neuchâtel, 1929), pp. 107-24, Paul Humbert gives one of the best demonstrations of the Egyptian influence on Ecclesiastes. In particular, he notes that whereas there is a realistic attachment to life in all of the Old Testament, Ecclesiastes questions the value of life (p. 110). Although in Egypt death is commonly seen as a remedy, and returning to death represents the only sure happiness ("Drink, for death is coming"), Ecclesiastes' texts on death constitute an exception in Israel (pp. 110-12). Humbert claims, characteristically, that there has to be an origin, a tradition; therefore, Ecclesiastes draws on sources (p. 112). Similarly, the continual recurrence of everything seems to Humbert to be of Egyptian origin (pp. 112-13). As for the term "God" in Ecclesiastes, it often designates a king (see 8:2), as in Egypt (p. 119). And Ecclesiastes' frequent use of the word "God" with the definite article (which we will examine later) comes, according to Humbert, from the deistic notion of the divinity, as we find it in Egypt (pp. 123-24). In a word, according to Humbert, Ecclesiastes has merely handed down Egypt's moral and didactic literature, which provided the content and the moral of the biblical book (p. 124).

the doctrine of wisdom as an attribute of the king and something he includes in his "will," for example. Other examples are the relationship of Ecclesiastes' themes with those of Babylonian wisdom texts, including the rather clear elements in common with the Gilgamesh Epic. In spite of such apparent parallels, Lauha concludes that the central problem of Ecclesiastes cannot be illuminated by such comparisons. Rather, Israelite thought itself must furnish the clues.

In short, we find a bit of everything in Ecclesiastes. I believe the search for a dominant influence to be vain. The book was written in a part of the world that functioned as a crossroads of various civilizations, so that many ideas and opinions naturally would have found their way there. In this sense, Ecclesiastes is certainly a syncretistic book, but it is precisely this characteristic that surprises me most. For it is above all a Jewish book! Hellenistic thought might well have presented a kind of alternative to the crisis that ran through Jewish society. Yet over against this practical and theoretical philosophy, Ecclesiastes rises up to witness to the specificity of the revelation to Israel.

4. Critical Agreement and Pseudonymity in Ecclesiastes

I do not propose to debate the matters treated in almost all introductions to Ecclesiastes and in the histories of Hebrew literature. I will limit myself to a brief summary of a few issues. While many points remain disputed, in at least four matters historians and exegetes of Hebrew literature agree: (1) The date of the book. After a time when the date ranged widely (between the 7th and 3rd centuries B.C.), experts have finally come to date the book between 350 and 250 B.C., with a preference for the period shortly before or after the conquest of Alexander the Great, around 320 B.C. (2) Therefore, Solomon cannot be the author of the book. We will return to this problem. (3) The etymology of "Qohelet," the name given to the author. (4) Specialists unanimously consider that Qohelet's Hebrew is very poor; he uses the adulterated language of an inferior period and has a bombastic, unpoetic style. Others call his language brilliant and "baroque," considering it has undergone foreign influence. They find that the Masoretic text contains important changes; in any case, the text is considered uncertain and not original.

Let's explore further the identity of the two supposed authors of this book: Qohelet and Solomon. Unquestionably, "Qohelet" comes from the verb *qahal*, which means "to assemble." This derivative form seems to have been created for this particular book. What does it mean? At this point we find all sorts of opinions. The term may designate one who convenes the assembly (what assembly?), or its president, rhetorician, or orator. According to Martin Luther, Qohelet was the preacher of the assembly.[21] Adolphe Lods calls the term an "honorific title" attributed to a teacher by his disciples.[22] So Qohelet becomes a sort of philosophy professor. But can we continue, in this case, to speak of an "assembly," which became *ekklesia* in Greek?

Lys seems to offer the most astute solution for this problem. He disconnects Qohelet from the institutional meaning of the Hebrew verb, suggesting that the objects he assembles are not necessarily persons (pp. 53-54). "Qohelet" could also serve to designate one who assembles maxims or ideas, who prepares a collection of *meshallim* (proverbs), which could represent this book and which corresponds to what is said in chapter 12. But like the others, this translation comes up against a difficulty: *Qohelet* is the *feminine* participle of *qahal* (and the word is clearly feminine in the text, as in 7:27). Consequently, *Qohelet* cannot designate a masculine convener or president of an assembly.

Furthermore, it seems that Hebrew institutions did not have a president or official orator of an assembly, and thus no title for such a person. H. Lusseau speaks of "the head of a group of sages" (p. 146). But in this case as well, we lack evidence for the existence of such an institution. On what occasion, and for what purpose,

21. Martin Luther, *Luther's Works*, vol. 15, ed. and trans. Jaroslav Pelikan and Hilton C. Oswald (St. Louis: Concordia, 1972), p. 12.

22. Adolphe Lods, *Histoire de la littérature hébraïque et juive depuis les origines jusqu'à la ruine de l'état juif* (Paris: Payot, 1950), p. 697.

would such a group have met? It would be amazing for no trace of such an institution to have survived.

The problem of the feminine form of *Qohelet* remains in any case. Could it represent the personification of wisdom? But Wisdom's words about wisdom in this book are not very encouraging! Maillot's interpretation seems the most promising: Qohelet represents Death, which summons and assembles us all (p. 8). How true! But in this case as well, how can we attribute Qohelet's words to Death, when he calls us to work, to act, to be joyful, to worship God? Death can speak only a very small part of Qohelet's message. For the rest of it, Death is an impossible solution. (Maillot also suggests a fascinating play on words: although not grammatically correct, could not Qohelet also be a derivative of *qalal,* meaning "to disparage, criticize, dispute"? In this way, with the innocuous name of "assembler," Qohelet gets away with a *qelalah,* a virulent piece of mockery.)

I must say that nothing I have read strikes me as very satisfactory. "Qohelet," it seems to me, represents neither a title nor a function. Rather, it is a gratuitous designation, probably due to the last author of the book, which has ironic and questioning overtones that the book as a whole expresses. In other words, we should understand "Qohelet" in terms of the book's content rather than in etymological terms.

For the most part this is a book of solitary meditation, of withdrawal into the self. It is composed of thoughts utterly impossible to express in an assembly. How many venture to preach on Qohelet from the pulpit, except for two or three oft-expounded verses? Which great theologians build on this book? We could mention Thomas à Kempis and Kierkegaard, for example: two preeminently solitary individuals.

This is a solitary book for solitary people. To me it seems consonant with the nature of this book to call its author the opposite of what he really is. He is called the "Assembler" because he is a solitary person. Thus the name is a pseudonym, but the reader fails to recognize this unless he faces up to the continual paradox of the book. The same can be said of the use of a feminine word to designate the author of a book that is singularly hard on women!

In order to insist on the irony of the pseudonym, then, we should use the name "Qohelet," untranslated, as the title of the book. In any case, we should not translate the title into Greek as *ekklesia*. This would amount to calling it a book of the Church—a remarkable idea, considering it suggests that the book could be useful for an institution! Keeping the title "Ecclesiastes" is even less appropriate, in spite of the long tradition behind it. Now that the original meaning of "assembly" has been lost, what can "Ecclesiastes" suggest to people? Only the most empty and trite message: "All is vanity." Custom has subjected Qohelet to the same indignity as the "Apocalypse," which people have turned into a book of catastrophes rather than the book of Revelation. Similarly, all that remains of the profound and paradoxical Qohelet is "vanity." We must preserve, rather, the pseudonym, antonym, paradox, and irony.

Now let us have a look at the second name connected with this book: Solomon. We have already mentioned that he cannot be the author, because of the book's date. There is no point, therefore, in resorting to such feeble arguments as the following (I mention them to show how mistaken they are): Barucq considers that the book is so violently antimonarchical that it constitutes a political manifesto against Solomon (p. 10). Similarly, Ginsberg finds that since the book speaks of oppression, a king could not have written it (p. 13). If he opposed oppression, he would put an end to it instead of denouncing it! Furthermore, the title of "Convener of the assembly" does not allow us to identify him with the king! Such nonsense need not take any more of our time.

Although Solomon is not expressly named in the text, there can scarcely be any doubt as to the intention of the author. He is son of David, king of Israel and Jerusalem; that is, he places himself before the division of the kingdom (into Israel and Judah), so that he can be no other than Solomon. No other descendant of David fits. We will have to see to what extent this text has Solomon in view and refers back to features of his reign. Lys has reason to say: "The author of Ecclesiastes places himself under the patronage of the man characterized by his openness to the world, who wanted to receive wisdom from God, and who is supposed to have said: 'It is the glory of God to conceal things, but the glory of kings is to search things out' " (Lys, p. 52; the quotation is from Prov. 25:2, RSV).

Of course, as I have mentioned, scholars agree that Solomon is not the author. The traditional explanation is that the ancients gathered under the name of a model author all texts of the same genre. In this fashion, all the laws were placed under Moses' name as the ideal lawgiver; Moses' name becomes a figurative designation for all legal texts. Thus everything dealing with wisdom is placed under Solomon's name, as the ideal model of the speaker of wisdom. This is surely correct, but it seems a bit simplistic for such an imposing text!

Solomon as the choice for symbolic author is quite important. Wisdom, of course, makes him a natural choice. Who could speak of wisdom the way he could? He was believed to be the author of 1,500 wisdom maxims, and is offered as a model of justice. Who, besides this wise one, could conclude that wisdom is vanity? Furthermore, the author had to present himself as someone with experience in exercising power, in order to give the impression of criticizing power from the inside rather than from the outside. Another reason for choosing Solomon was that the book deals with worship and religious service; who was better qualified to speak of these things than Solomon, the builder of the temple? Solomon was the great king, who built and inaugurated the temple, centralized sacrificial worship in Jerusalem, established Jerusalem in its central role; and Solomon's name, like Jerusalem's, includes the verbal root of *shalom,* peace.

This Solomon will be called into question in the book. Yet he brought wisdom and peace together so that it has been said that before Solomon and before Jerusalem, *shalom* was lacking in Israel's existence. Solomon also had exceptional experience with women; he had a thousand in his harem. This would give credence to what looks like the book's violently antifeminine attitude.

As we shall see, the word "vanity" (Heb. *hebel*) suggests idolatry, and can even be translated by the word "idols" (idols of emptiness). We must not forget that at the end of his reign Solomon became an idolatrous king. The proclamation that all is smoke, vanity, or idol, then, fits with Solomon's experience.

Thus within the text itself, everything converges in such a way as to suggest placing it under Solomon's authority. His name was not chosen by accident.[23] We need to go deeply into this matter rather than accepting the modern interpretation of it. Qohelet writes as if he were the king. He puts himself in Solomon's place, offering his book as if it came from Solomon. But the author is a king with no kingdom. He is not the great king, but he puts himself in the place of the king. His book expresses a relationship with the king (which could go so far as justifying the monarchy and calling the people to the aid of the king!). "Qohelet" designates the relationship of a subject with his king (and perhaps the relationship of the king with God, and of a person with himself).

The author is identified as Qohelet *and* as Solomon. Why two pseudonyms? And why two contradictory pseudonyms: one apparently the speaker in the assembly, the rhetorician, and the other the contemplative king of wisdom? The two do not go well together! At this point I inevitably think of Kierkegaard's use of "Climacus" and "Anti-Climacus," of which he says: "All the earlier pseudonyms are lower than the 'edifying author'; the new pseudonym represents a higher pseudonymity. It is to be understood, however, that the 'arrest' is accomplished by pointing out a higher ideal, with the consequence of forcing me back within the bounds of my limitations, condemning me because my life does not correspond to so lofty a claim, so that of necessity the communication is a poetic one."[24]

Kierkegaard's pseudonyms express the movement of the aesthetician or of the philosopher or speculative person toward a deeper attempt at Christian resolutions. It is the intersecting movement between reflection and the Unique One of faith: the author " 'has only willed one thing.' The discerning mind will at the same time recognize that this one thing is the religious, but the religious

23. We will return to the problem of the use of Solomon's name in chapter III below.

24. Søren Kierkegaard, "My Activity as a Writer," in *The Point of View for My Work as an Author,* trans. Walter Lowrie, ed. Benjamin Nelson (New York: Harper & Row, repr. 1962), p. 142 n.

altogether and utterly transposed into reflection, yet in such a way that it is altogether and utterly withdrawn from reflection and restored to simplicity—that is to say, he will see that the road travelled has the aim of *approaching, of attaining* simplicity."[25]

All this applies to Qohelet, I believe: the contradiction of the two pseudonyms expresses the basic contradiction in the work itself. It reflects the opposition between the writer who is the philosopher, skeptic, and poet, with all the details of his thought processes, on the one hand, and the affirmation of faith, on the other. This opposition is radical and unyielding: the appearance of the transcendent brings common wisdom to an end, as well as evasion through lyricism. But wisdom and lyricism have also constituted, time and again, an approach for returning to the simplicity of the proclamation of the unique and transcendent God, whose presence is the meaning, the purpose, the origin, and the end of the entire work.

5. Wisdom and Poetry

At this point we will tackle an even more ticklish subject. What kind of book is this, after all? It belongs to the "Writings" (the third section of the Hebrew canon), but this is too easy an answer. The books of wisdom, we know, belong to the least important category in the hierarchy of revealed texts. In simple terms, one could say that the Torah, made up of the five books of the Pentateuch, is entirely and directly the Word of God. Thus the Torah constitutes the basic book; all the rest must be understood in terms of what it says. Next, less important, we have the Prophets. They spoke under the inspiration of God, but these books include a human factor that can get in the way of the pure Word of God. Last of all, the Writings appear to offer us something quite different: a human being speaks, and God bears witness to this human word, adopting it and conferring on it the value of revelation. But it remains a human word, which must thus be understood in the light of the Torah.

25. Ibid., p. 143.

Douglas Knight emphasizes that "It is common for studies of Old Testament revelation to omit entirely any consideration of wisdom. . . . [G. E.] Wright is led to a highly problematic, even tendentious conclusion: 'Wisdom literature is not the center of the spiritual canon; it is peripheral to it.' "[26] H. Gese notes that "it is recognized that wisdom teaching represents a foreign body in the world of the Old Testament."[27] Yahwism functions as the norm for understanding wisdom.

However that may be, we have in Qohelet a book of wisdom. And this plunges us into difficulty, since wisdom is not a very clear concept. Qohelet's wisdom differs completely from what we understand by wisdom in the book of Job, and that in turn differs from the wisdom of Proverbs. This concept is subtle, iridescent, and polymorphous—difficult to grasp.

At the most elementary level, one could say that wisdom is a topic for study, with proverbs to help the memory. As a subject matter, wisdom could include didactic poems, such as the one on the circular movement of the elements (Eccl. 1:4-7), and the other on times and auspicious moments (3:1-11).[28] According to some scholars, wisdom amounts to a trite collection of aphorisms, like Proverbs: maxims with no relation to each other. They are "thoughts," flung out pell-mell, as they flow from the author's pen. We can compare Pascal's *Pensées*, which follow no order or coherent plan.

Some experts have come up with wonderful names for such maxims: "Sundry Small Fragments" (small fragments that raise the whole question of retribution!), or "Various Reflections," "Various

26. Douglas A. Knight, "Revelation through Tradition," in Douglas A. Knight, ed., *Tradition and Theology in the Old Testament* (Philadelphia: Fortress, 1977), p. 173.

27. Quoted in James L. Crenshaw, "The Human Dilemma and Literature of Dissent," in Douglas A. Knight, ed., *Tradition and Theology in the Old Testament*, p. 245 n. 15 (citing H. Gese, *Lehre und Wirklichkeit in der Alten Weisheit* [Tübingen: Mohr (Siebeck), 1958], p. 2).

28. Von Rad believes these poems to be very old, and used by Qohelet in a context that differs from the original one (*Wisdom in Israel*, pp. 121, 138-39, 263-64).

Maxims" (Barucq, pp. 99, 140, 153, 177). These demonstrate how hard put the exegetes are. Another remarkable suggestion: Qohelet as a "private diary," written day by day! These explanations fail utterly to convince me. The didactic poems strike me as very brief and unspecific. Contrary to the notion of an incoherent collection, I believe I find a deep internal coherence, including a point of departure and a point of arrival. Lauha also insists very judiciously on the unity and the coherence of the text (p. 6).

I can agree with the exegetes on two points: Qohelet is a poem, and a poem about wisdom. As for its poetry, we have mentioned that most exegetes find Qohelet's language very poor. It strikes me as strange that in translation we encounter such a wonderfully poetic text—evocative, rich, and moving. I am quite convinced we do not have the translators to thank for this! What could be grander than the poem "There is a time for everything under the sun" (3:1, JE)? Or "Remember your Creator during your youth. . . . before the sun grows dark" (12:1-2, JE)? These pages may be the most beautiful in the entire Bible. But according to the specialists, Qohelet is not first-class Hebrew poetry. I find this puzzling. I believe we find the explanation in the mystery of poetic creation itself. The truly creative poet forges his language at the same time as his message. There can be no separation between form and content. The poet does not have an idea to communicate, which he then puts into verse. By no means! We are faced here with something welling up from a deep spring; there is no distinction between the properties of the water and the underground path it has carved out to reach the daylight of expression.

The poet, then, is not a person who thinks *and* has a nice style. His thought cannot be expressed in any other way. He thinks as the words themselves come and evoke his thought. This double movement is beginning to be more widely known. I believe that it provides the secret of Qohelet's poetic grandeur. He does not give us philosophical, skeptical, or pragmatic thought, and then a heavy or baroque style. On the contrary, we sense here a spark of genius that overturns all norms, creating a language for itself at the same time that a total, harsh questioning springs up in all its relentlessness. This is a true creation, a *poiein*. Nowhere else in the world do we find the equivalent of Qohelet. His poetry reverberates in the reader, apart from linguistic opinion. For this reason, all his translators have ended up with a beautiful, harmonious text. They produce a poetic text because the original is poetic, and its language is beautiful, in spite of its carefree attitude toward grammar. The poetry comes from the language's being forged directly by the difficulty of the question in view.

This is a poem about wisdom. Since the book is grouped with the Writings, almost all scholars limit themselves to seeing it as a reflection within the limitations of the wisdom genre. But although wisdom plays an important part in this book, it does not explain the book's origin, purpose, or meaning, as I will clarify later.

Furthermore, this wisdom has posed unfathomable problems for historians and exegetes. What is it, after all? Does it deny all traditional Hebrew wisdom? Or, with all its originality, is it consistent with Jewish thought, serving to add deeper dimensions to it? James Crenshaw notes that the unusual character of Qohelet indicates its pagan spirit and content, according to some interpreters (pp. 245-46). Crenshaw believes that this "wisdom" originates in ideas shared by the entire ancient Near East. In this case, wisdom in Qohelet is nonconformist, and rooted in multiple traditions concerning the "High God theology." Thus the essential distinctives of Israel's belief fall from view: election, the covenant, the Law, and dialogue between God and his people, including forgiveness and promise. No revelation links the Creator with his creatures, in this view. Knowledge can come only through experience (but we will see as we continue that historians err at this point). According to this interpretation, the only means of discovering truth depends on the human spirit: God did not choose Israel, all people have equal standing before God, and all their ideas merit respect (pp. 247-49).

Qohelet's dissenting style is thus seen as expressing an original "point of view." But the cavalier manner in which critics like Crenshaw express such opposition surprises me: "Whereas the prophet [Amos] says: 'Seek the Lord, and live' (5:6), Dame Wisdom ventures the following invitation: 'Leave simpleness [including religious simpleness?], and live' (Prov. 9:6)" (p. 250). And Crenshaw gives an example he finds conclusive: "Whereas Gen. 1

spoke of creation as exceptionally good, Qoheleth concedes that God made everything appropriate for its moment, but goes on to place that judgment under a heavy cloud of divine neglect or mischief (Qoh. 3:11)" (p. 250). In this verse, however, Qohelet states that human beings cannot discover all that God has done. Crenshaw's "example" amounts to mere invention on his part. When we study this text we will see how biased Crenshaw is. He has just one end in view: to contrast Qohelet's skepticism with all the traditional values of Yahwism. How trite!

On this basis, Crenshaw simplifies everything. He declares that Qohelet despises life, that his "hatred for life grows out of his search for profit" (pp. 252-53). According to Crenshaw, this book presents a challenge to God's promises, to the glorious coming work of God promised by the prophets, since "none will remember former things *or* things yet to come" (p. 250). All this seems extraordinarily superficial to me. I find von Rad's thought much more profound and solid. He emphasizes that whereas Qohelet adheres carefully to traditional wisdom when he presents a problem, he differs from it profoundly by concentrating his attention on the whole of life rather than on isolated experiences. Moreover, von Rad demonstrates the existence of a deep internal structure and unity in the text (pp. 227-37).

6. Philosophy, Truth, and Reality in Qohelet

We need to eliminate two other frequent interpretations of this poem about wisdom: Qohelet as a book of metaphysics (or morals, according to some), and as a book of pragmatic thought by a concrete realist who limits himself to describing reality. The realist is said to present "the human condition viewed from the point of view of events."

First, Qohelet's wisdom is not metaphysical. This term involves us in a dangerous error, a common confusion of two different things: a given aspect of philosophy and theology, on the one hand, and the thought based on the Word of God, on revelation, on the other hand.

Naturally, for someone who does not believe in God or in a God who can reveal himself, or that the Bible can be the Word of God, anything about God belongs to the realm of metaphysics, whether it comes from Descartes or Aristotle. But the entire Bible challenges this term. The things concerning God do not amount to something "following physics." The revelation about God cannot be equated with a philosophical dissertation. The revelation deals with questions, disturbances, and confusion stemming from the insertion of a word of God into the flow of events. These do not fall under the kind of analysis we moderns draw from the physics of fluids to understand cyclones or the way disorder creates order. No philosophical reasoning based on observations of physical phenomena can bring us to the threshhold of revelation. Meditation on this revelation should not accept the label "philosophy."

In fact, we find no "wisdom" in this word of God. We cannot find anything metaphysical in the tragic questioning of Qohelet, because it has no "before" and no "after." Qohelet makes no reference to any human intellectual possibility of attaining or expressing the inexpressible, the unpronounceable, the ultimate, the unconditional. At most, we could concede that the "subjects treated" by Qohelet are also philosophers' favorite subjects—subjects that metaphysics has dealt with. But nothing more. Stars can be studied by astrology or by astronomy! Just because life, death, God, happiness, etc., have been treated by metaphysicians does not make anyone who speaks of them a metaphysician. Much less Qohelet! Let us leave metaphysics to the metaphysicians, then, so that we can listen to Qohelet speak without metaphysicians' discourse interfering. This way we will see that he speaks differently from them.

Even less can we call Qohelet a moralist! This book does not deal with morality. When scholars reduce it to the moralistic level, it is true that its morality (like that of Proverbs) seems very simplistic and elementary. "Work serves no purpose." "You cannot control the future." "Why accumulate wealth, when you can't take it with you?," etc. If that is all the Word of God has to say about our life, we can do better strictly on our own. We must carefully avoid taking this book as a collection of moral maxims!

On the contrary, it may well be the opposite: all these pious commonplaces come to grief with "all is vanity." Yes, of course— morality is vanity, too! We will get nothing more than this observation out of Qohelet's pearls of wisdom if we make them into an incoherent collection, instead of following the clearly indicated thread that leads us through the book. One end of the thread is vanity; the other, the presence of God. In Qohelet, then, we find neither metaphysics nor morality.

Other interpreters have seen the opposite in the book: concrete realism. They maintain that Qohelet, far from saying what should be, or what is desirable, tells us what is. "Here is human life," he appears to say. Instead of giving us a lesson, he presents us with facts. He rubs our noses in crude reality, with no illusions or anything to pretty it up, so that we must draw our own conclusions. Our backs are against the wall. "Let's not escape into dreams," he would say.

These scholars call Qohelet a "skeptic," because he gleefully demolishes values and illusions. I would agree with them on this, as long as we do not place him in a skeptic or sophistic "school" of Greek philosophers. We must not enter his name after Pyrrho or Protagoras. We will see the amazing difference between them and Qohelet. In another sense, he is not a skeptic at all, since after saying happiness is absurd, he encourages us to gather all the happiness we can on this earth.

Here we find one of the contradictions mentioned earlier. Qohelet most certainly is not a skeptic, since he never for an instant questions the presence and action of God. Everything is questioned, but at the same time everything is also the gift of God. No skeptic has ever arrived at such a confession. Qohelet the pragmatist? Yes, of course, that, too, since he conceives of life as a continuous action. We can act only in the context of a radical knowledge of reality. But everything does not take place on the level of action. Our action is in turn limited by the implacable words "all is vanity." These words are found on one side of the coin; on the other, we find "God."

Yes, Qohelet is truly realistic and pragmatic, but not in the usual sense. He describes reality, but never the way a human being can describe it. When we encounter reality, we always react in one of two stereotyped ways: either we cover it over, conceal it, brighten it up, so that it appears less harsh; or else, on the contrary, we make it so excessive and terrifying that it no longer threatens us. We say "No, it's not 'true'; it can't be like that." In the first case, we have the traditional myths, false hopes, shining futures, religions, praise of virtue, bourgeois morality, etc.—all transfigurations enabling us to escape the harsh dimension of reality.[29]

But today we see the opposite: our Western society finds itself so terrified by reality that, in order to avoid seeing it, we plunge into the atrocity and excess of images and representation. Thus movies, television, and novels provide us with a world more horrifying than the one we live in, and enable us to avoid seeing it. In this imagined world, everyone without exception is a despicable beast. Nuclear destruction devastates the entire earth. Cities are filled with unconscious, mechanical automatons. Robots run the universe. The ocean conceals monsters that rise up to annihilate all living things. The perversion of morals goes beyond anything human history has ever known, etc. Every reader can come up with the title of a "work" that illustrates each of these types. They enable us to say, as we leave the theater: "Whew! Life isn't like that: the weather is good for this time of year; women are very attractive; my children are nice," etc. We escape by means of squalor.

Qohelet falls into neither of these evasions. He speaks to us of the actual reality of human life. He does not speak of it with his personal wisdom, as a man of experience who looks at reality and tells it like it is; rather, he starts with God. Qohelet gives us a revelation from God.

At this point, however, we must take care not to misconstrue. Qohelet's point of view differs from that of Sirius, the representation of the star by that name [in Voltaire's *Micromégas*— TRANS.], and from God's point of view. Unlike Sirius, Qohelet cannot place himself at a distance and consider apparently random human activities as if he were examining insects. Qohelet cannot

29. As I showed in *Propaganda: The Formation of Men's Attitudes,* trans. Konrad Kellen and Jean Lerner (New York: Knopf, 1965), we find encounter with reality so painful that propaganda succeeds precisely to the extent that it provides us with a means of escaping reality!

adopt the point of view of a faraway star, a scrupulous or amused scientific observer. He says repeatedly: "I did," "I lived," "I experienced," "I was in authority," "I searched for wisdom." Qohelet does not speak of abstract human beings he sees from afar; he speaks of himself. Instead of taking Sirius's point of view, Qohelet plunged into every human experience. He saw what was possible, and he speaks of his experience with serenity, precision, and objectivity. He calls himself totally into question. Apparently Karl Marx took "Doubt everything" as his motto. He was not the first; Descartes' "De omnibus dubitandum est" came long before Marx. But Marx did not doubt everything. He doubted neither himself (consider his arrogance and hatred toward P.-J. Proudhon and Mikhail Bakunin), nor progress, nor the value of work.

Qohelet goes much farther than Marx in all these areas. At the beginning of his book he places himself on the stage, to show all he has done, and tells us it amounted to nothing. Qohelet is the dissenter par excellence.[30] But we must not take his point of view for God's! Qohelet knows perfectly well he is not God.[31] He repeats

30. So far as I know, the first scholar to emphasize Qohelet's dissent was Maillot, but Crenshaw gives us a very fine analysis. He considers dissent from six points of view: as "(1) a literary motif; (2) a structural feature of social change; (3) an ongoing phenomenon in Israel's history; (4) conflict between contemporaries; (5) a disintegrative force in society; and (6) Promethean attack against heteronomy" (p. 235 n. 2). Crenshaw emphasizes this last aspect of dissent, which seems to him to synthesize all the others. Such dissent characterizes prophets as well as sages, both of whom express themselves through "protest literature." Many sources contribute to this dissent: the institutional fabric, human nature (?), and the ambiguities of life (pp. 237-39). Crenshaw situates wisdom literature as follows: "Priests, as proud guardians of *ethos,* treasured sacred legal traditions. . . . Prophets, proponents of *pathos,* gave expression to their participation in divine suffering. . . . Sages, powerful advocates of *logos,* used rational arguments grounded in experience for the purpose of persuading society to maintain the order established at creation and to recognize the limits of all knowledge" (p. 237).

31. Qohelet is the stone upon which are shattered all the mystics and all the "enthusiasts" who go so far as to take themselves for God! (Consider Meister J. Eckhart, as well as the proclamation of his disciple, Sister Catherine, who said: "Sir, rejoice with me: I have become God.")

this continually: God is unknowable. No one can take his place, think as he thinks, or judge people (even oneself) as God judges.

Well, then, in whose name does Qohelet speak? How can he express on the one hand an implacable realism that never lets up and never tries to escape, yet on the other hand avoid despair or excess? I believe he provides us with a model of what a person in God's grasp can understand and know of humanity and society. God is Mystery. But this living God acts on a person, places him in a new situation, and from that situation, the person can see himself, others, and this world. He can see at the same time the *reality* of things as they are (this constitutes his realism) and also their *truth* (i.e., he can see their profound existence before God and for God).[32] In this case, reality prevents truth from being an escape into the clouds or into dreams (whether intellectual or aesthetic). And truth prevents reality from turning into despair, from leading a person to skepticism, then to nihilism, and finally and unfailingly, to suicide.

In reality, all is vanity. In truth, everything is a gift of God. This represents Qohelet's position, as I understand it.

7. Qohelet as Ritual Incantation

Another interpretation deals with this poem on wisdom as an important challenge. An ethnographic-psychological-sociological reading of the text permits a different interpretation and the formulation of an intriguing hypothesis. The book can be read as an incantation, as a text intended for reciting or singing (but not in a liturgical context). Several factors contribute to the book's potential value as an electrifying ritual: the repeated use of long, poetic phrases, the alternation of observations leading to despair with assurances of reason for hope, based on evidence from life, etc.

According to this view, Qohelet introduces four protagonists:

32. For a more detailed presentation of the opposition between reality and truth, see Jacques Ellul, *The Humiliation of the Word,* trans. Joyce Main Hanks (Grand Rapids: Eerdmans, 1985).

the king (called "Solomon"), the narrator (the author, the director
of the ritual), the people (the assembly), and a fourth personage:
breath, mist, Spirit. The work is intended for recitation before the
king; it comes at a time of crisis and means to effect a transformation
from a previous state to a later state. The text is thus turned toward
the future. Rather than describing objective reality, it speaks "for
the king," in order to help him recognize another distinct reality.
Consequently, this book could attempt to influence history (by
maintaining a society's unity, preserving the kingdom, etc.) through
a ritual incantation. A text destined to protect the monarchy! (This
interpretation would provide an explanation for later efforts to
include the book in the canon.)

Going deeper, this "royal" reading would suggest that Qohelet's contradictions reveal the point of view of someone for whom
all oppositions have disappeared: he no longer appreciates true or
false, good or evil. On a psychological level, all sense of direction
and discrimination disappears; on a sociological level, society
becomes lawless. Everything amounts to the same thing. To cure
this loss of the sense of distinction, the therapist uses the repetition
of contradictions: a kind of "logosociotherapy"! Our author tries to
remove the despair from the king, and to remove the king from
despair. The writer prepares a text based on the Socratic method in
order to exorcise the evil (and to bring the king back into grace,
although, of course, the text never admits this!).

The director of the ritual identifies himself with the sick king,
first entering his perspective, but then leaving it again. Then he
returns to the king's universe, nudging him toward progress. The
king's indifference stems from his satiation, his boredom, his sense
of uselessness. All appears to be the same; nothing makes any
difference. In view of these observations, the unexpected appearance of God in our text takes on pivotal importance, signifying that
reality regains control.

If this hypothesis of the book as ritual proves correct, the text
may well have originated much earlier. Unlike our books written
by an author with a central idea or a "message," this book could
then be a ritual related to the situation in which the sense of
discrimination is lost. This must have occurred more than once. The

book would then have grown by a process of accretion, authors adding portions dealing with new factors as they appeared. The original text may well have been written up when Solomon experienced bitterness at the end of his reign.

The reasoning goes like this: *if* a text had been created to be recited in ritual incantation before the king (Solomon?) and his assembly, to resolve a problem (whether personal, political, or dealing with the relationship of the king and the people), to mediate between opposing forces, or to ward off some future difficulty, such a text would have resembled this book of Qohelet.[33] If this is the case, we may be tempted to conclude that the book has nothing to tell us, since we must not generalize from one historical situation to another. But let us not forget that this text became part of Holy Scripture, thus rising above its historical context to take on a universal quality, since it was recognized as inspired by God. Thus it offers us truth concerning God, who reveals himself in it, as well as a revelation about all people, based on Solomon's unique personal experience.

8. Structure in Qohelet

Now that we have tried to understand what this surprising book is up to, and taken a look at the widely varying ways scholars approach it, we find ourselves faced with the question concerning its structure: do we have a series of poems, ideas scattered across the page pell-mell, or is there evidence for a certain coherence or plan? Many translators have tried to discover a design in it. According to A. Chouraqui, it has a prologue followed by three parts: (1) life and

33. Of course, the enormous length of time between Solomon's reign and our text means we cannot attribute it to him directly. But why not allow for the possibility that the book was the result of an initial ritual in Solomon's time, considering the vast capacity for transmitting memorized texts in Near Eastern cultures? Scholars have called this ability "mental writing." It might well explain many of the awkward spots and stylistic flaws in Qohelet.

death, (2) knowledge and wisdom, (3) retribution and love, and then an epilogue.[34] But although we can easily see sections we might call a prologue (ch. 1) and an epilogue (ch. 12), the rest of this outline remains quite uncertain. Pedersen finds a first section claiming life is not worth living (chs. 1–6); then a second part (chs. 7–12) suggesting the consequences of this idea (p. 321). Some scholars have chosen to move different sections of the text around, while others have tried to discover a rigorous logical sequence in it.[35]

Lys, who shows by far the greatest capacity for finding organization in the book, furnishes us with a coherent construction (pp. 64-66). In a long first part, he finds a theoretical view of the human condition (1:4–4:3), with two subsections: an overview (including an objective statement, a subjective statement, and a section on "Why live?") and a section on destiny (time, and God's justice). The second long development, parallel to the first, presents a practical review of the human condition, with two subsections: paradoxes (work, money, etc.), and relative ethics (women, philosophy, etc.).

Lys's outline is well constructed but is not at all convincing to me. For example, how can sections involving work or money not belong to ethics? How can injustice and success not be in the paradoxes? And how shall we explain the innumerable repetitions? Such outlines actually represent rational Western logic, but do not at all represent the traditional way of thinking.[36] Rational, scientific order did not preoccupy traditional thinkers and prophets. I have become thoroughly convinced that Qohelet follows no logical, coherent plan, nor does he treat a different question in each part.

34. André Chouraqui, *Les Cinq Volumes,* vol. 1 of *La Bible, traduite et présentée par André Chouraqui* (Paris: Desclée de Brouwer, 1975), p. 117.

35. For the former see, e.g., G. Bickell, *Der Prediger über den Wert des Daseins* (Innsbruck: Wagner, 1884). For the latter see, e.g., Etienne Glasser, *Le Procès du bonheur par Qohelet,* Lectio Divina 61 (Paris: Cerf, 1970), pp. 10-13, 179-87, 217-18.

36. In *The Technological Society,* trans. John Wilkinson (New York: Knopf, 1964), I showed that our eagerness to find a logical plan in a book begins with modern scientific thought, primarily (but not only!) with Descartes.

Could the book perhaps consist of sections placed one after the other? Nineteenth-century translators organized Qohelet this way. The problem with this view is that chapters such as 4, 5, 7, and 9 elude attempts to find titles for them and do not fit into a thematic scheme. Can we at least find places where the work seems to take off in a new direction? Many, of course, have tried to establish this. The most obvious approach involves seeing the phrase "vanity and a striving after wind" (e.g., 1:14) as the conclusion to each section. In this fashion, we distinguish eight different sections, but we can find no coherence within each one! For a time my approach involved finding another sort of articulation: I surmised that rhythmical invocations of God punctuated the text, indicating the beginning of sections (i.e., 3:11, 15; 5:18-20; 9:7-10; etc.). But finally I realized that such a hypothesis could not stand up to close analysis, and I have failed to find any similar workable theory.

How, then, does this book that follows no order give the appearance of granite-like solidity and coherence, of systematic thought? Does Qohelet perhaps follow some internal logic more persistent than anything we have come up with? Could he be following a "plan" infinitely more subtle than the sort we observe in certain university lectures? Does he perhaps enjoy covering over the tracks of his scheme, much the way some modern novelists do (e.g., J. Champion, A. Robbe-Grillet)? Should we compare him to a film in which flashbacks and symbolic film language lead us to associate two widely separated sequences, thanks to a symbol that appears in both? In this case, we would have an order we could not represent in outline form, because it does not resemble an erector-set model. It would consist of irony, metaphor, metonymy, anticipation, and winks from the author!

Following this "order" we find a kind of deliberate dispersal of some twenty central themes. Throughout the book the thoughts relate to each other from within variegated sections. The author raises questions and only several chapters later answers them, in an interplay of echoes. By means of this subtle intermingling, Qohelet aims at nudging the hearer toward an unavoidable conclusion, not at some artistic effect. I believe he does everything in view of a predetermined purpose. If I am right, we must above all avoid skipping over any part of the text or reducing any of it to some vague moral or metaphysical lesson. Every step counts, and we must take each one along with the author.

I find that the coherence of this text stems from a kind of woven texture rather than a logical plan, and I believe I can perceive a texture in Qohelet something like that of a complex variegated piece of cloth. You cannot find the beginning, the end, or the direction of the pattern, but such a weave blends its components in a surprising way. Our surprise does not spring from any tangling of the threads (since this would ruin the cloth), but rather from the threads' appearing here and there. These strands surface, suddenly cropping up from their surroundings, but we realize they were there all the time, underneath. Because of their presence (visible or not), the whole is coherent and is not just a collection of proverbs, recommendations, and occasional trite sayings. Such an arrangement would explain why we find the same themes repeated in such a way as to defy forcing the text into an outline. We find work, for instance, in chapters 1, 2, 4, 6, 9, 10, and 11. Happiness appears in chapters 2, 3, 5, 7, 8, 9, and 11; power, in chapters 1, 3, 4, 5, 8, and 10. And I could add the lists of chapters dealing with money, property, death, and language.

A further remark must be made. We find major and minor themes in this texture. We have only one text on women, but about twenty on work. We find two or three texts on justice, but fifteen on power. The number of passages does not necessarily indicate the importance of an issue but can force us to ask significant questions.

Everything passes in review in this book, under the author's ironic gaze, but certain themes stand out. Two of them seem to dominate from the outset: vanity and wisdom. They contradict each other. Wisdom is subjected to vanity, true! But wisdom also constitutes our only weapon against vanity. We witness a kind of debate between wisdom and vanity. On the one hand, wisdom demonstrates the vanity of everything, but is itself vanity. On the other hand, vanity loses its sharpness and bitterness, since the wise person has passed beyond all vanity. At this point, I believe, we begin to see one of the possibilities of Qohelet. But the book does not limit itself to this immanent and uncontrollable circle, since it also refers to God.

As far as positivist exegetes are concerned, these references to God amount to pietistic insertions, intended to make a spicy dish more digestible! But as we persevere in a meditative approach to the book, instead of indulging in a rapid, superficial reading (assuming we already understand it quite well), it dawns on us little by little that the reference to God is central: that is to say, decisive and pivotal. The theme of God gathers the dispersed elements, at the same time presenting us with an additional contradiction. As our study deepens, we see that the unexpected appearance of God in this text cannot be seen as a later supplement or pious veneer. On the contrary, God's presence at every turn signifies a righting of the situation.

Furthermore, I was surprised to discover that my comparison of Qohelet to a woven texture had been used long ago: "In what sense does the Torah constitute an explanation of God's name?" Joseph Gikatila answers that "the Torah is *woven* from the name of God."[37] Gikatila seems to have been the first to use this term (*'arigah*) to show how God's name continually appears in the *texture* of the Torah. "Know the manner in which the Torah has been woven in the Wisdom of God. . . . The whole Torah is a weaving of God's attributes, which are woven in turn from the different names of God," he says.

Furthermore, Lusseau anticipates this idea of a woven fabric when he suggests that two series of ideas overlap in Qohelet: one revolves around the vanity of life (as in Job); the other consists of maxims like those in Proverbs (Lusseau finds these "maxims" much briefer than the ideas related to vanity, but I disagree with him; see pp. 147-48). Lusseau thus finds "soliloquies" and "maxims." But, on the one hand, these are not soliloquies, but rather expressions that follow a definite expository method: Qohelet puts forward a common theme, then criticizes it. On the other hand, the contrast here occurs not in the literary form but rather in the substance of the book. We can make a diagram of the interweaving in Qohelet:

37. Cited in Scholem, pp. 85, 109-11.

Vanity	Wisdom	God
1:1-11		
	1:12-18	
2:1-11		
	2:12-19	
2:20-23		
		2:24-26
	3:1-8	
3:9		
		3:10-17
	3:18-22	
4:1-16		
		5:1-7
	5:8-17	
		5:18–6:2
6:3-12		
	7:1-12	
		7:13-18
	7:19-25	
		7:26-29
	8:1-9	
8:10		
		8:11-13
8:14-18		
		9:1
	9:2-6	
		9:7-10
	9:11-18	
10:1-20		
		11:1–12:7
12:8		
	12:9	
		12:10-13

9. Contradiction as an Essential Principle of Qohelet

Here we return to one of the main difficulties in the interpretation of this mysterious book: its contradictions. These have led many writers to accuse Qohelet of incoherence, or to carve up the text. I find it remarkable that the different aspects of human life are not treated at all similarly in the various chapters. We cannot synthesize all the passages on money or wisdom, because the statements on these topics contradict each other. As we have seen, Qohelet contradicts himself continually. He affirms happiness is worthless, yet elsewhere maintains that the only thing a person can reasonably do with his life is to take joy and pleasure, and live as happily as possible. He declares that wisdom and folly are identical in the long run, but elsewhere finds that wisdom is more precious than all else. We find contradictions on each of the above subjects.

Such contradictions do not represent gross oversights; on the contrary, they may be one of the keys to the book. Sometimes we find an amazing consistency in biblical books written over centuries (as I have tried to show in *The Meaning of the City*), but at other times we find contradictions. Often these are not due to incompetent or negligent authors, but have the purpose of putting our backs to the wall, so that we must become aware of something different. Few books contradict themselves as much as this one, and I believe one of its main meanings resides precisely in these inconsistencies. They guide us to a point where we must recognize the true character of human existence, and not just its reality: human existence is essentially self-contradictory.

Qohelet's contradictions are more subtle than the issues we usually dwell on: the contradiction between humanity and God, sin and holiness, nature and revelation, for example. Our author does not deny these, but he penetrates deeper into life, into existence and society, bringing to the surface our unresolvable and incomprehensible contradiction, at absolutely every level.

Qohelet is not one of those desolate thinkers who lets his head and arms droop down, exclaiming "vanity," which we understand to mean "What's the use?" Qohelet is a skilled surgeon who opens wounds, including the one wound that dominates human life, and reveals the incredible confusion in our beliefs and assertions, our absolutes and our occupations. Unresolvable contradiction forms one of the guidelines of this book. No separation can be made between good and bad, between "true to God" and "untrue to God." All we are left with is contradictory human nature. This contradiction, surfacing at every turn, makes it possible to say "vanity" in a generalized way. But such a response does not amount to discouragement or surrender. On the contrary, Qohelet constantly exhorts us to live.

Consequently, instead of applying the principle of noncontradiction to this text, we must read and understand it on the basis of the principle of contradiction, which is the key to its mode of thinking. The meaning of the text resides precisely *in* the contradiction. We must interpret the two opposing views on that basis. Consider, for instance, the famous contradiction so often cited: the author of "All is vanity" cannot also have said "God creates and controls all." We will see how one side of this contradiction reveals the meaning of the other. The harshness and bitterness of "vanities" find their value, perspective, and true light in Qohelet's proclamation of the God of Israel. A superficial reading sees this proclamation as "sugar to make the pill go down," as a toning down of the text. But, on the contrary, this proclamation concerning God represents the sharpest point of the text, since it gives us a different revelation of the God of Israel.[38] Those who interpret the text's invocations of God as "sugar pills" seem to me to follow a presupposition that all invocation of God amounts to rather primitive, sentimental pietism.

We must get to the point where we understand that contradic-

---

38. Crenshaw takes up the rational interpretation: "Traditionists even found ways to incorporate a work that rejects everything they stood for. . . . Tradition found ways to baptize radical skepticism . . . by the addition of neutralizing observations" (p. 257). But Crenshaw sees correctly that the force of Qohelet lies precisely in his contradiction: "The effect of juxtaposing creedal affirmation and profound denial electrifies. . . . Concealed within the human shriek is an awful recognition that God alone in all the universe is worthy of supreme devotion. Precisely here resides the power of dogma and its opposite. In a word, truth resides in creed *and* in skepticism" (pp. 257-58). But why do many scholars fail to see this truth in the book?

tion alone can enable us to move ahead. The principle of noncontradiction relates to death. Contradiction is the necessary condition for communication. Only contradiction allows for understanding a person, and, finally, for union (not a fused unity!). *"Union between identical things is impossible. . . .* Only between contrary elements *(haphakim)* is there relation *(yaḥas)*, activity *(peʿullah)*, and association *(shittuph)."*[39] This is the lesson Qohelet teaches!

Finally, as Jürgen Moltmann points out, contradiction squares with Miguel de Unamuno's "tragic sense of life," which is "a fundamental existential experience, for it is the experience of the death of human existence. 'Life is a tragedy, and a tragedy is a perpetual struggle without victory or hope of victory—simply a contradiction.' "[40] All of Qohelet parallels this thought. "Everything living is involved in this contradiction and is only alive as long as it is involved in it" (Moltmann, p. 36). For this reason Qohelet progresses by moving from contradiction to contradiction. In this structure of the contradiction, I believe we have discovered one of the essential principles of Qohelet. For this reason I refer so often to *irony* and *paradox.*

We must go further, however. One of the serious flaws in the commentaries I have read (Vischer, Maillot, and Lüthi are fortunate exceptions) is their habit of reducing this entire problem concerning contradiction to a few simple, general ideas: everything is absurd and we are all searching for meaning in life. Some scholars err on the side of taking Qohelet's statements too positively: "he clears the ground, demolishes false wisdom, etc., to make way for grace." Such reasoning may satisfy the reader, but it involves a very dangerous generalization. The text does not say such things! Qohelet does not limit himself to affirmations or to general ideas.

39. André Neher, *Le Puits de l'exil: La Théologie dialectique du Maharal de Prague (1512-1609),* Présences du Judaïsme (Paris: Albin Michel, 1966), pp. 175, 176. Other references to Neher are to his previously cited book, *Notes sur Qoheleth,* unless otherwise noted.

40. Jürgen Moltmann, *The Trinity and the Kingdom: The Doctrine of God,* trans. Margaret Kohl (San Francisco: Harper & Row, 1981), p. 36. Cf. Miguel de Unamuno, *The Tragic Sense of Life in Men and in Peoples,* trans. J. E. Crawford Flitch (London: Macmillan, 1921).

As I already indicated, I do not take this book as a collection of maxims. Consequently, if we want to know what it says, we must carefully avoid the practice of most hurried readers, who conclude: "Ah, yes, of course. All is vanity! Money, wisdom, power, family, pleasure, glory, and youth." Having recognized this fact, they move on to something else. No, on the contrary, in this book the concrete reason for each statement is the important thing. The reader is convinced at every point by the inclusion of a given idea (on love or the future, for example) within the whole and within a given context, as related to a given perspective. In other words, we must not pay attention so much to general ideas or abrupt statements (e.g., "There is a righteous person who perishes with his righteousness," 7:15; or "Wisdom makes the sage stronger than ten authorities who are in the city," 7:19), as to what he shows us: "Look, this is how things are—I have seen them." Rather than scientific proof, Qohelet offers us his observations. We must observe how this evidence relates to a context that renders it beyond challenge, in spite of the fact that we have just read the opposite, two chapters before!

Qohelet does not say "All is vanity" because he has measured human achievement in the light of death (although he does that also). It would be extremely easy to arrive at such a conclusion this way. Every sophist has arrived at the same conclusion. No need for great wisdom to see the point. Still less does such a notion have any place in the Word of God! The context of each word and the well-constructed whole are the important thing. The whole is designed with a view to highlighting human contradictions. Instead of memorizing the "conclusions," therefore, we should meditate on the connecting links of Qohelet's reasoning. These connecting links, I believe, constitute the second basic element in his weaving.

10. Qohelet and the Feast of Sukkot

To conclude this brief review of basic issues, I must add that Qohelet was one of the main readings during the days of the Feast of Sukkot, also known as the Feast of Booths or Tabernacles or Tents. The precise meaning of the term is "feast of thatched huts" or "booths." A many-sided event, celebrated in the fall as an agrarian harvest festival (thus the thatched huts, for the grape harvesters), it became something completely different through gradual theological development.

After a time, this festival constituted a very complex affair: commemoration of the dedication of Solomon's temple, of the dedication of the Bethel sanctuary by Jeroboam after the division of the kingdom, and of the resumption of the cult in Jerusalem after the restoration of the altar. Three cultural events were thus involved, and many modern scholars consider the festival of the dedication of the temple and altar as the main focus. This background confirms that Qohelet is also a ritual book.

Another dimension exists, however: the festival of the rereading of the divine Law (by Ezra) and the festival presented in Zechariah as the celebration of the messianic age. The latter involved the proclamation of Yahweh's universal kingship, the manifestation of light, and the presence of living water in the heart of the city. Based on these different factors many scholars have come to see in this celebration the festival of the covenant: a time when the people of God were faced with the divine requirements.[41] But how can we forget that it was also a royal celebration intended to affirm God's acceptance of the monarchy? This celebration finally came to be known as the "festival of the Lord."

What shall we conclude from the fact that the entire celebration is called by the name of "booths," and later, "tabernacles"? This name shows the connection between the celebration and the long, complicated journey of the people, the time when Israel lived in tents and confronted the desert. So the Feast of Sukkot commemorates their march through the place of testing, tempta-

---

41. See Albrecht Alt, "The Origins of Israelite Law," in *Essays on Old Testament History and Religion*, trans. R. A. Wilson (Garden City, NY: Doubleday, 1967), pp. 164-67; Sigmund Mowinckel, *The Psalms in Israel's Worship*, trans. D. R. Ap-Thomas, 2 vols. (Oxford: Basil Blackwell, 1962), 2:63-69; Gerhard von Rad, *Old Testament Theology*, trans. D. M. G. Stalker, 2 vols. (New York: Harper & Row, 1962-65), 1:17-18, 89.

tion, and deprivation: the desert—the place where they entered the dangerous sphere of freedom, where "everything is possible." The desert represents the time separating what was already given (liberation from Egypt) and what was not yet a reality (the promised land).

I believe we must read all of Qohelet in connection with each of the meanings of the Feast of Booths: as the royal book of Solomon; the book of the dedication of the temple; the book of an astonishing covenant; the book of the fragility of human shelter (the thatched hut); the book of the vanity of everything people possess (the desert); the book of God's absolute kingship. At the same time, however, it is the book of the end of the productive season (autumn) and of the beginning of winter. In spite of this, the people are joyful at this time and engage in a week of festivities. Thus Qohelet reminds the people of the vanity of these festivities in themselves. Through the very complexity of its symbols, the book also reminds them of the mystery of God's working, the meaning of which escapes us creatures.

How can anyone say that the parts concerning God have been "added on" to an originally skeptical book, in the midst of this central proclamation concerning the Lord at the Feast of Sukkot? Qohelet's presence at Sukkot thus testifies both to the covenant and to the wandering in the desert, to the instability of the wandering people and to their concentration around Jerusalem and the temple. The book involves the discovery that only by passing through the experience of such vanity can people enter into a covenant with the God who gives everything: harvest and grape gathering, as well as the temple and the Law. This discovery also involves a dimension that is hard to understand (because it works by opposition): the proclamation of a messianic era that includes all the times Qohelet enumerates.

At this point we have considered the first series of themes in Qohelet. Now let us look at the second series. The "booths" become home for seven days. The reader could profitably examine the admirable meditation of Albert Hazan on the seven nights of Sukkot, in which we learn how every Israelite each night welcomes one of the "sacred guests of [his] past history": Abraham, Isaac,

Jacob, Joseph, Moses, Aaron, David.[42] Abraham, who incarnates the virtue of love; Isaac, severity (hard virtue); Jacob, the man who hugged and cried, faced with unceasing provocation; Joseph, exile and the kingdom; Moses, the seal of Israel's eternity; Aaron, the great priest who can utter the unutterable name. Aaron thus unifies humanity, space, and time (Hazan, p. 177). Because of Aaron, "even under the reign of war you cannot eliminate Shalom, you cannot extricate yourself from the imperatives of peace" (Hazan, p. 182, quoting the Maharal of Prague). Finally, David, "the great Hosanna, the great salvation" (Hazan, p. 195). He marks the beginning of the proclamation of salvation. One must never forget these seven luminaries when reading Qohelet, since they also illuminate it.

No chance or historical accident is involved in the choice of Qohelet as a reading for this decisive week in the life of Israel. He speaks of nothing and of everything: heaviness and grace; zero and the infinite. Qohelet is spoken and proclaimed (rather than *read* individually!) for all the people during the festival of restlessness and duality. Amazingly, this Festival of Sukkot, after seven days, gives way to an eighth and final day, really a night, of special festivity, called *simhat torah,* "joy in the Torah"—as if this reading of Qohelet ought to lead to a celebration of joy.[43]

Sukkot is the Festival of Booths or Huts: temporary, fragile shelters. Each person must erect his "ridiculous sukkah [hut] under the stars, in order to shelter life and joy in life, because the Torah recommends that I remove restraint during the week of Sukkot— that I give myself over to joy" (Hazan, p. 69). In this festival of fragility and the precariousness of human shelter, Israel understood that only God protected her. All security, all solid foundations, were called into question once a year. "When civilizations stagger and die, it is not because they are so old they can no longer respond to the challenges history flings at them, not because they have ceased innovating. They die because they have utterly surrendered their

42. Albert Hazan, *Yom Kippour: Guerre et prière* (Jerusalem: Koumi, 1975), p. 75.

43. Lys emphasizes that the feast of Sukkot is a time of celebration and rejoicing, and that Qohelet commends joy (see pp. 79-80, 186).

future to *their own* granite-solid foundations. They have staked everything exclusively on the rigidity of the 'original' meanings of their myths. 'Egypt's error, the error of the nations,' is that they did not move their belongings into a simple hut, for a week's time, once a year" (Hazan, p. 67).

In this light, we see clearly the essential link between Qohelet and Sukkot. What book speaks more eloquently of this fragility, challenges everything, requires we examine our conscience, sweeps away all our rock-solid certainties? It leaves us alone with our precarious destiny, stripped bare to experience the only genuine security: the security offered by the sovereign Master of history.

Any study on vanity must be placed under the heading of Georges Bernanos's words:

"In order to be prepared to hope in what does not deceive, we must first lose hope in everything that deceives."

This is Qohelet's whole message.

CHAPTER II

Themes of Vanity:
Vapor, Smoke, Unsubstantiality, Fragility, and Evanescence

I saw that the meaning of life was to make a living, its goal to become a councilor, that the rich delight of love was to acquire a well-to-do girl, that the blessedness of friendship was to help each other in financial difficulties, that wisdom was whatever the majority assumed it to be, that enthusiasm was to give a speech, that courage was to risk being fined ten dollars, that cordiality was to say "May it do you good" after a meal, that piety was to go to communion once a year. This I saw, and I laughed.[1]

1. The First Word

Qohelet's first word stops us in our tracks (1:1-3)! How shall we translate *hebel*? Traditionally, over the centuries, the word has been translated as "vanity." But about twenty years ago, some scholars

---

1. Søren Kierkegaard, *Either/Or,* Part I, ed. and trans. Howard V. Hong and Edna H. Hong (Princeton: Princeton University Press, 1987), p. 34.

got the idea that its original, literal meaning was "vapor." This same word gives us Abel's name: vapor or mist. Scholars have emphasized this meaning of the word within the general context of "materializing" biblical interpretation. Earlier, we had the "spiritualizing" interpretation, related to a generalized idealist philosophy. Then the most specific biblical words, even coarse language, were transposed into a vocabulary filled with spiritual meaning. *Ruah* provides us with the most classic example: the word means "breath" or "wind," but was translated "spirit." Now that the trend has moved to materialist thought, we observe the opposite tendency! Scholars try to bring everything down to a concrete, material concept. Often they take texts from the Prophets or the Gospels and render them as trite sayings, so as to make them more common and relevant. At times this process coarsens and disparages texts for no good reason.

Translating *ruah* these days by "breath" is not preferable to the previous tendency to translate it by "spirit." Following the common trend, many scholars now translate *hebel* as "vapor." Does this translation represent an improvement? After all, the word also has a figurative meaning in Hebrew. We Westerners did not invent this meaning of "vanity." Why, then, should translators decide to write "vapor of vapors"? Personally, I fail to understand what such a phrase could mean.

Chouraqui prefers "smoke": "smoke of smoke, all is smoke" (pp. 113-14; unfortunately, this time I disagree with him). But he justifies his choice: "Vanity is 'something devoid of value.' To speak of 'vanity' implies a value judgment concerning a given reality. *Hebel* is a concrete word. . . . Qohelet makes no value judgment concerning reality. He makes an observation: all is smoke. The word must be taken, in Hebrew and in French, in its double meaning, both concrete and figurative. Concretely, everything proceeds from the original smoke, and everything returns to it. From this process we get the figurative meaning of the word, which designates any fleeting, vanishing reality. Qohelet takes his place . . . within the order of objective observations" (pp. 113-14). I disagree with this interpretation. In the first place, as with "vapor," I fail to see the meaning of "smoke of smoke." All I see in it is a silly redundancy. All this talk about original smoke is the rage nowadays: order born from disorder, between crystal and smoke, etc. But I cannot see that this idea has anything to do with Qohelet's content. The argument that we should reject "vanity," because the term implies a value judgment, so that one would not begin an action recognized as "vain," seems pointless. Qohelet makes judgments continually!

Indeed, the word *hebel* does imply a judgment rather than just an observation of "how things are." Saying that wealth is *hebel* amounts to a value judgment. How many times do we read the words "This is an evil under the sun," or "This is an evil task, an evil work"? We could multiply such examples. We noted above that Qohelet seems to give us a view of human reality revealed by God rather than the cold and objective description of what concretely exists. If we accept this view, how can we deny the presence of "judgments" of approval in the book? Of course, this is not the same thing as a value judgment in the strict philosophical sense, as we usually understand it. We are not talking about a scale of values: Qohelet does not offer us a dissertation on the things we might do well to appreciate. Rather, we find in Qohelet a certain connotation attached to every human work and activity, so that the false meanings attributed to work, money, etc., are eliminated. He gives us the means to measure each reality.

Finally, on this point I will follow the excellent exegetical work by Jacques Chopineau.[2] Jerome already recognized that *hebel* is commonly translated by "vapor, smoke, a faint breath quickly diffused." We find the same terms in the Babylonian Talmud, in Aramaic: "breath, nothingness," etc. Yet in the Septuagint we find the translation "vanity." Chopineau believes we can discover the word's meaning only by comparing similar words: "a linguistic element has . . . true meaning only within a given context and a given situation."[3] Thus he proceeds to study all the texts where *hebel* occurs, establishing the pattern of its relationships with other

2. Jacques Chopineau, "Hèvèl en hébreu biblique: Contribution à l'étude des rapports entre sémantique et exégèse de l'Ancien Testament," doctoral dissertation, University of Strasbourg, 1971.

3. Chopineau, p. 18, citing André Martinet, *Elements of General Linguistics,* trans. Elisabeth Palmer (London: Faber and Faber, 1964), p. 44. See also Chopineau, pp. 8-17.

"rival" words. In any case, this word has a diversity of meanings and a very rich power of suggestion.

We must remember that, as author of a later book, Qohelet knows how *hebel* was used in Job, the Psalms, and Genesis 4. He reads the Genesis passage, including Abel's name, in the light of the others! The tabulation of words used in association with *hebel* is quite revealing: in Isaiah, we find all the words indicating fruitless effort, illusion, idols, and death, but also wind and breath. In Jeremiah, the word is found almost always in association with idols, idolatrous practices, everything involving nothingness.[4] This relationship is so constant that we can say that *hebel* in the plural designates idols. Qohelet knows all this. We could perhaps translate "vanity of vanities," then, as "vanity of idols," or "idols are wind"! In any case, in Qohelet as in Isaiah, everything concurs to suggest the idea of uselessness. This idea is so strong that we might conclude that *hebel* suggests the idea of nothingness: from the point of view of reality, unsubstantiality; from the point of view of the truth, a lie; from the point of view of efficiency, uselessness; and from the point of view of security, deceit.

In Job, *hebel* means essentially something illusory because it is fleeting, deceptive, and without result. We find this regularly in the Psalms also. But of course, we also find *hebel* related to *ruah* in the sense of faint breath, light wind (mist, vapor?). We do not usually find these terms used as synonyms in Qohelet, since he wants to put *hebel* in a dazzlingly preeminent position. But he is clearly familiar with all the former usages of the word.

At this point a debate occurs: for some scholars the primitive meaning of *hebel* was abstract (to be translated "vanity"), and gradually it became more concrete. In Qohelet's time, it meant only "mist, smoke, breath." Such a development would be astonishing, since it goes counter to the normal evolution of the meaning of words, from the concrete to the abstract.

For other scholars, on the contrary, the primitive meaning of the word was concrete, and it gradually became abstract and sym-

4. Lauha specifies that the word *hebel* has a nearly specialized use in the polemic against foreign gods in Deuteronomy, Kings, and the Prophets (p. 18).

bolical. In this case, one would translate sometimes by "wind," and other times by "uselessness, vanity." But I think Lys (who translates it as "smoke") is right to insist on the fact that this translation does not amount to "nothingness" or "zero." Smoke or mist diffuses; *it has no result:* it is not nothingness! Furthermore, Chopineau studies the word's context in Qohelet, and finds "evil": the evil that one observes, speaks of, commits, or suffers: the pains one takes in doing work or the physical pain one feels. These expressions suggest the illusory effort to which all human activity is reduced, so that such activity is an evil! Nothing remains. But we cannot call our activity "nothingness," since a small part of it lives on: joy (2:10; 3:22; 5:18; etc.). Existence supposedly contrasts with joy, yet underneath joy still exists!

Chopineau also shows another significant aspect of this word: that "all is *hebel.*" But this "all" is One. A single destiny remains for everything and everybody. Only one breath, which is vain: everything is heading toward the same place. This globality forms a unity: "I have tried everything," "All people," etc. Thus the All is One, and enclosed within *hebel,* which reduces everything to One.

Another essential point: *hebel* also expresses destiny. Clearly, the whole book of Qohelet is affected by the presence of death (Maillot originally entitled his commentary "Brothers, we must die"). Everything is headed toward death. The wise person dies like the fool, people like animals, etc. *Hebel* appears like the word of destiny, in that it applies to all human activity. Everything is subjected to the same destiny of insignificance. Hence Chopineau decides finally to retain the traditional translation, "vanity," rather than following the trend of the most modern versions.[5] I believe he made the right choice. Chopineau says we must avoid translation with a concrete term such as vapor, mist, smoke, breath, etc., since these give more weight to the etymology of *hebel* than to its use in context. Furthermore, such concrete terms fail utterly to give us the equivalent of the Hebrew *hebel* in our language, which does not attach the same connotations to these words as Hebrew. This is

5. Lauha also translates *hebel* as vanity (p. 30; see pp. 18-19).

especially true because *hebel* in Qohelet is more than a word: it is a theme for meditation.

We must keep in mind the earlier usage and the context of Qohelet. The meaning of *hebel* in Genesis is especially important, since Qohelet continually refers to Genesis. We see, then, that *hebel* evolved from a concrete to an abstract meaning: it is a "lexicalized metaphor." Its concrete sense occurs in Syriac and Aramaic, but such references do not prove that the word remained concrete in Hebrew. Neither do the numerous parallels in various languages (mentioned by Lys, p. 89), in which a word with the same root means "vapor," "breath," etc.

We must not give these primitive meanings precedence; but neither can we eliminate them. Consequently, we must hang on to *both meanings:* the concrete and the abstract. Mist: everything dissipates like a mist that rises from the ground in the morning and disappears in the sun. This meaning relates to reality, as long as we limit it to reality—but a reality in the process of transformation. And vanity: that is, it is vain to commit oneself to one path rather than another, to look for gain in this or that. We must say "vain"; "devoid of value" is not sufficient.

"Vanity" is stronger than "devoid of value." First, vanity is illusion. One follows a mirage (note the direct relationship with "mist"!), labors under illusions, envelops reality in them. Next, vanity is ostentation (related to illusion!): we present ourselves in such a way that we create illusions in the minds of others. Our exterior, the front we put up, fools them. A woman with makeup, a man wearing a mask—both indulge in vanity. Throughout his book, Qohelet pulls off masks and lays illusions bare. In this sense, vanity also involves taking oneself seriously, being fooled by one's mask, becoming vain in the midst of other people. For this, Qohelet offers us a mirror: look at yourself as you really are; what remains of your overblown self-satisfaction?

Finally, vanity applies to things with no solution, no future— utterly useless things. Qohelet says of them: "What's the use? You work, enter politics, earn money . . . and then? *Finally,* what good do you get out of all this? Is it vain or not? Is it useful *(in truth)* or useless?" For this reason, I prefer to translate *hebel* by "vanity," provided we also keep in mind the ideas of mist, vapor, and smoke.

I fail to see in what sense this approach contradicts *hebel* as a tragic notion (see Neher, p. 72). Qohelet's is indeed a tragic proclamation of the vision of everything as both transitory and without value. I repeat, however, that he does not say everything is "nothing" or "emptiness." "Vanity" gives precisely the sense we need here: it tells us that our destiny is primarily characterized by failure. Nevertheless, when we use the word "destiny," it in no way implies the idea of *ananke, fatum,* or *moira.* Destiny is not God, or above God; rather, it comes from us, and is in us. It is part of our condition. Qohelet tells us that destiny may be known, but not mastered.

The diversity of these viewpoints appears even more significant when we consider that Qohelet fails to ask at least one question: "What is the use of a thing?" From our utilitarian perspective, this is always the first question. But Qohelet does not take the utilitarian position; he does not ask "What is the use of work or money?" The basic vanity of the things of life goes much deeper than concrete usefulness or uselessness. True, referring to work, he asks: "What good [or what advantage] does the person who works get out of it?" But Qohelet's question has nothing in common with the utility of technique or economics.

Why does Qohelet fail to ask this question? Not because it is strictly foreign to his culture, but because it is strictly foreign to God's revelation to Israel! I believe this distinction we have observed is a fundamental one. On the one hand, then, I think Qohelet takes exception to our modern question: "What is a thing good for?," in the sense of daily utilitarianism. On the other hand, he asks the question: "What's the use?"—"What profit is there for us in all our work?" (1:3). This same questioning comes up continually, throughout the book. "What advantage does a person get from this?" But this is not the same question as a thing's usefulness. Qohelet does not concern himself with gain in the sense of money (he had all he needed, and spent large sums). Rather, he has in mind the possibility or impossibility of answering the basic question about meaning.

In order to grasp clearly the difference between our modern

question ("What is a thing good for?") and Qohelet's question ("What does it profit?"), all we have to do is change the word "What" to "Who(m)." *Whom* is it good for? This is precisely the teaching of our texts. The first concern has to do with "Who?": the person, the one who acts, the living one. Qohelet has absolutely no interest in the "What?": the neuter, objective, established, or acquired thing, the means. For us, this primacy of the object predominates. Qohelet displaces our questions; throughout his reflection, "displacement" describes what he is about. This baffles us as much as any of his other accomplishments. "What profit for a person?" means "How can one become more of a person, and how can one answer the questions that are inevitably asked?" We will run into this question constantly. And just as constantly we will encounter the negative answer: the thing we are talking about is useless for finding wisdom or going beyond death.[6]

The first verse of Qohelet has still more surprises in store for us. First, when we hear "vanity of vanities," we find the expression moving. But what does it mean? Actually, Hebrew normally expresses the superlative in this manner (Lys, p. 90, etc.). It is a kind of absolute superlative (this idea is confirmed by the word "all"): absolutely vanity, vanity without exception.

This absolute superlative construction preserves "vanity of

---

6. Lys rightly emphasizes realism and pragmatism when he summarizes this problem of Qohelet under the phrase "What gain?" ("What profit is there for us in all our work?," 1:3). "The root *ytr* designates what else remains: the surplus . . . , the difference between the effort and the product" (p. 97). We find this root 18 times in the book, an indication of the importance of the issue. Lys also rightly dismisses Dahood's idea that this notion of profit shows it was written in a commercial environment (p. 97). How simplistic! However, I am not at all sure that "Can life be a good deal?" is the basic question of the book, its reason for being written. For me, Qohelet does not see this as the heart of the problem. He poses the question, however, and follows it through, precisely because it is the question everyone has, on the very simple level of immediate experience. But Qohelet questions something else: throughout his development, we notice he shifts the argument onto different ground. He seems to displace the center from this first, natural question, toward a renewing of the whole field of inquiry. From the question of gain or profit, the center of interest shifts to "for nothing" (one serves God for nothing).

vanities" from suggesting any *value* judgment. There is no more or less, no scale of values, more or less "valid." Here, everything is vanity, so that when I take hold of the sheaf, when I gather together everything about humanity and its activities, I can say that I have a bundle of vanities. Thus, vanity of vanities, the sheaf itself is vanity. Among all these things, I find only vanity; I survey it all, and it is a vanity among vanities.

Thus the phrase has a double explanation: as an absolute superlative and also as a genitive construction: "vanity" describes all vanities. If we accept this construction as a genitive, this understanding involves remarkable consequences. Declaring that "all is vanity" can be in itself another vanity. But the construction can also suggest the negation of negations, the disappearance of disappearances, the end of ends, the death of death, and finally, the vanishing of vanity or vanities.

Such a conclusion would prohibit the search for a limit to vanity. This idea comes from the text itself: "*All* is vanity." Consequently, no more distinctions can be made! Qohelet demands that we drop all sorts of distinctions: what is useful vs. what is useless, real needs vs. artificial needs, things of value vs. things without value, meaning vs. lack of meaning, what is legal vs. what is illegal, the righteous person vs. the unrighteous, just war vs. unjust war, the class that moves with history vs. the class condemned by history— all is vanity. *Under the sun* there is no differentiation (we will return to this limitation).[7] Except for this proviso, we must harbor no

7. Lys tells us that this expression, "under the sun," occurs 29 times in Qohelet, but nowhere else in the Old Testament (p. 102). It means something like "under heaven," or "in this world"; in the terrestrial universe, but not beyond it. This is the sphere of the person who makes no claim to have God's realm in view. "Locating" God in heaven does not indicate the place where he might be found, but his utter transcendence and inaccessibility. Some scholars have seen a Greek influence in the phrase "under the sun." Although it is true that a comparable Greek expression exists, the Egyptians, the Babylonians, and the Phoenicians also had similar images. Thus the figure is as Semitic as it is Greek. Where the sun shines is where human observation and investigation are possible. But the sun cannot illumine what would give meaning to human life and work. Such enlightenment can come only from the outside.

illusions. Only one class or category exists. We have no frontiers to
stake out, no concessions to grant. We will see this again, for
example, when we note how for Qohelet evil is concrete rather than
ideal or theoretical. Everything, under the sun, is enclosed within
the category of vanity.

Qohelet's judgment, however, is not the vain harangue of
someone who is by nature a pessimist. The author does not make
this judgment on his own. He tries to make intelligible the secret
that the wise person should receive from God. But at every turn the
author rams up against the same wall; all his experience, searching,
and reflection lead to the same conclusion: either there is no
wisdom, and everything is vapid, in which case the search for the
secret of the universe is chasing after wind. Or else wisdom exists
but cannot be communicated, in which case all is vanity, since
nothing has meaning—except for knowing that there is a meaning
we search for in vain.

I believe we must also take the relationship with Abel into
account. *Hebel* is the Hebrew word we translabe as "Abel." When
Qohelet read Genesis 4, clearly he knew all the meanings of the
word. Abel was mist, breath, or smoke that melts away; his name
predicted all the rest of his tragic life. He was not created to survive,
vanquish, or have posterity; he was innocent and righteous, and he
died. (Don't we read "Abel the righteous" in Heb. 11:4? The modern
works attempting to show that Abel was unrighteous and
thoroughly deserved what poor Cain did to him appear to me as
tortuous justifications of present-day humanity; they run up against
the indisputable judgment of Heb. 11:4.) Abel was executed by his
brother. It was in his name. I believe we must take this example into
account in order to understand Qohelet's message.

All is vanity, but not just in the sense we have detected. Beyond
what we have seen, all is Abel: that is, condemned beforehand, just
like Abel. Everything bears Abel's name. Here we see an aspect of
Qohelet's intransigence: everything that we see as power, grandeur,
success—all this belongs in advance to the category of vanity. It is
all condemned to disappear, to vanish, without any kind of posterity.

However, Abel is also righteous and godly: he offered a sacrifice. That also was useless. The righteous one died, assassinated.

He did nothing to deserve his fate, but he vanishes. Nothing of him remains—neither his piety nor his religiosity. In this as well, Abel is a model. You will not avoid death, suffering evil at the hand of others, or assassination. In the last analysis, you will not even avoid being the cause that provokes your assassination, because of your piety and sacrifices. All of us belong to Abel's race, not because he was weak and innocent, but because he was condemned to die and disappear—even the Cains, those who acquire power, weaponry, and domination. Qohelet has the capacity to show us that Cain and Abel form an inseparable couple within vanity's realm. Therefore, Abel's name is associated with this first step in Qohelet's determined march through the totality of the human domain.

Neher, indeed, shows that *hebel* designates *primarily* a person rather than a thing (pp. 71-91). In choosing this word, Qohelet binds destiny to the myth of someone who from the outset was given a role. Abel was born "a brother, a footnote to someone else. Something already existed before he came into being. . . . What . . . welcomes [Abel] at his birth" is what finally will kill him (Neher, pp. 74-75). Abel is breath and mist, beginning with his birth. His whole destiny is to disappear. His name coincides with his person: the mist rises (like his sacrifice) and disappears! Abel's "disappearance is complete: he dies childless" (Neher, p. 76). Abel has nothing, and no longer amounts to anything. But "God hears the voice of Abel's blood" (Neher, p. 77). That too we may see in Qohelet.

Neher goes on: Cain acquires and possesses. "Cain is permanence, whereas Abel is collapse. Whereas nothing remains of Abel, more always belongs to Cain" (p. 79). Cain is a person who acquires. Remarkably, Neher shows that Cain is also present in Qohelet, in chapter 2: when all the great works are described, they are designated by the verb *qanah* (2:7), the root of the name "Cain" (Heb. *qayin*). His name means "Faustian desire for pleasure" (Neher, p. 81) and power (we find the word again in 2:11).

Qohelet declares that Cain's great accomplishments of acquisition also are *hebel:* Abel, or vanity! Actually, we all are children of Abel. Seth, representing all of humanity, replaces Abel. "All is a striving after wind" is interpreted by Neher: "Under the sun, all of us are companions of Abel: as substitutes for his children, we walk with him and represent him" (p. 86). This idea gives us the key, Neher believes, to a difficult verse, which he translates: "I have seen all who live, who walk under the sun: with the second child, the one who stands in his place" (4:15). So all who live walk with Abel, and with Seth, who stands in his place. In this fashion, Qohelet sees all humanity in the person of Abel, and consequently, no faith in humanity is any longer possible.

2. The Myth of Progress

Progress does not exist. Here we find Qohelet's first great certainty (1:4-10). The identification of history with nature in this passage constitutes a terrible judgment. We usually think the contrary. The sun rises and sets, rushing eagerly toward its dwelling place; once there, it rises again. It remains the same. The wind heads south, then turns northward, only to return again to the south. The rain drains into the sea, but the sea is not filled up: the rain begins again from the sea.[8] This seems like a trite observation.

However, it is not trite for Lys, who sees in it a desacralization of the sun: "This verse emphasizes, then, (1) the ridiculous side of this sun-slave, of which no god can be made . . . ; (2) the sun's repetition as desperate rather than salutary as in the mystery religions, which try to escape the misfortune of history; (3) the sun is involved, rather than fire (i.e., unlike fire, the sun is not an eternal element, but an exhausted creature in a tired and tiring world). The sun's work appears to have no meaning, and is apparently absurd" (p. 113).

Podechard insists correctly that here we have a continual beginning over again rather than a circular movement (pp. 235-41). In that case, Qohelet points to the lack of meaning in this perpetual movement. What is the point in beginning something useless all

---

8. We should point out Qohelet's unusual knowledge in this passage: he writes as if he knew that water evaporates from the ocean and then rains on the land, thus feeding the rivers!

over again? Maillot underlines the stability of nature in this passage, in contrast with human fragility (p. 15).

Lys, however, makes the most extreme point based on this passage: "Qohelet uses Greek myths about humanity (Sisyphus, the Danaides) to ridicule Greek speculation concerning the elements.... Qohelet's demystification follows two lines of thought: (1) the explication of the world based on what constitutes it is insufficient; (2) the universe does not concern itself with human affairs. Those elements of the universe that move lack meaning just as much as human beings do. These elements simply move about without consequence, like the succession of human generations" (p. 118).

This recognition of rhythm in nature constitutes more than a trite observation. It is also the discovery that nature is not characterized by unchanging permanence, since it is subject to insignificant change. The wind whirls about like someone insane. Perhaps people were seeking a solid reference point outside religious myth. Qohelet informs us in passing that nature cannot provide this reference point. People may look for permanence, but nature is also subject to impermanence.

Qohelet jumps from this "trite" observation concerning the cycles of nature to humanity (he could have added the seasons). Words become wearisome. A person gets to the point where he cannot talk any more, but the eye does not get its fill of seeing, nor the ear of listening. This is the first step: as creators or producers of speech (of truth? of information?), we are limited: we reach a stopping point. But in our reception, as consumers, we are unlimited: we keep on looking and listening. This "consumer persistence" does not signify change or progress, however.

Here we have the point of departure for a basic reflection. Qohelet gives the image of a "natural" order here, at the beginning of his book. Nature obeys a rhythm. In itself, it is an order. Nevertheless, the entire argument that follows is devoted to revealing that the order (and the wisdom) we believe in (the order of our work) is in reality disorder. Order in the sociopolitical world is merely an appearance of order, revealed effectively as disorder by Qohelet's *paradoxical* thought. Only a paradoxical way of thinking could achieve this.

Finally, Qohelet's thought leads to the only possible conclusion: "Remember your Creator. . . . Fear God" (12:1, 13). Here we find true order. In this connection I cannot help but recall Kierkegaard's passage from the aesthetic stage to the ethical. His "alternate culture" serves as a wonderful illustration of most of Qohelet's themes (although Kierkegaard fails to mention him here). Kierkegaard's amazing analysis of anxiety corresponds precisely to vanity; and his refusal of all hope gives us a precise parallel for "pragmatic pessimism." Nothing is worth anything; we must on no count hold public office, or arbitrarily enjoy anything. All that is vain. "Something accidental is made into the absolute."[9] Qohelet reveals the same confusion. This will stay with us, until we reach the reference to the only absolute that is not accidental. But in the meantime, things will merely repeat themselves. We listen, but in the end, we always hear the same words.

Today we are tempted to label this as simple-minded wisdom, rather trite and outmoded. "What has been is what will be, and what has been done is what will be done: there is nothing new under the sun. There may be something of which it is said: 'Here is something new!' It already existed in the centuries which preceded us" (1:9-10). This seems utterly untrue, and especially so in our time. Nothing has ever been seen to equal our inventions! What about electricity, and the splitting of the atom?

But there is no point in enumerating the discoveries of science and the applications of technique! Today everything is new: we have economic crises without precedent, a new standard of living, medicine, a population explosion, political regimes, etc. I could solve this problem ironically by recalling, for example, Edgar Allan Poe's wonderful "Some Words with a Mummy."[10] Having awakened a mummy, scholars think they can dazzle him by showing him all that has been discovered since his time. But each time the mummy explains disdainfully that the thing was very well known

---

9. Kierkegaard, *Either/Or,* 1:299. See also 1:282-300; 2:157-333.

10. Thomas Ollive Mabbott, ed., *Collected Works of Edgar Allan Poe: Tales and Sketches, 1843-1849* (Cambridge, MA: Belknap/Harvard University Press, 1978), pp. 1175-1201.

three thousand years before Christ. Then suddenly he changes his tune because Dr. Ponnonner asks if the Egyptians "had comprehended, at *any* period, the manufacture of either Ponnonner's lozenges, or Brandreth's pills"—unknown items in the mummy's time (pp. 1194-95)!

Qohelet, of course, is nobody's fool. When he writes that there is nothing new, in the third century before Christ, he knows perfectly well that there have been new things, in the Near East where he lives, over the previous three thousand years! The wheel, irrigation, agriculture, navigation, the taming of animals, etc. Progress has been continuous. Qohelet knows all this, of course. Progress did not take place then as fast as today, but it was just as basic for humanity's future.

Yet Qohelet says there is nothing new under the sun. Undoubtedly, he does not have the above sort of progress in mind. He is not talking about science and technique, or gadgets. He speaks of humanity, as we see in 1:8. Remember that in the middle of the nineteenth century, a period with bustling progress, at the time when Marx based everything on his certainty concerning progress, we find the expression of the common conviction: "Something new, something new, even if not of this world!"[11]

It is impossible to find anything new. We travel, admiring what we see: changing landscapes, the wonders of the world, differing light and customs. Travelers' eyes (or, more likely, their cameras, in our time) are filled with new things. But if we look deeper, our response changes: everywhere, the men are hard conquerors, pitiless and cruel. Women are vile slaves. Charles Baudelaire comments: "We saw everywhere, without seeking it, . . . / The tedious spectacle of immortal sin. . . . / 'That's the unchanging report of the entire planet.' "[12] For Baudelaire, only death offers a way out.

Should a present-day preacher dare to say such things theologians would put him sternly in his place. But Baudelaire repeats

---

11. Originally from Jean de La Fontaine, *Clymène* (1671).
12. From "The Voyage," in Charles Baudelaire, *The Flowers of Evil*, trans. William Aggeler (Fresno, CA: Academy Library Guild, 1954), pp. 459, 461 (lines 86, 88, 108).

Qohelet! Qohelet knows about shimmering decors: Solomon surely must have been as good at creating them as the Pharaohs or Louis XVI. But behind the decors we find the same scene, as in H. Hesse's *Steppenwolf*.[13]

Thus, according to Qohelet, the human race does not progress. We may develop more perfect instruments, pull more strings, engage in more activities. But we *are* nothing more. Our life does not change. We remain trapped in our condition, by our time and space. People today are no more intelligent than five thousand years ago. Nor are they more just, or superior in any other way. We are not even better informed, since today's mass learning is largely offset by what we lose with respect to nature, instinct, intuition, and relationships. Furthermore, the things we learn these days fail to become part of our culture or personality.

We citizens of lightning twentieth-century progress cannot make ourselves believe this warning, but it should lead us to take very seriously what is probably the fundamental question of our century: What is the effective cost of each step "forward"? What do we lose each time we think we gain something? What disappears with every invention? What new danger lurks in every technique? As Qohelet would say, what is the ultimate "profit"? Until we can respond thoroughly to these questions, we must stop talking in a way that exalts progress.[14]

No, those of us who live in the 1980s are in no way superior. We are not even new; we simply arrive and pass on. This is all we can say about ourselves—the same that was said about previous generations. We leave no trace after we are gone. No one remembers ancestors. True, we leave the traces of things we have used, but what about us and our generation? We will not be remembered by those who come after us (1:11). We must become aware of the signifi-

---

13. Hermann Hesse, *Steppenwolf,* trans. Basil Creighton, rev. Walter Sorell (London: Alan Lane, 1974; German ed. 1927).

14. See Jacques Ellul, "Réflexions sur l'ambivalence du progrès technique," *Revue Administrative* 18 (July-Aug. 1965) 380-91. Available in English in somewhat abridged form as "Note on the Theme: Technical Progress Is Always Ambiguous," appended to Ellul's "The Technological Order," trans. John Wilkinson, *Technology and Culture* 3/4 (Fall 1964) 394-421.

cance of this fact with respect to our triumphalist ideologies. As Christians, we need to recognize that we in no way "progress" toward the Kingdom of God. History does not produce the Kingdom. The Kingdom will not come when the world at long last is Christianized, converted, or when society becomes more just, etc.

This enormous heresy persists today, especially perpetuated by the works of Pierre Teilhard de Chardin, who believed that spiritual, religious, and cultural progress propel us toward the Kingdom of God—as if it were the normal result of our history, like a river emptying into the sea. Yet repeated warnings contradict this idea: the entire book of Revelation, Matthew 24, 2 Peter 3:10—all warn us that we are headed toward a final catastrophe that will annihilate the world and the Church, before the Kingdom of God appears in the new creation. First comes chaos, in which all our religions, piety, cultures, and institutions will collapse. No continuous progress follows the stages so carefully outlined by our good Father Teilhard!

Qohelet goes even further, however: not only does a passage from history to the Kingdom of God not exist, but there is no progress in the course of history. True, history exists. But as it unfolds, humanity by no means moves from an inferior to a truly superior stage. This challenges our entire Western society: both the common interpretation of societies and that of Marxism, based entirely on belief in progress (which Marx never criticized).

Let me repeat that the absence of progress does not result in sameness or stagnation. "What has been is what will be, and what has been done is what will be done" (Eccl. 1:9). These words do not amount to a *quantitative* or practical assessment, but, as we have said, a judgment concerning *being* ("What has been . . . what will be"), and the way people carry out their action—not the *means* of human action. There is an enormous change in the way Genghis Khan killed (with the saber) and our way (with nuclear bombs), but the behavior pattern is the same. Murder, envy, domination—these do not change. Truly, there is nothing new under the sun.

To use a classic distinction, we can have (quantitative) human *growth*, but this does not indicate (qualitative) human *development*. As noted earlier, we need to look at reality in terms of what God reveals to us. We may live in the "illusion of progress," but God's revealed truth shows us what it really amounts to.

At this point we run up against another objection: "After all," someone says (with great wisdom and a degree of condescension), "we have here a well-known philosophy widespread in ancient times—the cyclical view of history, corresponding to cycles in time." Then he may cite a number of Greek philosophers: empires and societies are born, develop, reach maturity, decline, and die. Then it all starts over again. But this is not what Qohelet says! He has not spoken of decline and renewal at all; he does not mention the classic example of vegetation. He does not give us the cyclical model. Even with respect to the sun and the streams, rather than pointing out their cyclical character, he shows the ceaselessness of the same motion. Qohelet does not follow the sun in its course and its rebirth—not at all. He observes the brute fact of its rising and setting. There is nothing new in what happens!

At this point Qohelet speaks of a person's identity with himself, rather than of the repetition of events or circumstances. Events change, as do the conditions of life and standards of living, but people are basically the same. Thus Qohelet does not point out a cycle, an "eternal return," but a line of time punctuated by varying or comparable events. These events are reduced to insignificance because of the sameness of life! If we think we have discovered something new, it is because we have forgotten what happened yesterday.

Qohelet enables us to challenge our ideology of progress, but he does not fall into the trap of the opposite ideology: the marvelous past, the former golden age, and humanity's present decline. That kind of thinking dominated an entire school of thought in Qohelet's day, but he avoids it: "Do not say: 'How is it that the old days were better than these?' It is not because of wisdom that you ask this question" (7:10). Qohelet simply refuses that point of view. He finds it absurd to believe in an original golden age, a blissful past. Instead, what is now is what used to be! No more, no less. Moreover, that past age has been forgotten, both in its reality and in its truth. We should not seek to turn the clock back, either individually or collectively.

We have not exhausted the complexity of Qohelet's thought at this point. In a move that seems contradictory, he takes special note of the unforeseeable. If what will be is what has already been, we should be able to foresee it. Not at all! First, there is no true memory (1:11) of the truth about what happened previously. When Qohelet tries to study everything that is done, he concludes that this is an evil occupation under the sun. You cannot draw any conclusion or lesson for the future from what happened in the past, because you know only the outer shell of things: piecemeal testimonies that enable us to tell stories but not to know the truth.

Everything is forgotten.[15] True, what was is what will be. But what was has sunk irreparably into oblivion, be it the life of a wise person or that of a fool, whether it was a good example or a bad one (2:16). If the person "who comes after" ends up repeating what was done previously, certainly he fails to realize it. His repetitious action does not result from reflection or knowledge (2:12). A successor, the coming generation, will be lord of everything, but we cannot know whether it will be wise or foolish. What we can be sure of, unfortunately, is that the new generation will in no way profit from our experience, which will be forgotten. Thus the future is unforeseeable, the past forgotten; only the present remains.

A second limitation awaits us. Only the present remains, but the Hebrew language *never* conjugates the verb "to be" in the present tense (indeed, many scholars maintain that the Hebrew verbal system has no tenses at all). No one can say, absolutely, in Hebrew, "I am" (except, appropriately enough, "He who Is"!). Therefore, although we have nothing left for our life except the present, we cannot even claim proudly that we have Being itself in the present. Nor do we possess eternity, as the trite saying might suggest ("eternity dwells in the present moment").

Does everything amount to nothingness, then, and does everything we undertake end up as nothing? No! Here we have Qohelet's

15. The basic theme of universal forgetfulness calls to mind Milan Kundera's *The Joke,* trans. David Hamblyn and Oliver Stallybrass (New York: Coward-McCann, 1969), in which he announces this terrible truth: "All men commit a double error: they believe that nothing of what they do will be forgotten, and at the same time that all will be forgiven. The truth is that *everything will be forgotten, but nothing will ever be forgiven*" (fresh translation—TRANS.). In this sense, Qohelet serves as a preface to the gospel.

answer for the first time, but he will repeat it often: "What was, is; what is to be, already has been; and God seeks what slips away" (3:15). God gathers up forgotten time, lost works, all that has taken flight. He gathers up what takes flight into the past as well as what takes flight into the future. He looks for it, and we can be sure he finds it.

God's memory is a fundamental constant, as F. Mussner has shown.[16] In God nothing is ever lost. He "remembers" individuals (Noah, Abraham, Samson, Jeremiah, etc.). He remembers the covenant; the rainbow is the sign of God's constant memory. He "remembers" his covenant with his people Israel (Ezek. 16:60; Ps. 105:8-11). This verb "to remember" has a "theological-historical" value, as Mussner explains. In the context of Ezekiel 16:60 (16:53-63), twice "there is talk of the 'turn of fate,' three times of 're-establishment' (of Sodom, Samaria, Jerusalem), five times of 'covenant.' . . . God 'remembers' his 'covenant' which he once concluded with Israel, and this remembering moves history, drives it forward, leads to the 'turn of fate' " in Israel's destiny. "The 'remembering' of God is the expression of his loyalty" (Mussner, p. 97). For this reason, nothing is ever lost. God seeks out what has disappeared.

God loses and forgets nothing, but we cannot say the same about ourselves! The New Testament uses the word "recapitulation," which may seem enigmatic to us.[17] This concept may lead us to say, in discouragement: "If we have to wait for the end of time, if everything depends on this recapitulation God is going to bring about, this 'additional inventory,' if nothing is in our hands and we can expect nothing to get better, if our triumphant progress in science and action amounts to nothing, why not let ourselves go and take a fatalistic attitude?"

I could respond negatively to this all too human question by referring the reader to the theology of grace. Everything is grace. This

16. Franz Mussner, *Tractate on the Jews: The Significance of Judaism for Christian Faith,* trans. Leonard Swidler (Philadelphia: Fortress Press, 1984), pp. 96-98.

17. See Jacques Ellul, *The Meaning of the City;* idem, *Apocalypse: The Book of Revelation,* trans. George W. Schreiner (New York: Seabury, 1977).

theology, rather than promoting passivity and giving up, encourages us to strong activism (as we see in Paul). But here we must remain with Qohelet. His response astonishes us, since he said so forcefully in the first chapter that nothing new exists, that everything is useless, there is no progress. Then immediately afterward, he commits himself profoundly: "I applied my heart to everything that is done under the heavens. . . . I have caused wisdom to grow and progress more than anyone before me. . . . I made my works great: I built houses for myself . . . I accumulated wealth . . . I became great," I developed the arts, "I obtained singers for myself, and human delights: a cupbearer and stewards" (1:13, 16; 2:4-9). The author undertakes all this after saying "There is no progress, no brilliant creation."

In other words, only an idiot or a proud person can be stopped in his tracks by observing the truth of vanity—because he hopes to make his name immortal, to change the course of events, or to change humanity. No contradiction is involved. On the contrary, as we will gradually see, profound consistency is evident here.

At this point of convergence, where people forget the past and cannot penetrate the future, the first "moral" lesson of Qohelet's wisdom comes to life: all that remains to us is the present. We must live in the present. Qohelet will repeat this point endlessly. We must not escape into memories of the past or into some glorious future. Today, you must be what you are. And that is all.

3. Meditation

Having experienced both the vapor of *hebel,* on the one hand, and the lack of progress, constituting a heavy burden, on the other, we may now proceed to a different level of reflection. Nothing new exists—what was yesterday will continue to be tomorrow. Yesterday is completely forgotten. It is as if this past had never existed. We have no way of knowing what will happen tomorrow; no foresight is possible.[18]

18. We will consider the impossibility of foresight in chapter III below.

Thus we can expect no "lesson from history." No "meaning of history" exists: to establish such a meaning we would need landmarks, reference points along the way, some sense of the past that would enable us to decide what to aim for in the future. But history does not repeat itself.[19] No situation is ever comparable to another. We can never calculate what we must do today by using yesterday's events as a crutch.

At the same time, there is nothing new under the sun. What will happen tomorrow is not new: we already experienced it yesterday. Everything changes, like the wind that shifts and whirls. One generation departs; another comes on stage. And that is all. The rivers move on, and then begin their course again. Each instant is a moment open to everything—everything and anything. One moment is never like another, and can never be renewed. Each is without origin and without a future, since its opposite is identical to it.[20]

The above statements obviously contradict each other, yet we cannot deny them. At this point we find ourselves faced with the dilemma Kundera has revived.[21] The "eternal return" is madness: "to think that everything recurs as we once experienced it, and that the recurrence itself recurs ad infinitum" (Kundera, p. 3)—that is insane. "If every second of our lives recurs an infinite number of times, we are nailed to eternity, as Jesus Christ was nailed to the cross. It is a terrifying prospect. In the world of the eternal return,

19. For a time scholars claimed to draw lessons from history, or to find comparisons and equivalents by examining historical periods and developments (A. Toynbee provided historians with a fascinating model; comparison of our modern age with the decline of the Roman empire was a tradition). But presently the opposite approach prevails: such comparisons and equivalents are seen as impossible; too many factors are at work, and we have too many "parameters" we cannot compare, too much diversity of mentality. Each culture is specific, and each age unique. No resemblance exists between what we can know about one period or another, unless we remain on a level of insignificant generalities.

20. In chapter IV we will study Qohelet's poem on "A Time for Everything."

21. What follows is based on Milan Kundera, *The Unbearable Lightness of Being,* trans. Michael Henry Heim (London: Faber and Faber, 1985).

the weight of unbearable responsibility lies heavy on every move
we make. That is why Nietzsche called the idea of eternal return the
heaviest of burdens" (p. 5).

But this myth tells us, negatively, "that life which disappears
once and for all, which does not return, is like a shadow, without
weight, dead in advance, and whether it was horrible, beautiful, or
sublime, its horror, sublimity, and beauty mean nothing" (p. 3). If
an event repeats itself an incalculable number of times, it becomes
a "solid mass, permanently protuberant, its inanity irreparable"
(p. 4).[22] But "if the eternal return is the heaviest burden, then our
lives can stand out against it in all their splendid lightness. But is
heaviness truly deplorable and lightness splendid? The heaviest of
burdens crushes us, we sink beneath it, it pins us to the ground"
(p. 5). But at the same time it is "an image of life's most intense
fulfillment. The heavier the burden, the closer our lives come to the
earth, the more real and truthful they become. Conversely, the
absolute absence of a burden causes [a person] to be lighter than
air, to soar the heights [like breath, vapor, Abel], take leave of the
earth and his earthly being, and become only half real, his move-
ments as free as they are insignificant. What then shall we choose?
Weight or lightness? Parmenides posed this very question" (p. 5),
which separated the world into two polarized camps: one positive
and the other negative.

"Which one is positive, weight or lightness? Parmenides re-
sponded: lightness is positive, weight negative. Was he correct or
not? That is the question. The only certainty is: the lightness / weight contradiction is the most mysterious, most ambiguous
of all" (pp. 5-6). And Qohelet places us precisely in the middle of
it. This contradiction crops up endlessly in connection with all
possible themes, until at last we arrive at the ultimate discovery.

Let us return to Kundera: if life does not repeat itself, if there
is no "eternal return," then each situation is new, and we must make
decisions without depending on the past. "There is no means of

22. We can choose any historical event, and see that it seems horrible,
once we know its effects. Who would choose to begin World War I, realizing
what it produced?

testing which decision is better, because there is no basis for comparison. We live everything as it comes, without warning, like an actor going on cold. And what can life be worth if the first rehearsal for life is life itself? That is why life always appears like a sketch. No, 'sketch' is not quite the word, because a sketch is an outline of something, the groundwork for a picture, whereas the sketch that is our life is a sketch for nothing, an outline with no picture" (p. 8).[23] Hence it is vanity.

Einmal ist keinmal: "what happens but once, says the German adage, might as well not have happened at all. If we have only one life to live, we might as well not have lived at all" (p. 8). "Unlike Parmenides, Beethoven apparently viewed weight as something positive" (p. 33). He associated the weighty resolution with the voice of Fate: *Es muss sein* (It must be). "Necessity, weight and value are three concepts inextricably bound: only necessity is heavy, and only what is heavy has value" (p. 33).

"But is not an event in fact more significant and noteworthy the greater the number of fortuities necessary to bring it about? Chance and chance alone has a message for us. Everything that occurs out of necessity, everything expected, repeated day in and day out, is mute. Only chance can speak to us. . . . Necessity knows no magic formulae—they are all left to chance. If a love is to be unforgettable, fortuities must immediately start fluttering down to it like birds to Francis of Assisi's shoulders" (pp. 48-49). What a mistake would be involved if we believed chance was comparable to lightness, or to the uniqueness of life or of an event. Nor is it true that chance is the opposite of destiny or necessity. We know, on the contrary, that, even without grace, chance and necessity unite.

Qohelet speaks of neither chance nor destiny. Yet in his tenacious struggle everything takes place as if he wanted to destroy both chance and necessity, left and right. As if he wanted to remove any

---

23. For this reason, no trial marriage can exist, for example, contrary to the foolish ideas of Margaret Mead. Marriage is not merely sleeping together, but the commitment of a whole life, until death, for better or for worse. Until this commitment has been made, no marriage exists; and when it has been made, there is no more "trial"!

hold they might have on existence. "Human life occurs only once, and the reason we cannot determine which of our decisions are good and which bad is that in a given situation, we can make only one decision; we are not granted a second, third or fourth life in which to compare various decisions!" (Kundera, p. 222). *"Einmal ist keinmal* [once is the same as never]. . . . History is as light as individual human life, unbearably light, light as a feather, as dust swirling into the air, as whatever will no longer exist tomorrow" (p. 223). This is the heart of the problem, the only question worth asking. And the question must be formulated the way Qohelet asks it.

Two sorts of people stand confronting each other. Those who accept this lightness of life and history (who must accept, nonetheless, that once is the same as never, and that all is vapor or vanity); and those who do not accept the lightness of life and history, but prefer solid foundations and wish to calculate history's path. With Beethoven, they repeat: *"Muss es sein? Es muss sein!"* ("Must it be? It must be!" See Kundera, p. 32.) Such people act as though history were a finished painting rather than a sketch, as though everything they did had to be repeated numberless times. They are convinced they are right and feel certain they will never question their acts. Qohelet radically challenges such people, however, because they are models of what we now call the totalitarian person.

The totalitarian person's mindless repetition is never affected by the slightest question. The only thing he does not know is that all is vanity! But opposite this totalitarian individual who never has the slightest doubt about anything, someone else struggles against the totalitarian regime (here we prepare for the following text, on the vanity of power!). The struggler stands armed with only questions and doubts; otherwise, he also would represent a truth and simplistic certainty. And in that case he would be just like his opponent.

Can we be sure that Abel, smoke, and vapor are negative designations? What about *habel hebalim* (vanity of vanities)? We have already mentioned that this does not mean "nothing is worth anything." Here, following Kundera, we reach a final test. Lightness provides the very possibility of love. Only what is unique and transitory (what will be seen only once) can give rise to love in the miraculous instant that has so often been called eternity. "Love what will not be seen a second time" (Alfred de Vigny, "La Maison du Berger"). Why love something that will last indefinitely, that repeats itself in identical fashion? Why love something fixed, since it can be transcended? Jesus, unique and fragile, provides us with an example of a love object. In the context of destiny, fatality, and the immutable, no love is possible. Love possesses no reality or truth outside the fleeting moment. "Weeping like Diana beside her springs / Her love silent and forever threatened" (Alfred de Vigny, "La Maison du Berger"). No love is possible in a circular situation—nor in doubt, repetition, destiny, or fatality. The "eternal return" negates all possibility of love. How should we look, then, at Abel's fragility?

This issue of lightness is central to Qohelet and pops up often during his meanderings. If all is vanity, if lightness is only wind and striving after wind, utter uselessness, should we say Qohelet favors heaviness, solidity, fixity? The problem with this analysis is that precisely the heavy weight of "nothing new under the sun" is what shows that all is vanity! In other words, Qohelet takes particular pains to show that everything we consider stable, solid, or established amounts to wind: not the joyful lightness of dancing dust, but rather smoke that vanishes in a windstorm. Nothing is solid. The only stable thing is the fact that "there is nothing new," that what is essential cannot be changed. This fact leads Qohelet to reject the great human project as useless. The immutable shows just how vain everything is. Vanity reveals that nothing is immutable.

Vanity and changelessness seem mutually exclusive, but we are composed of both; we are both at the same time. We produce stability and we create lightning flashes. We are vapor, yet sameness; lightness, yet heaviness. We cannot escape from our essential duality: this is the lesson of Qohelet, until the final act, when everything changes: lightness turns into grace, and heaviness becomes eternity, because God is always eternal and new: "God himself young as well as eternal" (Charles Péguy, "Eve"). This is Qohelet's intention.

4. Power

Qohelet says that he was king in Jerusalem, and sought power. He assembles a mass of judgments concerning different forms of power. We must not be misled by his claim to be "king." This is either the conventional designation associated with the name of Solomon, or else an expression meaning simply "possessor of great wealth in Jerusalem." After all, we still remember the "kings of steel" and the "railroad barons" of a century ago! We should not make too much of the word "king." Nonetheless, I believe it has a meaning: Qohelet means to say "When I speak of power, I do not do so in an abstract, theoretical manner, like someone inexperienced in the corridors of power; I was king. Therefore I know from experience what I am talking about."

On this basis, Qohelet proceeds to give a striking analysis of the reality of power. This king's first radical observation: power is always absolute. The word used in 2:19 ("He will be master of all for which I toiled") confirms that Qohelet views power as absolute. The word translated "be master" indicates an absolute master, with unlimited authority and the capability of destroying! No one can argue with him! As interpreter of the king, Qohelet says: "Keep the command of the king, and because of the oath made before God,[24] do not be in a hurry to go far from his presence. Do not persist in an evil cause, for he will do whatever he pleases. Since the word of the king is authoritative, who will say to him, 'What are you doing?'" (8:2-4).

These verses form a contrast with the preceding verse, on wisdom: "The sage *knows* the explanation of things . . . a person's wisdom lights up his face" (8:1, JE). Qohelet thus takes his stance as a scribe in the king's service—an intelligent scribe, who knows how to interpret the laws and who also knows that no wisdom or intelligence can hold its own in the king's presence. The scribe must seize the propitious moment! He must take advantage of every fragile opportunity.

---

24. This oath could be the promise of fidelity to the king, in which case one must respect it as an oath sworn before God; or else it refers to a promise made during a trial, also sworn before God. So there is reason to obey carefully.

The wise person has no power—and the king is not wise. It is pointless for the sage to challenge the king's decision, since the king does whatever he wants! No one can insist that the king justify his actions. "Just like a dictator," you say, "an absolute monarch"? Not at all! Qohelet could just as well have in mind the board of a multinational corporation, or modern administration and bureaucracy. They are just as authoritarian, arbitrary, absolute, and without explanation as dictators and kings. No point in challenging them or demanding an explanation. Power is always power; whatever its constitutional form, it always takes the form of absolute power.

Can't power change, though, depending on who exercises it? Qohelet seems to say so: an experienced king is preferable, after all—one who has settled down, surrounded by virtuous princes who do not spend their time in banquets and orgies, and who work. And it is best if the king is "freeborn" (10:16-17).[25] But we dare not place too much stock in such preferences, since the wisdom of Qohelet immediately contradicts them in two ways!

Is an experienced king better than a child? Not necessarily. This question is raised by the enigmatic passage that seems to describe the contrast between an old, stupid king and a poor, wise child in prison. Then (after a coup?) this child leaves his prison and, although he was born poverty-stricken, he comes to power (4:13-16). This passage may also refer either to Solomon's accession to the throne, or to the fact that at the time when the author lived (let's say the 3rd century B.C.), the monarchy no longer had any value, and "criminals" had come to power. In this case we need a different translation, indicating, for example, that the one who came out of prison to reign remains *base* in spite of reigning. And everyone— the crowd, public opinion—follows him, acclaiming him. He was in prison (but why then does the text refer to "the *second* child, the one who rose up in his place"? [4:15]), but he becomes king, with everyone's support or at least with everyone's consent. This is good;

25. This allusion may have to do less with Israel than with Greece, where freed slaves were beginning to be "ministers." This practice increased prodigiously in Rome under the Principate, where all power rested effectively in the hands of former slaves.

and the people are happy and numerous: "There was no end to all the people, to all those before whom he was" (4:16a).

Do we really grasp the terrible demystification of royal power involved in this text? Just look at the conclusion: "Nevertheless, posterity will not rejoice in him! And this also is vanity and a striving after wind" (4:16b). Here we have the sum total of the judgment concerning the wise king who replaced the foolish one— concerning the child who drew the united cheers of his people. Doesn't this description bring to mind many political adventures we have witnessed or heard about? What happened to the image of Louis the Beloved after his death, for example? He came to the throne as a child amidst the enthusiasm of the people who were finally rid of that horrible old man who had himself called the Sun-King (Louis XIV). Louis XV mounted the throne after having almost no possibility of being crowned; he seemed to possess every virtue, to have exceptional intelligence. But his funeral procession met with widespread indifference. Vanity, a striving after wind.

In the long run, then, a wise king is no better than a foolish one! This is all the more true because one must think of the future: you have a good king, yes, but who will succeed him ("what will the successor of the king do?" 2:12b)? This enigmatic phrase may recall the unfortunate memory of Solomon's successors![26] Perhaps it means "who can say that power will not produce anything new, and that we can expect nothing good from a new king?" Or perhaps "who can say whether the successor will limit himself to running what the former king ran?" In any case, there is no reason to hope in this new king.

26. Lys gives us a remarkable survey of the various meanings of this verse, which has nine possible translations (pp. 232-37)! However, they seem to me to boil down more or less to the same thing. Lys's own translation is intriguing: "The successor will be what his predecessor has made him." Unfortunately, this does not square well with the succession of Solomon. Lys resolves this problem by saying the text is a kind of *mea culpa* spoken by Solomon! But we must not return to the idea that Qohelet is a pamphlet circulated by an anti-Solomon political party. In any case, the text gives us one more proof that wisdom does not guarantee a worthy successor and that education is not sufficient to prepare the succession.

Regarding the vanity of power, we must also take into account what Qohelet says concerning fame, reputation, and glory, qualities associated with the popularity of the young king (4:13-16). People will quickly tire of him. "Fame is better than perfumed oil." Many consider this proverb trite and empty (some have compared it to "Better fame than fortune"), but such a judgment assumes the simplistic notion that Qohelet gathered all sorts of texts, including old saws of no value. I must admit my surprise at those who so readily accept this saying as too "obvious," coming from such a hard, lucid author. I fear that when we interpret such a phrase as trite, it is we who are superficial and trite!

This verse as a whole, with its two lines, should snap us to attention: "Fame is better than perfumed oil, and the day of death than the day of one's birth" (7:1). Fame, glory, and reputation—why compare them to perfume or ointment? I believe we have a terrible irony here, confirmed by other texts. What is special about perfume? It smells good, gives a pleasant impression, but . . . it evaporates quickly![27] If you leave the bottle open, soon you have nothing left! Fame is similar: it also evaporates quickly and dissipates. Perhaps less quickly than perfume, but similarly; it does not last.

This is what Qohelet continually repeats: the dead are forgotten. No memory of them remains; and those who follow them will not leave any more of a trace (1:11). If someone has done evil, no one remembers it, and later the person is honored; the person who did good things is blotted out of our memory. No one remembers the great politician filled with wisdom and integrity who saved the city (9:15). Thus the people turn their back on the sovereign they had acclaimed. Public opinion is fundamentally unstable. Moreover, popular wisdom, convictions, and opinions die with those who cling to them.

Perhaps we should compare the above with a trenchant statement Job makes to his friends: "You are the people, and with you wisdom will die!" (Job 12:2, JE). Thus wisdom, along with all fame and culture, is essentially relative and temporary, fragile and uncertain, and only lasts for one generation. The people are not God. They

___

27. Unless the perfume has an oil base, in which case the oil turns rancid.

never say the last word, neither in politics nor as regards the truth. And fame and "glory" offered by the crowds amount to nothing, and have nothing to do with God's revelation. *Vox populi, vox dei* (the voice of the people is the voice of God) is a lie. We should understand "Fame is better than . . ." (Eccl. 7:1) in the light of this consistent perspective. Considering how short a time they last, it is perfectly ridiculous to aim for glory and world repute.[28]

Hence, death is worth more than life; first, because this life keeps vanishing; and second, because power (including the infatuation of the people and the public) is a trap. Qohelet manages to convey all this with his "trite" saying! Again in this case he shows us objective reality: Take a survey of glory and fame. Whose name endures? Try to think of someone who has not sunk into oblivion. Do politics offer glory? Who remembers Raymond Poincaré or Edouard Herriot? As for literary glory, who remembers Anatole France? We do well to follow Qohelet by reflecting along these lines. I strongly suggest to anyone who believes in the glory of our media stars that he read the *Grand Larousse of the Nineteenth Century.* There you will see hundreds of names of eminent persons who had a considerable reputation in 1890, but are utterly unknown less than a century later. Qohelet is right: why waste one's life seeking fame, which is part of power?

Next, a brief sentence will hold our attention: "A king is subservient to a field" (5:9b). Here we have the limit on royal grandeur! Our text speaks of the land, but, for good reason, ironically reduces it to a mere field. This may also have called up memories of ancient stories, such as the one about Naboth's vineyard (1 K. 21:1-24). First the land with the field, then the country, and finally the nation: the basis and limitation of power. Power can do anything, but it is subservient to the need to preserve the land and conquer more of it. "Subservient" carries a lot of weight. With a single word, Qohelet brings into view

---

28. Thus I utterly part company with Duesberg, who gives this explanation of Eccl. 7:1: fame lasts after death, whereas perfumed oil was used to wash newborn babies (cited by Maillot, p. 102)! But I also take issue with Maillot, who replaces "fame" by "name." He interprets the verse as meaning that existence matters more than appearance (pp. 102-3). But this fails to harmonize with the second half of the verse! How can existence be parallel with death?

the vanity of a reality that people attempt in vain to ennoble. We cannot dispute that political power is subservient to defense, conquest, and the security of a given territory, since without it the power would not exist. This shows the extent of power's vanity. Territory is involved in the very definition of the state, the nation, and power. Territory helps demonstrate both the vanity of power (think of French colonial conquest) and its fragility (which also is vanity). In spite of all its powerful infrastructure and terrifying means, power is subservient to a field. This is still true today.

But Qohelet goes farther. Power not only operates within the sphere of vanity but also is evil, and that in two senses: injustice and oppression. You may think this is hardly new, since the prophets dwelt on it. But Qohelet's radicalism is more extreme: "Moreover, I saw under the sun the place of judgment: *there* is wickedness; and the place of justice: *there* is wickedness" (3:16). Where justice should be handed down, where a power has been established to dispense justice among people, precisely there we find "wickedness." Evil has been installed as judge.

Nothing moderates this observation to make it less serious. Qohelet does not say "If the king is evil, let him repent; if there is injustice, the king should return to the path of justice," as the prophets usually did. Nor does he say "Sometimes power is unjust; at other times, we are blessed with a good and just political regime. We should make an effort to make our government good, by trying to create good institutions, etc."—that is the hope of all our political pundits and philosophers.

Qohelet makes no distinctions, offers no half-measures or alternatives. Things are this way and not otherwise, and Qohelet follows through relentlessly on this denunciation. Do you perhaps think that wickedness is on the bench of "justice" only by chance? Not at all—Qohelet paints a starker picture: "If you see . . . the violation of right and justice in the province, do not be amazed by this, for above a high official a higher one watches! And higher officials than they, over all" (5:8). So the problem is not with some rascal who gains power and does evil by accident. No: he obeys those who are above him, and they are worse. They in turn are under a still worse, higher placed person, and the higher we climb on the ladder of power, the worse the people we have to deal with (how naive of us to think a court of appeals will hand down a better decision than a lower court!).

At this point Barucq offers an intriguing translation and interpretation of 5:8: "If you see the oppression of the poor, do not be surprised. Indeed, a high-placed person covers another one like him, and above them, there are still more authorities" (p. 100). In other words, the collaboration of the "political and administrative class" constitutes one of the basic factors of oppression. An unjust administrator can always find a superior to cover for him! Here we see Qohelet's *experience* with power, and his determination to show that the evil in power does not spring from faulty organization or despicable people: "The higher you go, the worse it gets." This viewpoint may provoke some "amens" among those who have seen such a spirit of power and pride at work.

Evil reigns precisely in the places of human justice. Things cannot be otherwise, since we have a reference to God following Qohelet's radical denunciation in 3:16: "I said in my heart, God will judge the righteous and the wicked" (3:17a). In other words, no justice is possible, except for God's. Justice can be expressed only by him. This leads us to think that humanity has no idea what justice is. Wicked people are established on the seat of power. How could they possibly judge rightly? Such is the impasse.

This power also expresses itself as oppression (4:1; 5:8). In this case, we are not dealing with an incidental aspect of political power or kingship, but rather with any power one person may exercise over another, whatever its form and means. Qohelet makes this strange remark: human power has its limits where things are concerned (no human being has power over the wind, or the power to determine the day of his death; in our day we see this differently, since we have obtained nearly unlimited power over things—but we are no better off!). But we have power over other people. "All this I have seen, and I applied my heart to every work done under the sun, in the time when one person has power over another, to do evil to him" (8:9).[29]

---

29. Maillot makes a profound reflection on this text: "Are we devoid of all power as we are of all true knowledge? No! Qohelet will discover that we

Many other passages confirm the idea that any power of one person over another leads to evildoing. In the final analysis, we have only two sorts of people: oppressors and oppressed—no one is neutral! Oppression not only produces misery and the tears of the poor, but also "being oppressed drives a sage mad" (7:7). Here we reach bedrock: Wisdom cannot stand up against oppression. The desperation of the poor and oppressed should not astonish us. In Qohelet's view, both massacres in the course of a revolt and the undiscerning acceptance of absurd ideologies and vain beliefs stem from oppression. We must not have any illusions, either: the author suggests that profound wisdom, wisdom related to God, can also be perverted by oppression.

We see that whereas the perversion of wisdom used to be one of the spontaneous results of oppression, today the same result is purposely sought for by our modern means of psychic oppression. Nothing escapes this unbounded evil, since even wisdom itself cannot resist it.

Nothing on earth compensates for this evil, since the oppressor who has made evil use of his power is honored in the long run: "I have seen the wicked carried to their tomb [surrounded by an honorary procession], . . . and people forgetting in the city that they [the wicked] used to behave that way" (8:10). After their death people no longer speak of the evil they did! Adolf Hitler and Joseph Stalin are beginning to be rehabilitated. Qohelet declares this too is vanity, since hope in some judgment of history or in the return of justice after the death of a tyrant remains an illusion. But we need to understand that Qohelet's words apply to *all* oppressions (4:1). All are characterized by their absence of limitation (people go from one to the other, and there is no reason this process should come to an end); no one is around to comfort people in this situation.

Qohelet's choice of words in this passage is remarkable. He does not say "they have no comfort," but rather "they have no

have power at our disposal after all—power against our neighbor. We cannot dominate our life, our future, or our death, but we can dominate our brother, and we do not hesitate to do so. Our greatest power is that of doing evil" (p. 143).

comforter" (4:1). Abstract comfort in such a situation would amount to still another illusion, or vanity. A *person* is needed. Furthermore, Qohelet does not suggest "an administrator of justice" (we have seen that judicial power is vain!), or "someone who would improve the situation" (we have learned that this way you just exchange one oppression for another). No—he speaks of a comforter. This person will offer the oppressed the essential answer to their oppression, which does not lie in the vain agitation of an equally vain hope. In the midst of suffering, violence, and tears (4:1), the comforter is both their protector and the one who brings hope—not condolences, but something belonging to a different category. This hope is fully incarnated in a person. Instead of offering works of charity, he is himself full consolation.

Since Qohelet does not know such a comforter, and observes that none exists, he concludes: "The dead who are already dead are better off than the living who are still alive" (4:2, JE). This is one of the rare biblical passages in which death is preferred to life (but we will see how Qohelet makes up for this later!). In this context, the reference is directly related to oppression. Since people oppress each other, and the oppressed have no recourse, since no one cares about their tears, and violence spreads everywhere, since there is no one to comfort, death is preferable to life. Under such conditions, life is not really life.

We have seen how vanity and wickedness have triumphed over power; now we come to foolishness. We saw that a foolish king is an evil rather than vanity (4:13). "Folly has been set in the highest places" (10:6a). By whom? This text is strange and ambiguous: some have suggested that the author may refer to an "error" committed by the "Sovereign." Others have concluded this "Sovereign" points to God himself, so that God is said to allow an imbecile to come to power (or to empower a foolish person). After all, why not? In any case, this hypothesis overturns that lovely system whereby political power rests on the will of a God who is always just and who grants legitimacy to the king. Not here! Even God is said to make mistakes (the text cited is: "like an error proceeding from the Sovereign," 10:5). Thus we have power, but we have just observed that foolishness can exercise power.

Now we have played all three cards: vanity, oppression, and foolishness—these apply to all human power. In conclusion, we must note that this issue involves no counterpart, no dialectic. Contrary to what we will see in the case of almost all the other vanities, *all power* is vanity, oppression, and foolishness—without reservation or shading! One last remark remains. Taken as a whole, our last text may appear awkward: "Folly has been set in the highest places and wealthy people remain in lowliness. I have seen slaves on horseback and princes on foot like slaves" (10:6-7). This offends our idea of egalitarian democracy, of course. But why should the rich get the high places? And the slave riding a horse while the prince walks is thoroughly satisfying, after all.

To explain this text, some have suggested that according to Qohelet the rich person was one who had obtained his wealth by wisdom (thus contrasting wisdom and foolishness). But I think this interpretation adds to the confusion. The rich person and the wise person are by no means to be identified. The wealthy individual also has power, the difference being that he has acquired his wealth through his *intelligence* (which is not the same thing as *wisdom*!). The texts says, therefore, that it is better to have an intelligent person in power, after all (although he will of course be wicked), than an imbecile! Along the same line, a slave certainly has none of the ability needed for leadership, whereas a prince would *appear* to have more of it, especially for leading in warfare (on horseback). Nothing more. The author in his realism and radicalism eliminates from consideration the question of which person deserves more to exercise power one day. Qohelet limits his argument to the choice of the person least likely to use his position as oppressor to do harm. This interpretation seems to me to fit Qohelet's utter pessimism concerning power.

Qohelet shows the vanity of power, but also the failure of royal power—specifically, of Solomon. Our author considers at some length the failure of the great, wise king. We can easily understand why he chose Solomon. We can deepen our comprehension thanks to a recent study showing that wisdom was a specific attribute of the king in the societies around Israel.[30] The Egyptian king was inspired by Ra, whose intelligence made him the protector and guide of the universe, as well as the first king of Egypt. The current king is wise in turn, and shows his intelligence to his people so they will be united and live in peace. In Babylon, wisdom is a divine prerogative revealed only to the king. This king "does great things"; that is, he translates his wise thoughts into action. Finally, in Ugarit, justice and wisdom are the king's main virtues. But in this case these qualities lead him especially to care for the poor and to protect widows and orphans.

Thus, when 1 Kings shows us the wisdom of Solomon, we see this quality in the historical context of the neighboring cultures. But Qohelet calls this wisdom into question. It was already questioned lucidly by the last days of Solomon's life, but our author uses an extremely harsh tone! We cannot help noticing the difference: Egypt's Pharaoh and the kings of Babylon and Ugarit were assumed to be wise. They were wise mythologically, by definition. No other possibility was considered. One did not test this presupposition on the basis of experience, history, or concrete, theological judgment. But all this changes when we come to the kings of Israel. Only two (David and Solomon) are called "wise," and we see that their wisdom is severely measured by reality: David's sins, Solomon's idolatry.

How does wise King Solomon come to understand that wickedness reigns in the seat of justice? He recognizes that he is tied to a single small parcel of the earth, and that his "great works" amount to nothing. Furthermore, the protection of the poor and the defenseless, which was supposed to exemplify the king's wisdom, does not seem to have concerned him overmuch! Thus his wisdom leads him first of all to recognize the vanity of power, and finally to see that there is no "wise king"! Hebrew realism can be very harsh. Thus

30. See Leonidas Kalugila, *The Wise King: Studies in Royal Wisdom as Divine Revelation in the Old Testament and Its Environment,* Coniectanea Biblica 15 (Lund, Sweden: CWK Gleerup, 1980). See also Serge Guilmin's review of Kalugila, "Les Pouvoirs et les dieux: 'Le Roi sage,' " *Foi et Vie* 83/5 (Sept. 1984) 52-54.

we perhaps witness, as S. Guilmin rightly suggests, in biblical prophecy, "a *transfer* of the mandate that most kings failed to honor" (p. 54). Since the king is not wise, perhaps wisdom must become the responsibility of the community as a whole. The whole Hebrew people become bearers of wisdom, as the prophets show.

Wouldn't the above idea provide one (but not the only) explanation for the name "Qohelet"? Since Solomon cannot speak and act with wisdom, Qohelet, who incarnates the assembly as the people's voice, will express it! Solomon is present as the designated wise king, and Qohelet is the response: this king is not the wise one; wisdom is vanity, just like the works of this king. Thus Israel becomes more and more distinct from the religious structure of the surrounding world.

5. Money

Money is the second great vanity.[31] This proposition holds less surprise for us. Since Qohelet's thought concerning money is more familiar to us, we find it easier to accept. His basic idea involves us in a contradiction: money makes everything possible—and money is vanity. Here is his radical statement: "Money makes everything

---

31. Vischer interprets Qohelet's first experiences, as described in Eccl. 3, in *Valeur de l'Ancien Testament: Commentaires des livres de Job, Esther, l'Ecclésiaste, le second Esaïe, précédés d'une introduction* (Geneva: Labor et Fides, 1953), pp. 112-13. According to Vischer, these are metaphysical experience, sentient experience, and cultural experience. In connection with cultural experience, Vischer speaks of a "civilizing work." Lys, who follows Vischer's interpretation (p. 32), takes the third experience, beginning in 2:3, as one that synthesizes meaning and pleasure; neither philosophy nor enjoyment gives meaning by itself—each needs to be made fertile by the other. Furthermore, according to Lys, the "great work" is the creation of a culture (2:4-11). In spite of my respect and admiration for Vischer and Lys, I cannot agree with their reading of these verses. The passage deals with all money can provide, and not at all with a cultural effort. The issue is power and wealth, nothing more, so that Lys's question, "Is culture possible, after all?," finds no basis in the text.

possible" (10:19). Nothing can escape from money; it can buy and possess everything. We find no moralism or spiritualizing here, no evasions or illusions.

Qohelet's view finds its echo hundreds of years later at the end of Revelation, where money makes it possible to buy people's bodies and souls (Rev. 18:13). But in the above quotation our author makes no value judgment: as king of Jerusalem, Solomon, the wealthy builder, indeed used the unlimited power of money. He tells us so at the beginning, just so he can later say "I know from experience that all these things amount to nothing": he has experienced money and happiness; money and architecture, palaces; money and plantations, gardens, and orchards; money and great works and irrigation projects (Eccl. 2:6);[32] finally, money and the arts—musicians and singers (2:8).

We should note the admirable development in the above passage, from the "material" to the "spiritual." Solomon did everything with his great wealth. And he observes with satisfaction that after accomplishing so much, "my wisdom remained with me" (2:9). This very wisdom then leads him to conclude abruptly: "All is vanity and a striving after wind" (2:11). All of it amounted to nothing.[33] But we may ask, then, "In what sense is it all vanity?"[34]

32. The term "great works" is no exaggeration. Solomon's irrigation system was so significant that Marx used it to construct his model of "Asiatic production."

33. Obviously, I have taken these verses (2:3-11) at face value, whereas others take them as allegorical. In the word "garden" (v. 5), translated in the Septuagint as *paradeisos,* some see a reference to creation ("The Lord God planted a garden," Gen. 2:8); in "fruit trees" some find an allusion to the tree of knowledge. This leads to meditating on our nostalgia for the garden: can humankind replant God's garden? Others take "vineyard" (Eccl. 2:4) as symbolic of Israel. Whereas others broaden the meaning of this text, I take it to refer to human organization of the world. Does the passage allude to God's creation? The case for allegory here seems quite weak to me.

34. If one accepts my proposed interpretation of this text as cathartic and Socratic (see above, chapter I, § 7, "Qohelet as Ritual Incantation"), we must understand these texts quite differently: having done his "great works," the king declares that they are all vanity. But the point of the passage is to show him, on the contrary, that his works truly exist and do not amount to nothing.

The first reasons given are somewhat commonplace. (This fact should remind us that the Scriptures do not consider originality the criterion in every case! When common sense indicates the truth, the Scriptures do not hesitate to uphold it!)

First, our desire for money is never satisfied. Our pursuit of money is infinite. We can never say: this is enough: "The one who loves money will not be satisfied with money" (5:10a). There is no such thing as an abundance acquired once and for all with money. Money's indefinite quality does not stem from something in us, but rather from its very nature, as purely quantitative. Once a person has amassed his first billion, why shouldn't he add a second billion to it? There is never any limit, since in order to set a limit or a stopping point, one would need self-control and wisdom. And if one had these at the outset, he would not have had such a passion for money. From the beginning of the development of the relationship between a person and money, then, we find either wisdom or excess. If one has wisdom, money fails to interest him overmuch; without it, nothing will come into play to stop him at a given point.

This same text, however, becomes ironic as it continues: "the one who loves opulence has no income: this, too, is vanity. Where wealth abounds, those who devour it abound, and what profit is there for its owner, apart from the spectacle it offers to his eyes?" (5:10b-11). We cannot stop accumulating more and more, true. But what will our money be good for? Indirectly, Qohelet suggests it will bring opulence, luxury, abundance—and then hangers-on! In his time, these were the only things money could buy: gold tableware, jewels, and palaces. But after buying them, according to Qohelet, one has little money left (so he starts pursuing money again!), a rather amusing touch! In our day, we have returned to this point: we must keep earning more and more in order to consume more.

All he has done finds its place in society, in the world's development. Thus the king can say "I began to despair in my heart" (2:20a), but the narrator of the ritual shows him that this attitude is fictitious: merely an image the king has of himself. The narrator of the ritual recalls this attitude only to point to the reality, which is the opposite of the king's point of view. This may be a correct interpretation, but it would imply a conflict between the truth as proclaimed by the king and the call to reality coming from the narrator of the ritual.

On the societal level, this situation looks even worse: we must accumulate an indefinite amount of collective wealth in order to buy arms, equipment, highways, and airports. Finally we find ourselves in debt, so that we have no way to shore up our security or deal with the debt of countless countries in our world. All this constitutes modern-day "opulence," replacing antiquity's jewels and palaces. But the root of the problem has not changed. The issue remains the same: *loving* money. When he speaks of money, Jesus calls love into question: "Where your treasure is, there your heart will be also. . . . You cannot love God and money at the same time" (Matt. 6:21, 24, JE). Qohelet holds to the view that such conduct is absurd. Enough said!

A second irony in the above passage results from the fact that an abundance of wealth inevitably attracts whose who "devour" it: parasites, hangers-on, people in business. We know all this, of course. Qohelet's irony is sharp, however: in the long run, our rich person possesses only one thing: the spectacle before his eyes, of those who are eating up his money. We have no difficulty visualizing this text's allusion to banquets, etc. But for our opulent society, which has staked everything on the conquest of money, the result is the same! In the end, what remains of these gigantic sums we have produced, accumulated, and squandered? A spectacle. The consumer society, the opulent society, is a society of spectacle.[35] Likewise, this spectacle-oriented society in which we live, the only society we care to live in, implies a thirst for money and love of it.

So we see Qohelet's first reason for saying money is vanity: no amount of it can satisfy. Second, money is like smoke: it disappears into nothing (5:14-15). One bad business deal, and you have nothing left. This is what happens when you carefully save your money instead of spending it on opulence (as in the previous case), according to our text. Wealth is kept by its owner to his own detriment! Keeping it in this way shows that one loves it, so that losing it becomes a disaster. So whether you spend it or save it,

35. See Jacques Ellul, *The Humiliation of the Word*, e.g., pp. 114ff.— TRANS.

money is an enticement, smoke, or mist. It is vanity to attach any importance to it.

Qohelet's third reason for calling money vanity is as common-place as the previous reasons, but he returns to it throughout the book: "You can't take it with you." You spend your life in the conquest of money, and at the end, when your life is over, you will have nothing left. As a rich person you will die as if you had been poor. Your money will not benefit you in any way, since on the other side of death money means nothing.

Qohelet may intend a swipe here at the religions that sur-rounded the dead with food, weapons, and chariots, believing that people continued to need them after death. He maintains, on the contrary, that such objects have no value after death. They are worse than nothing, since while you are still living, doubt gnaws at you: "I hated all my work, because I will leave everything to the person who comes after me—who knows if he will be wise or foolish? He will be master of all my work, for which I have worked wisely under the sun. This also is vanity. And I began to despair in my heart concerning all the work I had done. For here is one who has done his work with wisdom, knowledge, and *success*—and a person who has done nothing will reap the rewards" (2:18-21, JE).

Why bother to gain wealth and leave it to others, since we have no idea what they may do? This leitmotiv is the counterpart of "You can't take it with you." If you don't know how the money you leave will be used, why devote your life to accumulating it? As we will see, however, a small amount of money can be useful for achieving a degree of happiness in the course of one's life. In reality, money's only justification lies in making this possible, in the present. Money is directly related to happiness on earth. But we must beware: it makes possible a purely material, concrete happiness: eat, drink, and be merry. Money fails to go beyond these things or to make anything else possible. In the final analysis, this is not so bad, since, as we will see, no other sort of happiness exists, and material happiness is in no way condemned.

But when Qohelet attacks wealth in this way, we must remem-ber that in his day sages believed wealth to be a sign of God's grace. In fact, even Qohelet recognizes that God gives wealth (6:2). In his desacralization of money, then, we have an attack on the thought of his time (this attack is confirmed in the same context, since Qohelet considers it vanity to live a long life and have many children [6:3], and this was the most tangible proof of God's blessing, according to Jewish thought).

We know all this today (although we fail to *live* it!), so that Qohelet's reflections seem at first to be lacking in originality. But they bring us to an observation that may be worth thinking about: Qohelet does not consider money to be evil in itself. Money is not condemned in its concrete reality. In gathering together his texts on money, we find that the evil lies in the fact that *money makes everything possible, yet it is nothing.* You can do anything, but by using this thing that amounts to nothing. You can give your all to money, which seems to be everything, but this means that you have tied yourself to a mere nothing. This amounts not only to irony and misfortune but also to evil. On the one hand, money is vanity, smoke, and absolute uncertainty; on the other hand, we find this relentless fact: money is precisely what makes everything possible. So the medieval devil called Nothingness is also the one that makes everything possible. He granted wealth, success, honors, etc. Something worth thinking about, as is the reverse: what makes everything possible and provides all the means amounts to nothing—it is just wind.

Two related reflections: first, being and having, a commonplace distinction in our day. The more you add to what you have, the less you are. Accumulating more, concentrating all your effort in the quest for things you can have, means losing your being in the process. Marx had no need to wait for Gabriel Marcel's arrival on the scene to describe this terrible play of forces in detail. You cannot escape from it, not even using all the efforts of modern thought and science. Being involves something different than the quest for having. Adding to what you have means losing your being. Jesus said it this way: "What, then, will anyone gain by winning the whole world and forfeiting his life? Or what can anyone offer in exchange for his life?" (Matt. 16:26, NJB).

Second, a scandalous observation: in our day, money is not all that makes everything possible. Technique (no reason anyone should lose patience with me at this point!) is the means for having and doing everything. But technique cannot concretely come into play and develop without money. At this point we come back to our previous observation: what makes everything possible amounts to nothing. Technique is also wind, smoke, and vanity. All we have been saying about money can be applied to technique. This is particularly true of the fact that money cannot be considered evil. Technique is no more evil than money; the evil resides in the fact that it has, like money, become the *mediator of everything,* whereas in itself, it is nothing. In an earlier time, the allurement of money dominated people. Today the allurement of technique plays this role.

A final reason for considering money to be vanity lies in the guiding principle of all Qohelet's reflections on money: success always depends on time, whether it be success with money or technical success. Here is the basic text: "I also saw that under the sun the race does not belong to the light of foot, nor the battle to heroes, neither food to the wise, nor wealth to the intelligent, nor favor to the learned, for time and mishaps happen to everyone. Nor does a person know his time: like fish caught in an evil net, like sparrows caught in a snare, people are caught by an evil time, when it falls on them unexpectedly" (9:11-12). We will return to this theme of time, so constant in Qohelet. But here we need only emphasize that nothing belongs to a person (a concept related to money), nothing depends on his abilities. Rather than referring to blind chance, on which everything depends, Qohelet speaks of time at this point.

We have seen that money eludes our grasp because of time. There is a favorable time and a bad time. Qohelet most certainly does not refer here to the indifferent majesty measured mathematically and indicated by our watches. He does not mean the mere neutral passage of minutes and hours. Qohelet qualifies time. We find two sorts of time in the Gospels, both well-known by the Greeks: time that passes, and appointed time. We say "My time has not yet come . . . it is not my moment." You may have every reason to win, but time, being unfavorable, prevents it. You will lose everything because the time is not right.

Time is the only thing we can in no way master. This is as true today as it was 2,500 years ago. You may call it history, contingency, circumstances, configuration, structure, or whatever. The reality remains the same: bad timing prevails over money, so that money's dependence on time shows its vanity. All human activity is subject to time, however, and we know nothing about it. Nor can we change it in any way.

6. Work

Money and work—unlike many other books of the Bible, this one dedicates much thought to both. But Qohelet does not treat work in the same way as money and power. With work, we enter a different universe—a world still dominated by vanity, but where meaning sometimes prevails. Qohelet speaks from experience here, as he did in connection with power and wealth. He can state: "I made my works great. . . . I turned toward all the works my hands had made and toward the work I had done to make them and behold, all is vanity and a striving after wind, and there is no profit under the sun" (2:4, 11).

In the long run, work is not worth it: what a person achieves is immediately dissipated like smoke. Consequently we are warned that work has no meaning or value in itself. It provides no justification for living. It is not everything in life.[36] Work has meaning only through what it produces in the final analysis; it is judged on the basis of this result. Thus the question posed by Qohelet: "What profit is there for a person in all his work which he does under the sun?" (1:3).

This question is the first to be raised in Qohelet. Work has a special place in human life, according to Qohelet. The society he lived in was not a work-oriented society like ours, however. For that reason this question is all the more important: it is a *modern*

36. A very good translation by Lys highlights this point: "Yes, what *being* is there for a person in all his work?" (2:22). He comments: "What truly *is?* What is the *being* a person can see resulting from all the trouble he takes? . . . Do human actions entail a participation in being, any presence of eternity?" (pp. 274, 275).

question. The importance Qohelet gives to work shows he does not concur in the contempt generally felt for work in ancient societies (and some call them "slave societies"!). Work matters to Qohelet— enough that we should ask ourselves about it. It is on a level with questions of happiness or power. This attitude is remarkable.

Suppose work gave meaning to life, after all—a modern concern. Qohelet finally concludes it does not. But when he asks "What profit can we show for it?" we must be careful! Our author by no means claims that work has no result. On the contrary, he shows that work gives money and power, and that one would have to be insane not to work. So it produces a material result, without any doubt. Qohelet merely denies that it is worthwhile to devote one's life to such an effort. To spend one's life working, to do "*all* the work" (1:3)—there lies vanity and a striving after wind.

We question this conclusion? But we have seen with Qohelet that the things we can obtain through work (money and power) amount to just that: vanity. Through work we can neither enable humanity to progress nor change anything basic or decisive. We cannot change unchangeable reality: "What is bent cannot be straightened, and what is lacking cannot be counted" (1:15).

Of course, we have techniques (so did Qohelet's time!) for straightening out twisted things, or for bending straight things into crooked ones! But Qohelet is not dealing with that sort of obvious issue, a piece of bent wood or iron, as we see from the second half of the verse: "what is lacking." Something "bent" means something involving a basic imperfection. You cannot straighten out what is intrinsically perverse, defective, gone astray, or, if we choose to include the "moral" level, hypocritical. You cannot "change nature." You cannot take communication that involves no message and make it say something. You cannot take a basically sinful person and make him just (before God). Work cannot change the way things and people are; it can only affect the exterior: behavior and appearances.

This is the meaning of "what is lacking cannot be counted" (1:15). True, you can know that a *given* lack exists; or in the case of a totality with which you are familiar, you can, depending on your ability, deduce that something you can count is lacking. But if the issue has to do with "what is lacking" with respect to infinity, you cannot count it. Trying to measure the distance between the edge of something and infinity is utterly futile.

A path stops just short of a precipice. You can count the steps up to there, but there is no measuring the path beyond that point. Work can change nothing about human limitations, which cut us off from the qualitative and from infinity. This observation enables us to see work within its limitations, which do not lead us to deny its existence or to despise it. But if work is so limited, it surely is not worth our sacrificing everything to it. Work for the sake of work makes no sense.

Qohelet intertwines two themes along these lines: "Again, I saw a vanity under the sun: there is someone alone, without another; he has neither son nor brother, and *there is no end to all his work;* yet his eyes are not satisfied with wealth: 'For whom have I worked and deprived my soul of happiness?' This also is vanity and an evil pursuit" (4:7-8). Note that in this text work eliminates happiness. Thus devoting oneself to work is unreservedly bad. Qohelet seems to slip in a positive dimension, however: working *for* someone. Apparently work *can* (but does not necessarily) have some justification. Working to help someone else, a partner, a brother, or a son, seems less absurd. Since the presence of the other is usually muffled in Qohelet, we need to emphasize it here. In any case, Qohelet gives us his categorical opinion: unless we work for someone else, work has no meaning.

Of course, we must once again avoid concluding that lazy people have the right idea! Qohelet simply leads us to recognize the limitations of work and its lack of value: "All human work is for the mouth, and yet the soul [or appetite] is not satisfied" (6:7). The author's point of view is clear: work enables us to eat (nothing useless about that!), but that is all. Eat—sleep—work—eat—sleep—work; work to eat, and eat to work. As I have shown elsewhere,[37] this approach coincides with the *entire* teaching of Scripture, from beginning to end. Work is a necessity. It is no virtue,

37. In *Foi et Vie* 79/4 (July 1980), an issue of the journal devoted to the question of work. Most of the articles are pseudonymous, written by Ellul. Two of them have been translated: "Work and Calling," *Katallagete* Fall-Winter

good, remedy, human expression, or revealer. It holds no value. This is what Qohelet means by "the soul is not satisfied"—although his stomach may be. A serious perversion of the truth takes place when a whole society claims to provide satisfaction for the soul through work! Such talk can produce nothing but a huge vacuum, which all the other passions will rush to fill up.

Work remains on trial: all work, all of a person's ability to work, and all his efforts provide no guarantee of even the smallest result! Hear Qohelet again in the passage we quoted when dealing with time; this time consider what he has to say about the vanity of work: "I also saw that under the sun the race does not belong to the light of foot, nor the battle to heroes, neither food to the wise, nor wealth to the intelligent, nor favor to the learned, for time and mishaps happen to everyone. Nor does a person know his time: like fish caught in an evil net, like sparrows caught in a snare, people are caught by an evil time, when it falls on them unexpectedly" (9:11-12).

In this text we see there is no relation of cause and effect between work, related to a person's qualities and effort, on the one hand, and the result, on the other. Everything just happens, depending on the "time." We will return to this idea that everything has its time, but that we do not know "our time": the auspicious time, the moment we should seize. As a result, all our efforts are useless, or simply depend on chance, and we end up caught in a trap, like a bird or a fish. Thus all our work becomes utterly futile, and if we are successful, we have not deserved our reward.

In this connection Qohelet teaches us a basic lesson. We always think success fails to crown our fine efforts because things are poorly organized: some injustice prevents our work from being completely and rightly rewarded. We are forever calling for "equal opportunity," "recognition of merit," "justice," and "the right to a fair wage." We suppose that a new political regime and a better organized society will result in salaries that represent the total value of what we produce.

(1972); repr. in *Callings!* ed. James Y. Holloway and Will D. Campbell (New York: Paulist, 1974), pp. 18-44; "From the Bible to a History of Non-Work," *Cross Currents* 35/1 (Spring 1985) 43-48.—TRANS.

But Qohelet says no: the problem goes deeper than you think, and is almost inherent in our being and in the world. You cannot avoid bad and ruthless times crashing down on a person, not even with the best possible organization of work and the economy. You cannot avoid "luck" and "chance." Even with the best organization, we now know that you cannot prevent "pull," either.[38] So our fine qualities and our work amount only to vanity and a chasing after wind. There is no possibility of our seeing the day when a true meritocracy is established.[39] However you try to provide equal opportunity and the fairest possible recognition of merit, you will

38. See, for example, a most important and edifying book by Michael S. Voslensky: *Nomenklatura: The Soviet Ruling Class,* trans. Eric Mosbacher (New York: Doubleday, 1984).

39. At this point I cannot avoid quoting at length from Maillot's excellent commentary on this text: Qohelet "does not denounce injustice so much as the fact that no one is in his proper place. There is a sort of basic disturbance preventing most people from obtaining what they seem to have a right to. Qohelet opposes [the liberal] optimistic philosophy . . . that teaches that every person will find his niche, since we all start out with the same odds. . . . An honest person has to admit that we experience . . . not only a disturbance but a kind of reversal, so that the slowest win the race, . . . and idiots get rich. True, this situation provides cheap consolation for those who lose races and wars. . . . But by following that route we forget that here again, in a negative, reverse fashion, Qohelet sounds the theme of Pauline grace. Everything is upside down in our world. For this reason God brings about in Christ a second reversal: he chooses the weak, foolish things, or the things that have no existence, to show his strength and wisdom, to give reality to things that had none. Furthermore, Christ proclaimed this double reversal in the beatitudes" (p. 164). In the following text, Maillot clarifies what Qohelet means by "sin": "a basic disturbance in the world that causes *no one to be in his proper place.* There is a kind of dislocation in the world that no one escapes. . . . Since the tares first began growing in among the good grain, no one and nothing is where it ought to be. . . . If people had meditated more on this text of Qohelet's, they would have avoided speaking of a basic, essential human depravity. The *relationships* between things and people are distorted, not their nature: relationships between people and God, people and the world, people and other people, people and themselves. So Christ's work consists of changing not our nature but our relationships. Slaves, we become children; enemies, we become b:others. This is the meaning of *katallagé* (reconciliation). It is in reality a change of place" (pp. 165-66).

never control the "accidents," the "chances," and the "imponderables" that determine success.

Alas, Qohelet takes us farther. This focusing of the issue to show how relative things are fails to satisfy him. He puts work in the dock and begins his accusation. Work becomes an evil—hatred, despair, jealousy. Its result is perverse. "I hated all my work at which I had labored under the sun and which I will hand over to the one who comes after me. Who knows if he will be wise or foolish? He will be master of all my work at which I have labored wisely under the sun" (2:18-19). We can sidestep the argument concerning what we leave when we die, since we have already examined it. But hatred is another matter: I hate my work because when all is said and done, it does not satisfy. It fails to measure up to my expectations. The more hope I placed in it, the more I counted on finding immortality in it, the greater my frustration, which causes me to hate.

What have I done? How will it be used? This is not a small matter! If Marx could see what Stalin did with his work! When Einstein saw what they did with his! One does not just react with "What's the use?"; he finds hate and despair welling up inside him. The two are joined in our text: "I began to *despair* in my heart concerning all the work at which I had labored under the sun" (2:20). True, this reaction stems partly from Qohelet's constant theme: "You leave things to an incapable or evil person. . . ." But despair adds another dimension. The lack of any meaning or progress in our lives and in society shuts out hope and joy. Faced with the sterility of our greatest efforts, we can feel only hatred and then despair.

We feel hatred for our work and despair deep within (as well as despair from writing so many books—Qohelet warned us about that!). These reactions are a far cry from a futile and superficial "What's the use?" Qohelet asks, "What return does a person get from all his work *and from the quest of his heart,* at which he works under the sun?" (2:22). We would all like work to be something besides a necessity for sustaining the body. We want it to be the means of finding an answer to our heart's quest—for truth? For eternity or goodness? Perhaps. In any case, we find no answer. Since work is the only means at our disposal for finding an answer, we despair when we recognize the vanity of this means. We move from hating work to hating life (2:17). This is normal if one's entire life has been taken up with work. Thus work becomes a destroyer of the person when it is too highly valued.

Next, Qohelet judges work not as the great means of human solidarity, but, on the contrary, as the source of conflict between people: "I saw that all work and all the success of a work are one's *jealousy* of another: this also is vanity and a striving after wind" (4:4). Work involves competition, the elimination of others, the triumph of the strongest, and provokes to jealousy when someone succeeds!

In this case also, realism wins out over pious idealism, showing that work corrupts human relationships. Instead of solidarity through work, we find domination and hostility. Work is vanity and a striving after wind precisely because in the final analysis it gives nothing to people: it offers no benefit, its result is futility and absurdity. It is vain because it provokes hostility and competition among people who fight each other—over something utterly vain.

One more argument remains in this trial where work is the accused: the negative effect on the worker himself. Not only does he begin to hate life, but he is also subject to what we might call "the perverse effect of work." Work turns against the worker: "Whoever digs a pit will fall into it, and a serpent will bite whoever breaks down a wall; whoever mines stones will hurt himself at it; whoever splits wood will run a risk" (10:8-9). Sometimes there is an advantage in not doing the work! "If the iron is blunt, and one does not sharpen the edge, he will increase his strength" (10:10a). This astonishing paradox calls into question our eagerness to use machines that enable us not to "increase our strength," since the machines work for us. Soon we will stop engaging in the fundamental steps of thinking because machines will think in our place!

All forms of work can turn against the worker. Instead of producing a positive effect, work involves danger or an impairment of the worker. The verses quoted above come between sections on the vanity of power and the ambiguous importance of the word. In this context, the meaning of these verses becomes clear, so that we come full circle: work has been examined from its deception to its danger. Consequently, we are advised to work as little as possible, so as to assure ourselves of the minimum we need (assuming work is a necessity, a theme to which we will return): "Better is a handful of quietness than hands full [of riches] or work and striving after wind" (4:6).

We also find ourselves faced with a decisive choice: either we work a lot in order to consume a lot (our Western society's option), or we work less and accept a lower level of consumption (this was sometimes the considered option of certain traditional societies). These days we would like to have it all: working little and consuming much. But all Qohelet's judgment against work still stands: all we have said up to this point concerning hatred of life, mortal competition, the feeling of emptiness, and work's inability to respond to our basic needs. Besides these arguments, we now know how far short excessive consumption falls from being able to compensate for work's emptiness and insignificance.

Having observed work on trial, should we now conclude that it would be best to condemn work and stop working? Not at all—this is not what Qohelet teaches. At this point we sound a different note than when we were dealing with power and money. In connection with these themes, we could not find a single positive word in Qohelet. With respect to work, on the contrary, he offers us a counterpoint within his series of accusations. This contrasting theme occurs throughout the text, at carefully calculated moments.

For instance, one would have to be crazy not to work: "The fool crosses his arms and devours his own flesh" (4:5). The lazy individual is no better off than the worker; his life has no more meaning, and he destroys himself just like the worker. Work may not be a virtue, but laziness is folly. Looked at from one extreme, it amounts to a kind of negation of one's being. And since we are to some degree subject to necessity, this judgment agrees with biblical thought generally.

Qohelet's positive comments on work suggest two modest rewards that go beyond the fact that work enables us to eat. First, satisfying work guarantees peaceful slumber. Yes, that's right: "Sweet is the sleep of the worker, whether he eats little or much;

but the rich person eats his fill and cannot sleep" (5:12). We should not write this advantage off as unimportant! Even if one's work fails to feed him really well, according to our text, it assures him of sleep, whereas the rich person never experiences rest. You can label this text folklore, small-minded morality, or even worse, morality of the "haves," who have reasons for instilling such notions in the "have-nots," and you may be right. We have heard this theory many times. But why not simply observe the reality involved? After all, any worker who does his work, who has responsibility and takes it seriously, knows the truth of our text: work we are satisfied with assures us of sleep.

Second, we have seen that the worker who does not sharpen the edge of the iron when it is blunt will increase his strength (10:10). But if he takes time to sharpen it, if he works at it, this is wisdom! So there is a kind of wisdom to apply to work. These days we appear to have nothing to learn from Qohelet's admonition. We have already learned to organize everything around the importance of work and to apply wisdom to it. This notion holds little significance for us.

Qohelet's essential stance on work involves a paradox: "All work is vanity and a striving after wind; however, we must work." But his "we must" goes far beyond vital, compelling necessity. We must work because work is *a gift from God:* "I have seen the task God has given human beings to work at" (3:10). How amazing! Qohelet does not deny any of his ironies or even his condemnations, but at this point he speaks of the "business" of work that God gives humankind. This text comes right after the question: "What profit has the worker from his toil?" (3:9). Immediately we find "work as God's gift." So we must work, not because work is *useful,* but because it is a gift! Not a compulsion, not an obligation, but a gift. We may not necessarily understand its meaning and value, but after hearing the word of God, we should accept that work is a gift.

Certainly not all work can be called a gift, since work is also vanity and a striving after wind. We must weigh any given work imposed on humanity on both scales. How difficult—or impossible!—we find it to distinguish the gift from mere wind. So Qohelet gives us this astonishing two-pronged advice: "Everything

your hand finds to do with the strength you have, do it" (9:10, JE).[40]
How can anyone accuse Qohelet of always being negative and
skeptical?

We must get to the bottom of this paradox: all is vanity; all
human work is vanity. But whatever your hand finds to do, do it!
In other words, do not worry about its being vanity; do not try to
guess whether it is useful. In any case, it does not matter very much.
This conclusion finds its confirmation in a text we will return to:
"Cast your bread on the face of the waters, for after some days you
will find it again. . . . Whoever observes the wind will not sow, and
whoever looks at the clouds will not reap" (11:1, 4). So you can act
as if you were throwing your bread into a torrent: someday you will
find it again. Do not worry about conditions, meaning, value,
possibilities, the final results of your work. In any case, if you start
taking everything into account, you will do nothing and arrive
nowhere. So do not worry overmuch. Do not get anxious ahead of
time (note how Qohelet prepares us for Jesus' "Do not be anxious"
in Matt. 6:25-33). Just do the work you find at hand, nothing else.

So one person sows and another reaps—so what? Here we find
ourselves at the opposite pole from today's careful reckoning of
rights and duties, from our continual claiming of our rights! Do
what you do as you would throw your bread into the rushing water.
The torrent of our life and of our world carries it off. You find work
vain and useless? In the final analysis, it surely is. We need to know
this in order to avoid seeing our lives as tragic. We must take our
distance and avoid caring passionately about our affairs. Why care
passionately about something vain?

At the same time, however, we must attempt everything: "In

40. Here again, Qohelet refers to Genesis. The biblical account of Creation
ends on the invitation to humanity to "do, accomplish" (Heb. *la'asot,* Gen.
2:1-3): "At this point the sacred notion of Sabbath rest is integrated into the
biblical economy; that is, in a final sense, the dignity of humanity's historical
existence. The entry of the Sabbath is marked by both a retrospective and a
prospective view of work. . . . According to Jewish tradition, imperfection is
the very mark of creation, justifying the necessary creation of humankind,
humanity's autonomous contribution, and its history. This imperfection invites
humankind to act" (Hazan, p. 86).

the morning sow your seed, and until evening do not let your hand rest [curious advice from someone who encourages us to laziness!], for you do not know whether this or that will succeed, or if both together are good" (11:6). You can never foresee the results of your work. So try things, commit yourself, discover, and act in one way or another, on the off chance that something may succeed. The results will not belong to you. "Everything your hand finds to do. . ." (9:10a).

So do not worry so much about determining if something is good and useful, if a given thing would be the will of God for you. You find something within reach? Do it. But, you exclaim, that could be terribly dangerous! The murderer might have his victim within reach! The soldier could make war! No, these conclusions are not justified: you must not separate a verse from what comes before and after it. Before this verse we find: "*God takes pleasure in what you do*" (9:7, JE), and the joy mentioned in this context is to be found *in the midst of your work,* according to verse 9. These comments constitute two limitations, so that "everything" (in 9:10) cannot mean "anything at all." On the one hand, what we choose must be work (and not crime or foolishness); on the other, it must constitute *pleasure for God.* We find a third limitation in the second half of 9:10: Do everything during your life, "for there is no work or thought or knowledge or wisdom in the dwelling place of the dead where you are going" (9:10b, JE). "Everything" thus means some work, thought, knowledge, etc. Within the triangle of these three limitations, all activities are welcome, and you need not weigh other factors. You should do whatever you find within your reach.

We must not neglect any part of this invaluable passage, however: "with your strength." The command given to Gideon comes immediately to mind. In the midst of the catastrophes that were overtaking his people, Gideon becomes convinced that God has abandoned Israel. Then God speaks to him: "Go in this your strength and deliver Israel from the hand of Midian" (Judg. 6:14, NASB). We must interpret these words in two ways, one positive and the other restrictive. Positively, you have strength. You are to accomplish your task with this might. You may not realize how much strength you have: you may think you lack strength or ability.

But Qohelet repeats "with your strength." Do not neglect this strength. And since Qohelet says that God gives you work to do, as he gave Gideon, you can count on strength being given you in what you undertake: enough strength to carry it out, strength that gives authority. But you already have might, just like Gideon, who felt so weak.

But this command also has a restrictive side, which I failed to take into account for many years: you are to accomplish this work you are about to undertake with *your* might, and nothing else. You must not undertake a task that is too much for you. For instance, you must not count on God to enable you to accomplish some heroic or athletic feat, to break a record or to create a work of art for which you lack the ability. No, you must use your strength, nothing else. You must know your ability and its limitations. Commit your might, but nothing beyond it (we must remember we are dealing with *work*). This command is personal. We must learn to grow old, then, and not attempt to overcome the aging process when our strength begins to decline, maintaining we can still do what we did twenty years ago.

Our text requires that we go further. "Do the work with your strength" involves a cultural problem. Can we multiply energy indefinitely? Can we substitute some unlimited source of energy for limited energy sources? Can we undertake projects that use up all the world's reserves for the sake of multiplying human capacity millions of times? True, we *can* do these things now—they have become possible. But do they fall within what is permitted? I know full well that this question will immediately rouse some people's anger and judgment against the backward attitude it supposedly reveals. I answer in the simple fashion of our text: in any case, your work is vanity and a striving after wind—all of it: your satellites and space probes, your nuclear plants, your billions of volts, your millions of cars and television sets. In the dwelling place of the dead, where everything is going, nothing of all this will be left, absolutely nothing.

To bring you joy, then, the work you find within reach is sufficient, using the strength *that you possess,* and not the might of nuclear plants. That handful of wheat you are holding, and fulfillment through small things—these are enough to bring you joy. Anguish only increases as our projects grow more lavish, and devouring the world for the sake of producing something useless only makes our conscience more sensitive to the vanity of such wealth and to the despair of losing it as soon as we earn it. Do all your work, but it is vanity! Qohelet's rather casual wisdom and his irony concerning things we take seriously angers you? What do you mean, work is vanity, and we must receive it as a gift from God? Work is absurd, but we should attempt everything? Yes, that comes from Qohelet, all right, but it is also God's revelation throughout the Bible!

We can conclude by considering three basic guidelines. The first comes from the text itself: "Give a portion to seven, or even to eight, for you do not know what evil may occur on the earth" (11:2). This text follows immediately after "Cast your bread. . . ." So work can take the direction of giving. If you work, in any case you have that possibility: give, share the result of your labors with someone else. This has at least one possible meaning: prepare yourself for future trouble and do not worry about much else. We see a certain parallelism here: God gives you work so that you can have something to give in turn. Again, how this contradicts our concepts of work and profit!

So we need to guard against overgeneralization. We have seen that Qohelet continually repeats that work, money, and wealth are vanity. Furthermore, their outcome is an evil, since you leave what you have accumulated to an unknown person. You do not know if your heir will be worthy of you, if he will be a capable person, etc. Whereas if you *give* something, all this becomes clear: you know the person you give it to! Death does not strip you of anything, since you yourself choose to act. Chance does not choose the fool who will come after you. You give, knowingly (perhaps), and with your gift you establish a relationship. Each idea clarifies the other, so that Qohelet is by no means inconsistent.

The second guideline concerns the "little things." Work is a small thing, a matter we can judge as having little importance. It belongs to this world of vanity and should not be taken too seriously.

But we must do it,[41] and even do it responsibly. Here as well, Qohelet coincides with the Gospel: "Well done, good and faithful servant! You have been *faithful over a little,* I will set you over much" (Matt. 25:21, RSV). Utterly uncompromising, Qohelet goes even further: "There are no big things—the little things make up life, and we must maintain life. Of course everything is vain and a striving after wind. Having acknowledged this, we must be faithful in our useless actions. But we must also weigh what we do according to this uselessness, so as not to devote everything we are to striving after wind!" (see 2:11).

The third guideline confirms the paradox of revelation, which Qohelet presents in its extreme form. This paradox takes its final form in Jesus Christ. We must live by this difficult truth: God does everything—and you must do everything. There may be a contradiction here in terms of formal logic, but not really: this truth sums up our entire relationship with God, and his entire revelation to humanity in the Bible.

7. Happiness

With the theme of happiness, we take another step in the positive direction, but here also we find the "positive" to be relative. In a word, happiness is nothing—it is vanity, too. But it is all a person

41. The necessity of doing "useless" things reminds me of narratives in which we see even God taking "useless" steps. In connection with Moses' useless effort in declaring peace with King Sihon and asking for permission for the people of Israel to go through his territory (Deut. 2:26-32), Rabbi Rashi (quoted by E. Levinas) says: " 'Since God knew my efforts at pacifism were useless,' Moses said, 'I did not receive from him directly the order to call Sihon to peace. But still I took this step.' Doesn't the Midrash tell us that God also took a step he knew in advance to be in vain? When he wanted to give the gift of the Torah to humankind, first he offered it to Esau (who refused it) and Ishmael (who refused it) . . . and thirdly to Israel, who accepted it. . . . This example inspires me."

can aspire to. Qohelet states that happiness is vanity like everything else, in his preface. Yet the quest for happiness was his initial inclination and became his first attempt: "I said in my heart: Come then, let me test you with joy! Taste happiness! And behold, this too is vanity. Of laughter I said: It is madness! And of joy: What does it matter?" (2:1-2). So in the search for the human condition, the first, most obvious step is the experience of happiness or pleasure. This shows, incidentally, that our modern world is not alone in making happiness an ideal, the center and purpose of life.

But whereas our world is incapable of judging happiness as a false value, Qohelet arrives rather quickly at an assessment based on his experience. Yet our search parallels his, even in its means: luxury, consumerism, servants, money, and pleasures. Our advanced, developed society fails to furnish us with anything different than his, if we consider the equivalents in the two cultures! I believe this is of fundamental importance in our day: remembering that the most obvious goal, the first thing we tend to aim for, is happiness. But we also need to remember that today, as formerly, happiness is vanity, folly, insignificance ("What does it matter?"), and a striving after wind. We have a long way to go to understand this lesson! Our world goes on as if it had not heard, as if only happiness and the "right to happiness" actually constituted our goal, our self-realization, and the revelation of the depths of our being.

Happiness is so important to Qohelet that he chooses it as the basis of his first attempt to find the answer to the question "Who am I?" He attempts to satisfy human desire by searching for happiness and experiencing it. But he undertakes his quest with an utterly clear mind, refusing to be taken in by the ease and passivity happiness produces. He comes immediately to a conclusion: happiness is absurd; it has no meaning in the long run. It amounts to "folly," the opposite of wisdom, and is vanity like everything else. Everything we read about happiness *after this* must come under this overall judgment, finding its place *within* this folly and this vanity.

Here we see the enormous error of the interpreters and historians who have tried to group Qohelet with hedonistic philosophers! They have to omit this headline, this initial judgment. But Qohelet's first conclusion enables us to see everything else he says in the right light, in proper perspective.

Even more important, this text shows us that Qohelet is not a philosopher belonging to this group or that group. His approach bears examination; chapter 1 ends with his declaration: "I caused wisdom to increase more than anyone before me in Jerusalem. . . . I applied my heart to wisdom" (1:16, 17, JE). His "experiments" begin right after this statement: What are the paths to wisdom? Work? Happiness? Qohelet searched for happiness, then, not simply because of the pleasure he might find in it, but as a sort of philosophical experiment to find the ways and means of wisdom. He was searching for the center or foundation of a philosophy. His conclusion shows that no philosophy can be founded on happiness and the quest for happiness.

However! Following this preliminary, fundamental affirmation, we find a whole series of positive statements! We could say the whole book is dotted with references to happiness: "There is nothing better for a person than to eat and drink and cause his soul to taste happiness through his work. . . . For 'Who will eat and have enjoyment *apart from me?*' " (2:24a, 25). "Nothing better," he says. But we must be careful: this is not a superlative. It is relative to the human condition "under the sun"; that is, it is vanity, but better than the rest. And if you fail to take the pleasure offered to you, who will take it?

As for the quality of this happiness, we dare not dig too deep: it is not the sublime happiness of the aesthete or the mystic, nor is it the blossoming of the soul, of thought! No, this happiness consists quite simply of eating, drinking, and working well! Qohelet consistently places himself within this circle of happiness—that of the ordinary person. He does not share Epicurus's elevated, demanding concept. Qohelet speaks of every human being's happiness (see 3:12).

He does, however, add two dimensions to this ordinary happiness. The first dimension is enjoying one's own works (3:22). We have already observed this well-known satisfaction, but it brings no ultimate happiness. How could happiness, which is vanity, justify satisfying work? And conversely, how could work, which is vanity, raise happiness to the level of an absolute?

We must take the second dimension into account: the relationship with the wife one loves: "Enjoy life with the wife whom you love" (9:9a). This is certainly good and worth experiencing. But unfortunately this, too, has a limitation. Qohelet goes on: "Enjoy life with the wife whom you love during all the days of your life of vanity" (9:9a). So this happiness does not eliminate vanity; it neither constitutes the meaning of life nor enables a person to escape from himself. No, this happiness occurs within the circle of vanity: during these days of your vanity, you do well to profit from the happiness that love gives. God approves of this, so long as we do not take it for an absolute or for eternity! If you try to escape from vanity through love or happiness, you will find that way lies a trap. Otherwise, it is not only good, but advised, even a commandment.

Qohelet is remarkable: he gives a kind of order to young and old: "Eat, drink, enjoy . . . be happy when pleasure comes." The consequence we draw from this seems essential to me: when days of happiness come, don't torment yourself with thoughts of all that could happen to wreck your happiness, of all the reasons this happiness is incomplete. Don't be discouraged by the fact that it is vanity. When you are happy, don't be on your guard: indulge in this simple pleasure. A holiday is a holiday—away with gloomy thoughts. The food and wine are good; do not look beyond them. This is the day for happiness. Live this moment to its fullest: evil will come another day. Do not be worried about tomorrow: "To-morrow will be anxious for itself" (Matt. 6:34, RSV). Thus Jesus confirms Qohelet's message. "Under the sun," then (not in an absolute sense), receive this unusual commandment from the Word of God: be happy with the simple means of simple human happiness. But with two reservations: in the long run, such happiness is vanity. This fact should not mar our pleasure, however! The second reservation: most important, you need to know that this is a gift from God. We will consider this matter at length later on. For now, this two-pronged judgment is the only one you need to bring to bear on your experiences.

We cannot consider ourselves superior to Qohelet's teaching concerning happiness. He speaks of the reality of all human life. We have no reason to believe we are better than others. Nor should we consider this reality to be something merely contingent, and thus avoidable. The two extremes, work and happiness, are an order, a commandment. We must be happy, with this simple, elementary happiness, not escaping into illusion (whether religious, political, philosophical, or ideological) or into sophistication (by creating artificial paradises). We must not hope that tomorrow will be much better, so that we try at all costs to fabricate some unexpected, perfect happiness. Qohelet warns us against this: "All that comes is vanity" (11:8). And your entire lifetime can pass by in this fashion: "If a person lives many years, *let him delight in them all,* and let him remember that the days of darkness will be many. . . . Delight, young person, in your youth, and let your heart make you happy in the days of your youth" (11:8-9).

So our whole life is involved: during our entire life, we can find and create this happiness we *must* look for! We must use nothing but our human means; we cannot do much more than that, and we need to know this is vanity. Even so, such a life is worth living, Qohelet tells us, if we accept it and desire it on these terms.

We must also desire it, if I am right in my understanding of Qohelet's last instruction: "Eat your bread with joy, and drink your wine with a glad heart. . . . and at all times let your clothes be white, and let not oil be lacking on your head" (9:7-8). Thus we find that this distressing Qohelet, who insists so strongly on the vanity of everything, including our lowly materialistic human happiness, recommends we take pleasure in such a life. Even more, he wants us to let our pleasure show. We should not only eat and drink, but also give certain outward indications of our pleasure that might seem to be unnecessary extras, such as special holiday clothes and perfume. These signs also give a message to others.

Do not despise this vain pleasure. It is worth the trouble. But since it is immersed in vanity, we should surely emphasize the useless side of such happiness, in a society like ours. The "happiness" of consumerism cannot give meaning to life, nor does Qohelet imply that it should. He simply tells us not to neglect happiness in a difficult universe, which depends to some extent on hard drugs to keep going. But in our day, we are so self-assured that we need to hear the opposite truth.

We shall conclude with three remarks. First, happiness is not connected with the accumulation of power and wealth. But, as we have seen, Qohelet's great text on riches does not conclude with hatred of everything. Rather, he maintains that happiness is based on the simplest things: eating and drinking, loving the spouse you spend your life with, and also having friends, as a background theme. The rest amounts to nothing.

The second remark has to do with Qohelet's deliberate scattering and repetition of these texts. His whole book is punctuated with the advice "Enjoy . . ." (which occurs roughly as often as his pronouncements of vanity), as if each sequence called for this advice after sounding its warning.

Third, we should take note of the relationship between happiness and the gift of God. There is nothing better for a person than to eat, drink, and experience happiness through his work: *"I have seen that this also comes from the hand of God"* (2:24). "Go, eat your bread with joy, and drink your wine with a glad heart; for God has already accepted your works" (9:7). We will return to both of these ideas. First, happiness is a gift of God, and you can rejoice because God gives. But, second, you can also rejoice because God accepts your works. Which ones? We do not know—we are simply to take this statement as it stands. I do not believe it means that happiness is a sign of blessing! The train of thought goes a different way: you can eat and drink happily and in peace, you can enjoy life with the spouse you love, you must show your joy by your white clothing (these are found in the same text!) *because* God has accepted your life. This is the good news Qohelet proclaims to you.

Learn that God has approved of your life, and on that basis, with your heart at peace, be happy with the material things that are only vanity in themselves, to be sure! This principle inevitably brings to mind the festival of the Kingdom, where Jesus shows that God invites people *first;* then the guests must show their joy and gratitude by their wedding clothes, like the white clothing in Qohelet (and the one who fails to wear them is thrown out, Matt. 22:1-14).

So that is all? We are just to manifest our joy for such vanities as a good meal, all throughout our lives? No: we are to manifest our joy and desire it because we have understood the importance of the invitation to eat and receive. Even more, because we have learned that God approves of our life. Why? No answer has been given! We have no need to know, but we are to receive this Good News, just because *it is proclaimed to us* (just as the invitation to the wedding was announced). And in the midst of all this vanity, it becomes possible to rejoice and be happy. Everything moves on and disappears, but that in no way changes the pronouncement God makes on our life. This is the meaning and the limit placed on happiness. Any other meaning given to it falls within the circle of vanity.

8. The Good

Qohelet is not a book on morality! Although he declares certain situations "evil," our author says almost nothing about "good." He neither suggests what we should do nor engages in praise of the good. On the contrary! We have seen the importance of happiness in this book, but the good is nearly absent. I am tempted to leave the matter with a quotation from J. Keynes: "Evil is useful, but good is not" (he was speaking as an economist!). All we see in Qohelet is that doing good, being just, etc., are useless and have no meaning in the long run: "There is a vanity that is done on earth: some just people are treated according to the work of the wicked, and some wicked are treated according to the work of the just. I have said, this also is vanity" (8:14). Of course, Qohelet does not approve of this situation. He does not even state objectively "that is how things are." No, he finds in such events an evidence of vanity.

This vanity takes many forms and turns up everywhere. The passage just quoted points up one of them: just and unjust people are treated in the same way. There is no justice—no reward we can expect if we do good and act justly. Everything is inverted, perverted, or muddled by the enormous effect of vanity: "Everything is the same for everybody: an identical destiny awaits the just person and the wicked, the good person [and the evil one], the pure and the impure, the one who sacrifices and the one who does not sacrifice. The good person is like the sinner; the one who takes a vow is like the person who fears to take an oath. This is an evil in everything done under the sun: that there should be the same destiny for everyone" (9:2-3).

At this point, Qohelet commits himself: the lack of justice is not just vanity but an evil, an evil that prevails. We must not think we can escape from it by means of good, virtue, justice, or religion. People's destinies are always identical in the long run, so that placing our hope in our goodness is mere vanity.

Take note that Qohelet's argument differs from the usual "everyone dies all the same." This idea certainly enters into what he says: the good person and the wicked person die alike, and their death resembles that of an animal (3:19). But the powerful notion of vanity conveyed by Qohelet seems to me to stem from another idea: "some just people *are treated according to the work* of the wicked" (8:14). In other words, neither God nor destiny brings this about: humankind behaves in this way. We do not recognize the just person. We treat him like a wicked individual, thus adding our human contribution to the world's vanity.

Do not expect any reward or renown; do not expect others to appreciate you because you are good and just. You will simply be wasting your time if you anticipate such a result. There is no justice on earth or beyond for us to look forward to, no human solidarity for the purpose of bringing about the triumph of the good, no struggling together against the vanity of the human condition or to set up a right scale of values. By means of one's judgments and criteria for deciding what is good, everyone only adds to the world's vanity.

This state of things wrecks the very foundation of our claims that human nature is good or to be followed. It topples our notions about the human capacity for discerning what is good and just, for weighing things soundly on the basis of morality and equity, etc. No just politics can be devised. History and society are founded on vanity and evil; they cannot possibly provide us with any guidelines. We must remember they are just wind, smoke, mist, vanity. History, politics, society, and the good amount to nothing more.

Do not protest that Qohelet is an unusual or unique book that we must not rely on for guidance, since elsewhere in the Bible we find something different, etc. In reality this book also constitutes a preface. If we fail to listen to it from the outset, if we do not start out penetrated with its rigorous approach, or if we refuse its radicalism, we are bound to turn the rest of revelation into a collection of children's fairy tales. Consider: if this pronouncement concerning the uselessness of goodness scandalizes us, how can we accept the crucifixion? Take Qohelet's words on "the just being treated as though they were wicked" (8:14), and "an identical destiny awaits the just person and the wicked" (9:2). Do not these harsh words find their complete and harsh fulfillment in the condemnation of Jesus, who was pure goodness, justice, and love, yet was "numbered with the transgressors" (Isa. 53:12), crucified with thieves (or terrorists, if you prefer!)? The problem is that the crucifixion belongs to our mental universe so that it fails to shock us. What shocks us is Qohelet's *generalization*.

Let us avoid confusion: when I refer to Jesus Christ, I do not mean that our text is exclusively prophetic, that its only referent is Jesus. This elegant maneuver is often used to get rid of a biblical text: claiming it "prophesies" something about Jesus, with the unspoken understanding that it does not concern *us*. I simply mean that this harsh affirmation finds its confirmation in Jesus' experience, so that Qohelet's statements become undeniable.

So we are all immersed in vanity. Qohelet certainly realizes the evil in this situation, but states things as they are. Doing good has no purpose. It does not enable you to escape humanity's common destiny or other people's hatred. Certainly Qohelet does not tell us we *must not* do good: just that we must not expect anything from it or be shocked by the triumph of the evil person and the defeat of the just person. We must not have blind faith in some triumphant future for humanity. We have already encountered this principle when we examined Qohelet's denial of progress. Here we find the same idea in connection with the victory of vanity over the good.

This lesson on vanity does not constitute pessimism, but rather a warning. Qohelet shows us the reality of what surrounds us so we will not take it seriously, so we will not *believe* in it. We must not attach our love, our truth, or our person to this reality. Do not devote yourself to all this, since that would amount to chasing after wind!

Nor is vanity a philosophy or a concept of human life. It constitutes a reminder and a warning for each of us as we live out our lives. Qohelet wants us to understand that our whole life, in all its aspects, is subject to vanity. But of course you may respond that this amounts to pessimism in spite of what I have said. If we give Qohelet a serious hearing, however, we come to an entirely different conclusion: recognizing my life is subject to vanity means that in the final analysis I cannot place *myself* in the center; not in the center of the world, not in the center of my circle of relationships, not in the center of history, action, or culture.

We need to reflect on the importance of this shift of perspective. It does not amount merely to a rejection of egoism and egotism (on the basis of the knowledge that my life is vanity, not because of morality and a proper attitude!). Such a shift also implies rejecting the belief predominant in the West that once we have asserted our culture and our economic concepts as the only valid ones, we can destroy other cultures and economic systems. Remember your culture and political system are vanity! And then listen to others and respect them.

Faith represents another area in which self-centeredness has made victims of us all. Our private understanding of Scripture is vanity. If I am to comprehend revelation, I must listen to others. I must also struggle against the nagging temptation to substitute *my* interest or *my* person for the center of revelation: the person of Jesus Christ! If I fail to realize that I am vanity, the ideas that preoccupy me (such as my personal salvation) or interest me (revolution, for instance) become the basis of my interpretation of Scripture. Thus the Bible becomes a sort of mine in which I hunt for *my* answers and arguments! Remember when you do this that you and your ideas are only vanity. Listen to something besides yourself.

9. Human Answers

In view of the above situation, can there be a more desirable, better-adapted human attitude? Let us begin by ruling out the solution that automatically comes to mind. For Qohelet, the human response to all this does not lie in religion. Later we will see what he thinks of religion! Useless, he will conclude, because the same fate awaits "the pure and the impure, the one who sacrifices and the one who does not sacrifice. The good person is like the sinner; the one who takes a vow is like the person who fears to take an oath" (9:2). So religion fails to stand up in the face of "all is vanity." We need to establish this fact at the outset!

Well, then, does Qohelet give us any advice? We will come later to what he continually says about wisdom. But even apart from wisdom, we can find a whole series of attitudes he considers to have some importance. First, however, I want to establish that for Qohelet (in reality, for the whole Bible) the real human adventure begins on the basis of the radical thought that "all is vanity."[42] It begins when we realize that basically nothing has any use, when all our illusions have been stripped away. Then, once the ground is cleared this way, the adventure can begin. But first we must be stripped and still manage to survive! Like the camel, we can go through the eye of the needle only if we take nothing with us: the camel must have neither saddle nor baggage. When we come out on the other side, we are naked and alone. Vanity affects us this way.

How can we respond to "all is vanity"? Perhaps with a kind of stoicism? We can find such an attitude underlying the pages of Qohelet: this is the way things are, no point complaining and lamenting the fact; hang your head and go on existing, in spite of everything. You will lose everything you have; every single memory of you will disappear after two or three generations (1:11). And you leave your work to heirs who may not deserve it or make good use of it. If you die leaving no heirs, that is equally bad. But you must accept that, in either case, this is vanity—no point despairing.

Let us note in passing the harsh sobriety of our text. No romanticism here! Qohelet does not bewail our sad human fate. He

42. Again I find I agree with Maillot, when he writes that Qohelet denounces human works only to the degree that we require them to resolve the mystery of our destiny (p. 27). It is not the realities but our relationship with them that is without value. Our human drama consists of our becoming the servants or slaves of things that should serve us. This fundamentally idolatrous tendency of ours motivates the biblical attacks on everything that panders to our idolatry.

tells it like it is, so that we are warned and can make our decision. We do well to be strong and courageous (since at the same time Qohelet invites us to work, even if work is vanity and its results offer us nothing). This is not philosophical stoicism, following the great Greek intellectual models.[43] Qohelet's is an everyday stoicism: "Do with stout heart your long and dreary task, / No respite look for and no mercy ask, / And in unbroken silence die like me."[44]

But Qohelet does not remain at this point of acceptance. We now enter an extremely ambiguous universe, in which we can never be sure we have fathomed the author's intention. He may mean what he says, he may be mocking bits of popular "wisdom," or, on the contrary, he may mean the opposite of what he says! This ironic tone underlies everything Qohelet says to us, in my opinion.

Irony has two forms, however: direct and indirect. Certainly, when our text states that work provokes jealousy, or when it describes a person who has accumulated great wealth without knowing who will inherit it, we have simple, direct irony. Other examples: "Do not be too wise" (7:16, JE); "The laughter of a fool is like the sound of thorns burning under the kettle" (7:6, JE); "Being protected by wisdom means being protected by money" (7:12). Or consider this amazing verse: "I have seen the wicked carried to their tomb; out of the holy place they go, with people forgetting in the city that they [the wicked] used to behave that way" (8:10). In other words, the wicked are praised and honored; they are lavishly buried—the whole city takes them to their last dwelling place, starting out from the "holy place." How many church burials resemble this one? All these examples involve direct irony.

---

43. The very diversity of the parallels scholars insist on finding between Qohelet and Greek philosophers makes such finds suspect. Since Qohelet is obviously an intelligent person, had he known the stoics (he lived a bit too early for that!), the hedonists, or the skeptics, he would have presented his thought differently. I do not deny all relationship with the milieu of Greek thought; on the contrary. But I take exception to the view that Qohelet was influenced in a major way by any school. Qohelet is Qohelet, not some Hellenistic by-product. See Lauha's introduction (pp. 11-12).

44. Vigny, "The Wolf," in William Frederick Giese, *French Lyrics in English Verse* (Madison, WI: University of Wisconsin Press, 1946), p. 179.

We must not become overconfident, however. Qohelet often gives us a text that looks simple enough but has a second meaning. For instance, the declaration "all is vanity" seems utterly direct. But can we be certain this is his last word? Should we not read this first thought in the light of what he says at the end of his text? I believe that throughout the book Qohelet alludes to a truth that differs from the one that appears so simple.

In reality, it seems to me that what Qohelet has to say cannot be communicated directly, as is. This is true, first, because truth can never be conveyed directly, and second, because if he blurted out his message in plain terms, it would lead us to despair. Rather than a book of despair, Qohelet is part of the Good News, as we have already seen. Furthermore, it seems clear to me that the message of this book is not the enormously hackneyed exhortation that has been repeated so often: "the things of this world do not count, so turn toward God." This book is not *The Imitation of Christ,* and Qohelet is not the author of an apologetic. But "that which is deep, deep, who will measure it?" (7:24, JE). So we are faced here with typical "indirect communication" and "veiled truth." The pseudonyms and opening verses prepared us for this.

Qohelet does not write this way because he enjoys communicating in code, but because he is dealing with truth, and there is no other way to express it. No direct statement of truth is possible, because it does not belong to the order of our intellectual capacity or to our dimension. This principle applies not only to God's truth but to everything that belongs to the order of truth. Indirect communication is the only possibility, because it is the only accessible, bearable communication.[45]

45. I have three comments to make on this matter: (1) I deal with this issue in *The Humiliation of the Word,* establishing the relationship between word and truth, which excludes images, just as images exclude truth. They belong to different "orders." In that book I explain that precisely because images are the exact medium, they deal with the most uncertain and fluid matter: reality. Conversely, since truth remains immutable, transcendent, and absolute, we can reach it only through the most easily misconstrued, unstable, and fluid medium: the word. (2) My comments above concerning indirect communication hold true not only for God's truth but also for what scientists call "truth" (or what

Although indirect communication is the only accessible, tolerable medium, it also proves misleading and scandalous. So when Qohelet gives us a radical description of the reality of the world, society, and humanity, he is neither reporting his observations nor deploring the lack of meaning in life. We arrive at these conclusions

---

everyone calls "truth" when speaking about science). It is impossible to convey directly the things scientists know and understand, whether they deal with galaxies or the composition of matter. To explain such concepts, we resort to mathematical symbols and equations, graphics, or diagrams (such as the well-known drawings of the structure of an atom, which of course do not represent reality). Absolutely none of these media involve the direct transmission of what the scientist wants to express. They constitute an imaginary, approximate representation: in other words, indirect communication. (3) Kierkegaard emphasizes that such indirect communication is the only medium possible in our relationship with Jesus Christ (see "Thoughts which determine the meaning of 'the offence' strictly so called," in Kierkegaard's *Training in Christianity and the Edifying Discourse which "Accompanied" It*, trans. Walter Lowrie [Princeton, NJ: Princeton University Press, 1947], pp. 122-44). Kierkegaard considers that indirect communication constituted Jesus' primary suffering, since he could not communicate directly to people that he was the Christ, the Son of God, God himself (this explains why he never applies these titles to himself, using instead "son of man"). Because of his indirect communication, this man who is God represents *both* the possibility of faith *and* the possibility of scandal. But Kierkegaard explains that "if the possibility of offence were lacking, direct communication would be in place, and thus the God-Man would be an idol. Direct recognizableness is paganism" (*Training in Christianity*, p. 143). Kierkegaard maintains that indirect communication is infinitely more difficult to sustain than direct communication: "Human beings need each other, and this is a direct need"; "only the God-Man is pure indirect communication from start to finish . . . he in no way shapes himself to conform to human ideas, and does not speak to people directly." He speaks in parables, and always reveals himself as the servant, the poor and suffering one (with one exception: the Transfiguration; and we know how that was misinterpreted!). When he seems to speak directly (to the rich, the Pharisees, the temple merchants), we fail to understand him, thinking he is a lawbreaker, a revolutionary, etc. We misconstrue his actions just as the people of his day did. This shows that his communication remains indirect. Thus we have two levels in Qohelet: direct and indirect communication. These make the book difficult to understand, since we tend to see in it either the hackneyed phrases of commonplace wisdom or incomprehensible references to a God who intervenes for reasons we cannot fathom!

if we take his words as direct communication. But Qohelet's words involve an indirect communication of the truth, which goes well beyond what he says. When he refers explicitly to this truth, we have the impression we are reading a useless, unrelated addendum.

When we discover that everything around us is vanity, this constitutes the indirect communication of something good. Such indirect communication sometimes appears as veiled irony. At other times it takes the form of antiphrasis or truism. The fragmentary form and woven thematic texture in Qohelet that we have already noted stem from such indirect communication. The continual recurrence of themes seen from differing angles in no way constitutes a string of maxims stuck together.

We should place Qohelet's indirect irony in this same context. Some of his catchy phrases amaze us. I will not go into detail at this point, since we will return to this theme when we deal with wisdom. But we should note the intertwining of utterly trite commonplaces and the eruption of a steel-tipped barb in the form of a statement that jolts and shocks us. The beginning of chapter 7 is typical of this pattern: "Fame is better than perfumed oil" (7:1); "the heart of fools is in the house of joy" (7:4b); "it is better to listen to the rebuke of a wise person than to listen to the flattery of fools" (7:5); "it is better to be longsuffering than proud in spirit" (7:8); "Do not say: The old days were better than these" (7:10, JE); "the advantage of knowledge is that it gives life to the one who has it" (that is, it earns money for him; 7:12); "a present can ruin a person's heart" (7:7, JE). What a string of pearls! These remind us of the stock phrases and worst platitudes of Job's friends.

But this series, an obvious reflection of current opinion, is carefully cut with a scalpel, with a harshness and a flair for scandalousness that bring false, rudimentary wisdom crashing down into ruin. Qohelet obliges us to search elsewhere, and contrasts this advice on good, sensible behavior with his radical finale. Indirect irony provides us, I believe, with the key for understanding such apparently incoherent texts.

Here we observe the same contrast one can observe between Job and his friends, except that here we find it within a single couplet: "Fame is better than perfumed oil" (7:1a). True, but Qohelet has emphasized that "fame" does not last: it sinks into oblivion. In any case, the effect of these words is ruined by what follows: "and the day of death [is better] than the day of one's birth" (7:1). So if everything depends on the illusion of a good reputation, if a person's life consists of what others think of him, life is not worth living, and it would be better to die immediately! The day of birth inserts us into a world of falsification as vain as perfumed oil.

Similarly, when we learn we must beware of "the house of joy," we should consider the counterpart of this statement: "The heart of the wise is in the house of mourning" (7:4). Only in the face of death can the wise person understand and receive anything. For that reason, grief and suffering have more value than laughter. Only suffering can enable a person to reach something more.

All this trite, parroted wisdom stumbles on the definitive "Better the end of a matter than its beginning" (7:8). The beginning amounts to a lie, illusion, folly, childish wisdom: a meaningless undertaking with no significance. Earth offers us no other sort of beginning (so that the wise person's rebuke amounts to a bad joke). It is wiser and more appropriate, then, to put an end to a matter. No point in thinking we can right the situation. Only indirect irony, by means of its convoluted progression, can lead us—not to the truth, but possibly to the place where the path to truth begins, perhaps to the edge of truth's woods, to the fork in the road where we must choose.

It seems to me that we need to maintain this same perspective as we read Qohelet's astonishing advice concerning the happy medium, worldly discretion, and political caution! Let us not forget that Qohelet's irony functions on two levels: he uses direct irony to counter habitual stances of ordinary people as they attempt to avoid the icy harshness of the truths he shows us. When he wants to introduce us to truth, he has recourse to indirect irony.

Two wonderful examples of the author's cautious half-measures will help us here: "Do not become righteous in the extreme, and do not make yourself excessively wise; why destroy yourself? Do not be wicked in the extreme, and do not become foolish: why die before your time? It is good that you cling to this and that you not allow your hand to let go of that, for the one who fears God will fulfill both" (7:16-18). Religion is all right, but not in excess; evil is useful, but we should not go too far. And then do not try to do two things at once. Such fine advice Qohelet gives us! Virtue lies in the middle! Be careful not to overdo it, be neither too pious nor too wise, but do not lack these qualities, either. Excess is always a fault. Too much wisdom would make you stand out from others, so that you might be judged, perhaps even by the authorities!

Can we seriously believe that such praise of caution and half-heartedness represents Qohelet's real thought? Would this writer who pours his acid-like sarcasm, without any reservation, all over everything we consider right and good, all our hopes and honor, promote such "wisdom"? Come now! Such pseudo-wisdom belongs to vanity and wind. It is utterly useless, both on earth and in the presence of God: "Because you are lukewarm, and neither cold nor hot, I will spew you out of my mouth" (Rev. 3:16, RSV).

I believe we need to take Qohelet's recommendations of obedience to the authorities and extreme caution in politics with the same grain of salt. He warns us to obey the king in everything: "If the leader's anger rises against you, do not leave your place, for calm prevents great evils" (10:4, JE). And be discreet and secretive: "Even in your heart, do not disparage the king, and do not disparage the rich person in your bedroom, for the birds of heaven will relate the word, and winged creatures will make the thing known" (10:20). These two passages offer us wonderful advice to be cautious, indifferent, and suspicious. Can we believe they come from the same writer whose attack on the rich and the king we have considered? The author who depicted the king as senile and mad, who called power an evil? We must get serious! Such a possibility seems highly unlikely—much more so than Qohelet's references to God, which hasty exegetes have found inconsistent.

Note that I am not suggesting some copyist added such lines of advice. That would not make any sense. Qohelet sifts through human absurdities, false wisdom, and cowardly caution, bringing all his irony to bear on them. In this way, when he gives "good advice" in the manner of Jean de la Fontaine, he trips up the reader who takes his words at face value instead of sensing the enormous contradiction involved. Qohelet's massive affirmation of vanity reduces everything mediocre, lukewarm, and cautious to silence.

The existence of vanity makes the person who tries to figure everything out in advance seem ridiculous (we can see this clearly when Qohelet attacks such attempts by saying, in essence, "if you examine the sky and try to tell what direction the wind is coming from and which way the clouds are blowing, you will never do anything" [see 11:4]).

In other words, we could arrive at a kind of ethic: on the one hand, we must relativize everything, measuring all by the standard of the absolute. Consequently everything looks like nothing, or perhaps, to take the extreme view, everything becomes a death warrant. What is left, then? Just relative things (happiness, work, justice), which we must undertake and live out *as relative.* That is, we must do them free from the crushing weight of anxiety and free from obsession with tomorrow. This constitutes the good. On the other hand, we should reject with savage irony all lukewarmness, lack of commitment and of boldness, the "wisdom" of small-minded bourgeois shopkeepers (see G. Flaubert's *Bouvard et Pécu-chet*), commonplaces and new commonplaces. These things are bad. We must maintain a sharply critical view of what people commonly think of as truth, yet not confuse this stance with the relativization of all causes.

But if vanity reduces everything to nothing in this way, leaving things with no meaning or value, is it worth the trouble to pursue something that leaves us empty-handed? Should we try to catch the wind? No, it is not worthwhile, but this is a time for living, after all, a complex time made up of many things. Although relative, these things are all we can manage. We find the highest expression of this relativity of everything in Qohelet's wonderful text:

> For everything there is a moment,
> and a time for everything under the heavens. (3:1)

We will return to this poem in chapter IV below.

This "time," which the author speaks of without giving it a preliminary definition, is to be lived and not done away with. Qohelet never suggests suicide as a possible response. He goes so far as to say that if life is like this, it would be better not to have lived: "And I praised the dead who are already dead more than the living who are still alive; and happier than both of them [I say] is the one who has not yet been, because he has not seen the evil work that is done under the sun" (4:2-3). The dead are happier than the living, because they no longer have to struggle with this vanity, with the unsolvable problem of finding meaning in life, with the unsolvable problem of the utter injustice of life, with the impossible riddle of wisdom. Why bother to exhaust ourselves for such things? Those who have never lived are happier still, he says, since they have never entered this circle of weariness and vanity. They have never run into the unsolvable and unfathomable problems of life. Most important, those who have never lived have no experience of the evil and injustice that take place under the sun.

Injustice is the issue here, since Qohelet's declaration (4:2-3) follows his condemnation of all oppression and his lament over the absence of a comforter and liberator. Under such circumstances, it would be better not to have lived than to run the risk of carrying the memory of oppression and the triumph of evil to one's tomb.

We find no happy people in this passage. "Happier," he says (4:3), but how can he affirm that they are happy, when the dead are those who feel and experience nothing? They most certainly are *not* happy! But Qohelet judges that they are: "And I declared that the dead . . . are happier than the living" (4:2, NIV). He adds nothing. In spite of this radical stance, Qohelet by no means advocates suicide. There is a time to live (we will consider its source), *and we must live it.*

As the author often states, we can work and indulge in joy and happiness (for a while!) during this time. This keeps us busy and helps the time pass, but not much else. Things are relative: folly reigns, but sometimes we can slip in a bit of wisdom; vanity reigns, but sometimes we can discover a hint of meaning. We must have no illusions, however. We are to do these relative things, rather than abolishing them, thus filling up the time allotted to us. You can do this; we can do good just as well as evil. But once we have taken a good look at vanity, we can never have the first blush of our illusions of purity and beauty back again: "One fly spoils the ointment." The fly lies there, dead. Nothing can give us back our innocence.

Time is not a kind of wealth filled with wonderful gifts. On the contrary! It is something to be filled up, nothing more. Baudelaire errs when he says: "Each moment, foolish mortal, is like ore / From which the precious metal must be wrung."[46] The moments contain nothing. They will be what you make of them, and you can make anything of them you like. Instead of crushing a nugget to find the treasure in it, you must bring your treasure to it so the time will be rich. But usually it is only vanity. Time is available, and you give meaning to it.

We have passed in review just about everything that goes to make up a person's life, everything that constitutes one's universe. We have found nothing but mist, smoke, lack of solidity, and vanity. Everything is either subject to the power of nothingness or situated between two voids. Paul takes up this idea in Romans (8:20): all of creation was subjected to vanity or to the power of nothingness, or situated between two voids. We see, from the fact that Paul takes up Qohelet's harsh view of the world, that our author in no way indulges in the cynical description given by a person "without God." On the contrary, he places in our hands the experience of a believer who bears the world's vanity before God, of one who takes it up as his responsibility.

By this radical act, Qohelet by no means condemns the world; he merely leads us to grasp the situation and to grasp our reality within it. He brings to light the deepest wretchedness of creation: the unpardonable and inexcusable wretchedness, the ongoing scandal of it. But Qohelet cannot hold out the hope so roundly affirmed by Paul. Qohelet lived during the time of waiting, and he took the first step. A person could do no more, then; the rest of what he was waiting for would come in time.

46. From "The Clock," in *Poems of Baudelaire,* trans. Roy Campbell (New York: Pantheon Books, 1941), p. 111.

10. Conclusion

We must keep trying to avoid misunderstanding. Everything we have just tried to express on vanity does not constitute a philosophy. It does not amount to a concept of human life, nor is it a treatise. At several points I have used the word "existential," which suggests a philosophical tendency these days, because of the development of existentialism. But when I use the word, I am attempting to avoid just such a connotation.

Qohelet does not attach the label of "vanity" to some trite generality about life. If we think he makes no value judgment in what he says, we have missed his point. He means to make each of us reflect on our own past life in its reality and concreteness. He does not say "life" is vanity, but rather your life, my life. Everything needs to be translated into the first person. Rather than using the currently fashionable and utterly childish expression "I is another,"[47] Qohelet says "I is vanity." This is no idea or opinion. What Qohelet says is true of "me" in every way. How can I be so radical and uncompromising in this attitude? I take my cue from Qohelet himself: he says "I" at every turn.

We need to look at this from another angle: Qohelet does not conclude that work or money is vanity based on his reflection alone. He bases his conclusion on his experience, which is his whole self. This discovery leads him to important consequences. If I am vanity, my life has very little importance, and I can by no means consider myself as the center of the world. My work and my experience also amount to wind and a chasing after wind.

If we apply it to a very concrete area such as biblical interpretation, for instance, this principle leads us to astonishing conclusions! It produces a rather significant shift in almost all biblical interpretation. Of course, everyone rightly repeats that we read the Bible with an interpretative grid, a cultural grid, etc. But I refer to a more serious matter: when I read the Bible I place *my* interests or *my* person at the center. I construct the biblical message on that basis.

47. A phrase from the nineteenth-century poet Arthur Rimbaud, more recently used by Jacques Lacan.—TRANS.

Let us examine two completely different examples that can clarify this slant we put on what we read. The first example is almost frivolous, and the second has basic importance. (1) Think of all the people (mainly women) who have as their main concern the feminist "cause" and its triumph. When they read Paul's letters, they will feel exasperation at his three "antifeminist" passages and will remember nothing else. Sometimes they interpret everything Paul says in the light of this exasperation; more often they throw out the whole revelation given to Paul, saying it holds no interest, since Paul was a phallocratic misogynist. You can substitute a person's political option or a scientific certainty in this exercise. The interpretation always comes down to our interests and opinions. But if "I" is vanity, perhaps I could forget "I" for a bit and listen to something besides the thing that obsesses me?

(2) Individual salvation constitutes a much more fundamental and weighty issue. What concerns me is *my* person, *my* salvation, *my* faith, *my* eternal life, etc. We always center the matter on ourselves. But we are astonished to find that Jesus did just the opposite. If "I" is vanity, then the main question is not my salvation, but the turning over of myself to the One who should be everything and in everyone. At this point I can let go of my preoccupation with self. My approach to the Bible changes immediately. I cannot continue to construct a theology of individual salvation. What matters is this Other, who is not vanity. I must not make use of the Bible for my own ends, but rather take myself out of the picture as much as possible, in order to listen and learn. This way I may hear a word that has never entered into the human heart and that will catch me unawares. This is how far the principle of vanity can take us.

CHAPTER III

Wisdom and Philosophy

A touching story will help to focus our search for wisdom in Qohelet and through his thought. Albert Einstein was at work when the bombing of Hiroshima became known. An American general rushed to inform him, telex in hand. Einstein took his head in his hands, remaining silent for a time, and then said: "The old Chinese were right: you cannot do whatever you want."

Wisdom appears in our text just as insistently as vanity, but readers tend to attach much less importance to it! "Vanity of vanities" appeals to our masochism, giving us the sensation of arriving at something profound. Vanity fits our gnawing anguish as moderns. But wisdom? So what? That is a dusty business from an outmoded culture. The concept holds no interest whatever for us in the age of computers and atoms. The French may have an even more negative reaction, associating wisdom with their childhood, when the word was continually used in the warning to "be good"—but it is true that few parents use the expression these days!

"Despair" (although we have just seen that Qohelet by no means preaches despair!) stirs up vibrations within us, but virtue or wisdom does not. Nevertheless, wisdom remains present throughout Qohelet, punctuating the text in a sort of counterpoint. We should recognize, however, that wisdom is also subject to vanity! Qohelet is not an apologetic that begins by showing the vanity of things in order to lead the reader to recognize the truth (of God or wisdom!). Can we consider wisdom as the answer, the solution, to the problem of vanity? Here we have one of the fundamental questions raised by Qohelet. The importance of this matter is underlined by the fact that wisdom, in its various guises, represents our finest human invention. In Qohelet we find it too has been corroded and eaten away. But a small part of it holds out against this process.

Not all wisdom is vanity. Yet we cannot fail to be struck by a disconcerting contradiction maintained throughout Qohelet. Sometimes wisdom is praised above all else, as the only worthy human occupation: "Wisdom is as good as an inheritance, and it is profitable to those who see the sun" (7:11). Unlike work, which provides no benefit, wisdom is advantageous. Yet at other times wisdom is brushed aside and rejected, like wind, along with everything else: "I spoke with my heart, saying: Behold, I have caused wisdom to grow and progress more than anyone before me over Jerusalem, and my heart has abundantly enjoyed wisdom and knowledge. I applied my heart to understanding wisdom and to understanding madness and folly, and I knew that this also is a pursuit of wind" (1:16-17).

Neher shows that Qohelet maintains two "registers" with respect to wisdom: an ordinary, trite "wise approach" recommending common sense and the happy medium, and a second level of terrible anxiety and doubt. I believe there are many more registers! Furthermore, we must now consider the subject of wisdom within the context of von Rad's overall study *(Wisdom in Israel),* and take into account Lys's discussion of wisdom as the equivalent of philosophy.

On the subject of wisdom, von Rad strongly emphasizes that Qohelet "stands firmly in the wisdom tradition" (p. 227), but that prior to Qohelet this tradition remained strongly confident about good and evil, how to act, etc. Qohelet breaks "the strong urge to master life. . . . Man has lost contact with events in the outside world. Although continually permeated by God, the world has become silent for him" (p. 232). "The essential element in the chance character of the temporal realization of destiny for men is the inscrutability of the future."[1] "Man never achieves dialogue

---

1. Von Rad, *Wisdom in Israel,* p. 232 n. 58, quoting E. Wölfel, *Luther und die Skepsis* (1958), pp. 49-50.

with his surroundings, still less with God" (p. 233). Qohelet's God carries on no conversation with humanity. Job rebelled, but "Koheleth no longer poses Job's question as to whether this God is still his God" (ibid.).

Between Qohelet and the teachings of Proverbs lies an enormous distance. Qohelet opposes the principal doctrines of wisdom, which lack realism on the one hand and are too dogmatic on the other. But we must go further: Qohelet "is turning against not only outgrowths of traditional teaching but the whole undertaking" (p. 233). Von Rad offers a basic explanation: "The experience in which the older teachers put their trust was of a different kind from that which finds expression in Koheleth. The former was an experience which was in constant dialogue with faith; reason was at work, reason which never set itself up as an absolute but which knew that it was based on knowledge about Yahweh" (p. 234). In Qohelet we find utter vulnerability, since he fails to share the older teachers' confidence. He no longer truly has faith in Yahweh: "Koheleth's greatest predicament lies in the fact that he has to set out to answer the question of the meaning of life . . . with a reason which is almost completely unsupported by any confidence in life. He confronts that question with the totality of life and simply makes it responsible for answering the question about salvation. The old teachers, in their search for understanding, were more modest and certainly also cleverer. They did not see it as their task to answer, by means of their still only partially valid understanding and experiences, the ultimate question, the question of salvation" (p. 235).

"Anyone who has listened carefully to Koheleth's dialogue with the traditional doctrines should not find it quite so easy to give one-sided approval to the lonely rebel" (p. 235). This is especially true for von Rad, who finds that

> in the radicalism of his questioning he has become completely the spectator, only observing, registering and submitting. In contrast to the older wise men, he has overstepped a limit which was drawn . . . for them. While they, in order to interpret the realities of their life, did not make use of any all-embracing, abstract terms, Koheleth immediately goes the whole way. In order to find the

definitive formula, he lumps the whole of life's experience together, and the result is 'vanity.' . . . His reason is on the look-out
for a final abstraction. . . . Koheleth has withdrawn from every
active development in life and has thereby excluded himself, from
the outset, from a wide range of conclusive experiences. . . .
Koheleth . . . was incapable of entering into a dialogue with the
world which surrounded him and pressed in on him. It had become
for him a silent, unfriendly, outside force which he was able to
trust only where it offered him fulfilment of life. The wise men,
however, were of the opinion that, through the medium of the
world as it addressed man, God himself spoke to man, and that
only in this dialogue was man shown his place in life. (pp. 236-37)

As the reader will note, in progressing through the following
pages, I am utterly opposed to von Rad's opinion, in spite of his
scholarship. I believe he, too, has been taken in by the massiveness
of Qohelet's "all is vanity," and has failed to appreciate the extraordinary complexity of this text.

Lys reminds us of the antiquity of wisdom and humanity's
universal search for it (p. 45). Wisdom in Israel incorporates some
aspects of pagan wisdom from various sources. Wisdom literature
finds its way into the canon on the basis of the covenant, which
proclaims that the Law is written on the human heart, assuming the
possibility of direct knowledge of God the creator of the world (pp.
49-50).

Lys establishes a fundamental distinction between wisdom
and salvation history (although Qohelet clearly belongs to the
history of revelation!). Wisdom in Israel deals more with the
destiny of individuals than with the lot of the elect people of God
as a group (pp. 47-48). Such wisdom might have led to a kind of
"natural religion," but Lys shows that nothing of the sort occurs in
Qohelet!

Barucq and others have tried to distinguish between Qohelet's
imitation of traditional wisdom's teachings and the points on which
he parts company with tradition: basic questions concerning the
problems of the human condition (Barucq, pp. 17-21, 57-61).
Tradition guaranteed success to those relying on wisdom, but

Qohelet denies it the right to such a claim. No wise person possesses the secret of success![2]

Moreover, we must distinguish three Hebrew terms: *ḥokmah* (wisdom), *byn* (intelligence), and *daʿat* (science or knowledge). But Lys translates *ḥokmah*, which occurs throughout Qohelet, as "philosophy," since the value of the term "wisdom" has eroded in French. The work of the wise person as described by Qohelet is certainly the equivalent of the philosopher's task: "he observes the world and tries to understand its meaning" (Lys, p. 153). The philosopher searches for "logos" in phenomena, in order to learn how to live. Although this is true, I would prefer the term "wisdom," since it implies an art of living rather than an understanding. Furthermore, Qohelet aims at something broader than what we now call "philosophy." Be that as it may, we should keep Lys's translation in mind.

As for *daʿat* (from the root *ydʿ*), its connotation varies. We find it forty-three times in Qohelet, sometimes praised (7:12; 12:9), sometimes questioned (1:18; 9:11). In any case, it suggests knowledge wilfully searched out, or science. This *daʿat* proves truly essential in biblical thought. For example, Hosea proclaims: "Because my people rejects knowledge [*daʿat*] since they refuse it, it is silent—and since you have rejected knowledge [*daʿat*], I will reject you from my priesthood. Since you have forgotten the Torah, I will forget your children" (Hos. 4:6, JE). Thus *daʿat* relates to the Torah and revelation, but it is a *science* or knowledge. And it is situated pivotally within the relationship between God and God's people, as in Qohelet.

---

2. Strangely, wisdom in Qohelet, according to Pedersen, amounts to resignation: not hoping for success, yielding to facts, contenting oneself with mediocrity, and being ready for anything. Such wisdom enables a person to make the best of life, according to Pedersen. But Pedersen may be the mediocre one here, since he limits himself to such a superficial conclusion. We should add that, in order to segregate contradictory texts, he contents himself with calling the book a collection of incoherent maxims (pp. 317-18, 323, 326, 362)!

1. Wisdom: What Is It?

An ambiguous word if there ever was one![3] We have so many books and commentaries on the Hebrew wisdom writings—filled with confused essays on the meaning of "wisdom." Still, we must try here to grasp what Qohelet is talking about when he uses this word, even if we fail to understand it fully or to define it.

From the outset I believe we must take two precautions, staking out two negative limits. (1) The first concerns method: I believe it is pointless for us to look for help in the other biblical books on wisdom, such as Job, Proverbs, Ben Sira, etc. In the last analysis, each of these books has its own characteristics. They do not share a common idea, a sort of common denominator we could use. Such a synthesis or collection would not enlighten us much, and would lose much of these writings' special flavor. If we want to know what Qohelet is talking about, we must find the different meanings he gives the word "wisdom" within the context of his book.

(2) The second basic limit has to do with the obvious fact that in Qohelet we are not dealing with the wisdom of God. Rather than delightful Wisdom who played before the Lord at the creation of the world (see Prov. 8), we have mere human wisdom: our creation, expression, and criteria, our way of living and thinking.

In Qohelet we are not in the presence of "divine," superhuman, hypostatic wisdom. We know that very early in Jewish thought, wisdom was hypostatized, idealized as a kind of celestial maiden, and transferred from humanity to God. Oddly enough, Qohelet does not share this conception of wisdom, but he retains at least one of its early facets: wisdom as experience in life, as the ability to straighten out life's complications. Qohelet does not conceive of wisdom as God's thought; rather, we might suggest the author deliberately resists the widespread temptation to identify idealized wisdom with the *logos* of Platonism. For Qohelet, wisdom is a human activity, with all the limitations that implies!

Knight states correctly that Qohelet, having observed the dis-

---

3. Lauha emphasizes that wisdom in the ancient Orient was a royal *function,* and that the king was surrounded with wise counselors (p. 12).

crepancies between the dominant Yahwistic theology and life's realities, looks for the means whereby he "would be able to continue" (p. 176). It would not do to hold out false hopes to people, "and thereby diminish the urgency of their coming to terms with their specific situation" (ibid.).

In this sense Qohelet is "creative," but he uses human means. This is precisely what later made it difficult to include Qohelet in the canon. The difficulty stemmed in part from the book's contradiction of standard theology, but primarily from the concept of revelation involved. Revelation from God was always thought of as his revelation of himself, as when a prophet speaks expressly and directly the Word of God. Modern theologians express a similar point of view when they consider wisdom literature as located on the periphery of the Scriptures rather than in the heart of them: "Wisdom literature is not the center of the scriptural canon; it is peripheral to it" (Knight, p. 173, quoting G. E. Wright). "The sage's word is not obviously revelatory. It is not oracular but is continuous with the world" (Knight, p. 173).

In order to understand that Qohelet's reflection of and about wisdom truly involves revelation from the same God who spoke through the prophets, we must remember that the sage belongs to the same covenant: he is part of *this* people. In particular we need to consider the entire book of Qohelet in the light of its final message: "Fear God" (12:13). Thus we discover that through Qohelet God truly addressed his people, and us, but differently. Revelation through the sage prevents tradition from congealing in phrases fixed for all time.

Wisdom in Qohelet is very complex. I find it comprises two important aspects that may be irreconcilable: knowledge and usefulness. (1) In the first sense, wisdom implies an examination of everything (1:13). Nothing must be neglected or left out. Wisdom is not found in things, however; on the contrary, it helps us understand things. We must not study wisdom in nature, but approach nature through wisdom. We must see, understand, and learn everything: "all the works" (1:14). This includes not just human works but also those that simply *exist.* More than a catalog or inventory is involved: this is an examination. As long as we have not seen and understood *everything,* we have no access to wisdom. No judgment or choice is possible. Consequently there is a close relationship between wisdom and science (1:16, 18).

Thus wisdom is not a matter of morality, religion, or belief; it does not consist of precepts for living based on some theory or insight. Wisdom must be based on knowledge. Some overall, general knowledge, even if presented to us by the book of Qohelet itself, will not do. Many believe Qohelet offers us a rather perfunctory judgment, a sort of bird's-eye view, but that is not the case at all. The judgment he gives is a result, which he offers without listing all his reasons. But he informs us that he has experienced and examined *everything,* attempting to understand everything.

Therefore the use of science in a quest of this kind is legitimate, so long as the phase of evaluation is included. When our modern scientists, then, following Jacques Monod, try to construct a morality for our age or a philosophy based on their science, they are not mistaken. They follow the path Qohelet has shown them. He merely sketches it out, of course, since he lacked the means for acquiring such knowledge, which goes deeper and deeper all the time. His science is limited to elementary, superficial knowledge. He has no scientific method or tools. But he shows the way.

Furthermore, for all their phenomenal devices, modern scientists find themselves faced with more and more insoluble enigmas. The more science advances, the more it discovers how much we do not know. So scientists today are not much better off than Qohelet when he declares that science amounts to a chasing after wind. Since we cannot grasp ultimate reality, each step we take shows us a vaster horizon. It shows how far we are from the boundary of possible knowledge. A chasing after wind.

Qohelet does not regret devoting himself to all this work, nor does he try to talk us out of taking it on. We return again to this central principle: we cannot say, *before we begin,* with a blasé, disgusted, superior tone, "All is vanity, so we will not do anything." Only *after* we have searched out, experienced, and tried everything do we have the right to conclude: "Well, it is true that all is vanity."

We have often reiterated this spiritual constant found in the Bible: a person can see himself as an unworthy servant only *after* doing everything commanded him. When we say "since God does everything, he has no use for my puny efforts and my tiny works; so I will do nothing," we show our hypocrisy and cowardice. The Bible never validates such an attitude, teaching rather that although God does everything, he chooses human beings to accomplish it!

Another pseudo-reasoning follows the same logic: "If everything is by grace, then no matter what I do, I am either saved by grace, or lost if I do not receive grace." But this amounts to more hypocrisy and cowardice. For only after we have done the whole will of God can we even recognize that we have not done it all, so that ultimately we have recourse to grace, and grace alone. We can know the proportions and the cost of grace only when we have tried to do everything that came "before" it. Viewed in this light, "all is vanity" offers us no pillow for our laziness and no pretext for giving up the search for wisdom.

Furthermore, this coming together of wisdom and science strongly suggests another principle: science must not be left on its own, to be autonomous. It is linked with wisdom. Of course, you may say we are merely dealing with a cultural matter tied to Qohelet's time, when science had not yet left behind all sorts of moral and religious prejudices. Pure science had not yet come into being, so that no one would have thought of presenting scientific knowledge or the search for it as something in itself. The science of numbers got its meaning from geometry, and astronomy's only end was astrology. So Qohelet's union of wisdom and science in no way enables us to draw conclusions or to understand the slightest truth that would be valid for our era, you maintain.

I realize full well that all this is true. But our era is precisely what I cannot help thinking about! What have we done with our autonomous, independent science? Certainly we have made enormous progress in knowledge and method. So? Have we not observed that we lack an additional truth, a counterpoint, or a way to measure science? Do we not see every day the harmful effects of science when considered as independent and of ultimate value?

Now scientists themselves are beginning to ask this question, from within the discipline. "Science with no conscience ruins the

soul"—is this merely an outdated notion? A saying so often repeated that it no longer hits home, especially since we carefully
avoid giving it any meaning, unconsciously shrinking from any
consequences it might have? No, in reality this is a *new* notion, on
the rise: Edgar Morin called one of his recent books *Science with a
conscience.*[4] Before that, we had Georges Friedmann's *Power and
Wisdom.*[5] We have come back to the old saying.

Qohelet warns us, however: separating science and wisdom
involves a serious error. But wisdom does not hold out a "solution"
either, since it is subject to vanity. Things are not as simple as we
think: we do not have science on the one hand, and on the other a
kind of sacred yardstick, a transcendent point of view that would
enable us to come up with a correct opinion—unfortunately not.
Wisdom remains inseparable from science in both its aspects. But
searching for wisdom is like chasing after wind.

Along the same lines, Qohelet shows us wisdom as the search
for an explanation: "Who is like the sage, and who knows the
explanation of a thing?" (8:1). This view is utterly modern, since it
has nothing to do with metaphysics or rhetoric. Rather, the idea of
explanation suggests "scientific" rigor and precision. After all, the
term "explanation" covers both of science's early objectives: the
why and the how.

Another aspect of the meaning of the word "wisdom" deals
with an enormous question that has roots in both philosophy and
wisdom: discerning between wisdom and madness, between intelligence and folly: "I applied my heart to understanding wisdom
and to understanding madness and folly, and I knew that this also
is a pursuit of wind" (1:17). How can we learn to discriminate?
Where is the dividing line? We do not have wisdom on one side
and madness or folly on the other. For Qohelet, apparently, the
matter is not that clear or simple. He is not at all sure the mad
person is mad or the wise person wise. What are we going to use
to classify people? These issues come up throughout Qohelet.

4. Edgar Morin, *Science avec conscience* (Paris: Fayard, 1982).
5. Georges Friedmann, *La Puissance et la Sagesse* (Paris: Gallimard,
1970).

They appear to be fundamental if we are to conduct ourselves correctly in the world.

Who is mad? The radical result of the effort to establish this shows it to be vanity and a chasing after wind—an utterly vain and superfluous activity, because of its impossibility. We see constantly how the wise person suddenly becomes the fool (a bit of money will do the trick), how the mad person can adopt a reasonable attitude toward life.

Moreover, we waste our effort when we try to distinguish clearly the mad people from the wise. One of the main teachings of Qohelet points out that even if we could tell the fool what he "should" do, he will not do it. Neither advice nor example can make a person pass from one category to the other. So why try to distinguish them? It is not madness that is mad but the desire to define the borderline: "I applied my heart to understanding wisdom and to understanding madness and folly, and I knew that this also is a pursuit of wind" (1:17). In Qohelet's double search for knowledge, then, all he has learned is that his very quest is absurd.

(2) Qohelet also understands wisdom in a second, completely different sense: a kind of practical, utilitarian, down-to-earth knowledge or intelligence. This "wisdom" appears in two spheres: politics and war. Wisdom proves useful for good government (2:12-13; 4:13). In this case, we are no longer dealing with science and moral reflection, but with pragmatic wisdom, which counts as wisdom just as much. The poor youth, although imprisoned, if he is wise, finally leaves prison and takes power, replacing the crazy old king (4:13-15).

He does not accomplish this through meditation, like Hamlet. Nowhere, and at no time, has metaphysics led to power and its effective use! Plato's experience shows how true this is. Political wisdom, different from moral reflection or science, is called wisdom, too, and rightly so. *Realpolitik* works better than the idealism of a Jimmy Carter. As a force, it teaches a person how to use force.

"Wisdom makes the sage stronger than ten authorities who are in the city, for there is not a just person on the earth who does good and who does not sin" (7:19-20). This enigmatic passage deserves our attention. The gift enjoyed by the wise person here does not make him better than others. His wisdom does not make him stronger than those in power. Rather, his superiority consists in knowing that everyone is unjust, a sinner, and that no one does right. This knowledge makes him stronger than ten city authorities.

Who can fail to recognize politics at work? It knows how to use others' sin, based on precisely what evil a given person has committed. The political person is not taken in by the authorities' magnanimous talk, but knows that all of politics' wonderful promises amount to wind. He does not place his confidence in a given party or leader. These basic "qualities" of the political individual show his wisdom. Such knowledge effectively makes him stronger than all others. In this passage the sage does not have the wise person's moral grandeur or the loftiness of his vision in view. Rather, he shows us the wise one's ability to understand human nature.

Qohelet goes even further when he extends the concept of wisdom to cover the ability to succeed at war. He does this in a remarkable parenthesis within a completely different teaching (9:13-18). His story has three parts: a city besieged by a powerful king; a poor wise man of the city who succeeds in saving it; and the result: no one remembers the poor man afterward, or expresses any gratitude. Qohelet offers us a two-pronged conclusion: first, the wise person's calm words have more value than a captain's shouts in a crowd of fools (this may allude to a composed person's ability to calm people where a leader fails to stave off panic). And second, "Better is wisdom than weapons of war" (9:18a).

We cannot easily determine whether Qohelet refers here to a concrete event. Generally (with the exception of Elijah's miracles), in the sieges of Samaria or Jerusalem, the prophets' efforts to save the city proved useless. Qohelet could not have known the story of Archimedes at the siege of Syracuse, although that would fit nicely. In any case, it seems probable to me that this story betrays a kind of Greek flavor. Skill in waging war, composure, perceptiveness, a clear head for tactics—these matter more than heroism, armaments, war cries, and trumpets.

For Qohelet, such practical ability amounts to wisdom, too. But he stops and becomes his old self again as he ends his story: the wise person is despised after he saves the city. Even worse, "a single sinner ruins much happiness [or success]" (9:18b). Precious little is needed to ruin what the wise person has done. Nothing is more fragile than political success or military victory. In this case folly or stupidity are not at fault, but the sinner. Wisdom's work is impaired and finally obliterated by a single sinner, who does evil and perverts God's work. Wisdom cannot overcome sin, even in this instance that seems purely human. We see in Qohelet's story the possibility of a certain solidarity: the wise person can be useful to others and save them. But in the end the weight of a single sinner in a group, in society, or in the state wins out, showing wisdom's limits and humility.

In any case, we find two concepts or formulations of wisdom here, and they do not overlap. I do not believe we find two differing ideas because of any oversight or careless expression on Qohelet's part. Both kinds of wisdom are subject to vanity.

Current thinking maintains that we find wisdom not only in a wise or distinguished person, but also in the people—a kind of grass-roots wisdom. Unfortunately, this insight goes up in smoke, like so many others. We have already noted the folly and fickleness of crowds. But we can go further: a crowd or a people fades into oblivion just as much as the philosopher! On this matter, Qohelet reflects Job, who declares to his friends: "No doubt you are the people, and wisdom will die with you" (Job 12:2, RSV). No, the people are not God, even in their wisdom.

Philosophy and all wisdom are subject to vanity like everything else.[6] And if we take "vanity of vanities" as a genitive expressing the superlative, then the ultimate vanity is to discover (by means of

6. We might wonder why Qohelet is so hard on wisdom. I agree with the authors who believe he directs his attack toward *Greek* wisdom. This explains why Qohelet deals constantly with philosophy, so that Lys translates *ḥokmah* as "philosophy" (p. 153). Hebrew wisdom was rather humble and flexible. We have noted the enormous distance von Rad finds between traditional wisdom and Qohelet's. But with many others, I believe this is just the issue: Qohelet clashes with *sophia:* a grandiose, conquering, subtle wisdom that tries to understand the whole world and explain everything. This Greek philosophy is the object of Qohelet's attack.

wisdom!) that all is vanity. Our declaration that everything is fragility and smoke amounts in itself to fragility and a "word in the wind." Saying that everything is folly is not wisdom but another folly in turn. So this cynical evaluation is not wisdom's deepest expression. Qohelet warned us at the beginning that we would see that everything is mist, but knowing this turns out to be without substance as well!

What can we say, then? That wisdom in the end is an enigma. We find just this thought in Psalm 49, where the concept of wisdom parallels Qohelet's: "My mouth will speak wise words, my heart murmurs intelligent things; I lend my ear to a parable; I will interpret my riddle . . ." (Ps. 49:3-4, JE). The verses that follow show that the riddle to be interpreted is wisdom itself!

At this point we are leaving privileged territory. Before we begin to examine the critical texts, we must understand that we are moving to another level. We have encountered wisdom on two planes: philosophical, moral, and intellectual on the one hand, and useful and practical on the other. Now everything Qohelet is going to say will be on the existential plane, and this approach will simplify matters. Instead of presenting what we know or do, we will be dealing with what we *are*. At this point wisdom collapses. There is no contradiction between these different planes of meaning; we must simply situate them where the One who reveals them does. We must move to his territory: the vital experience and profound reality of living people, in their actual existence.

2. Irony

Some writers have seen that Qohelet is ironic through and through.[7] His treatment of folly provides one example of his irony. We will

7. For example, Proudhon says: "Irony, you are true liberty! You preserve me from aspirations to gain power, from being a slave to parties, from pedantry in science, from the admiration of the great, from the mystifications of politics, from the fanaticism of reformers, from the superstitions of this vast universe,

have to base our thinking on the certainty that folly is evil. From the outset, though, we need to be aware that this does not mean we take the easy way out, giving in to the great temptation and perversion of our Western world. This temptation consists of choosing madness as our solution, since wisdom is absurd. Historically we have observed the failure of Christianity and philosophies, then that of politics, the absurdity of wars for justice and freedom, followed by the failure of socialism to bring about all we hoped for. Finally we witnessed the enslavement of all art, leading to the dead end André Malraux called the "museum of the imagination." The only thing left to us then was the solution of madness. At that point A. Artaud [a French writer who tried to cultivate his mental imbalance in order to delve deeper into thought—TRANS.] looked like our forerunner.

We went beyond the classical position that sees poet or genius as always on the verge of madness. We reversed the proposition: the mad person became our model and example, our way out. But Qohelet states clearly his disagreement: madness is an evil—nothing more, nothing less. Madness produces evil, so we must neither wish for it nor seek it (in any case, it comes easily, without any effort on our part!). The mad person ruins his life and other peoples': "Words from the mouth of a wise person bring him favor, but the lips of a mad person ruin him. The beginning of the words of his mouth is folly and the end of his talk is evil madness" (10:12-13). Qohelet states the way things are; his words do not represent a condemning judgment, a desire to exclude, or "racism." Nor does he seek to reject or refuse a relationship. The mad person is respectable but he produces evil. We see this daily in our society. We must watch out for such madness, avoiding it for ourselves, and helping others out of it (I don't say "curing others,"

---

and from self-adoration. In the past you appeared to the Sage on the throne when he cried out, before all the people who saw him as a demigod, 'Vanity of vanities'" (Stewart Edwards, ed., *Selected Writings of Pierre-Joseph Proudhon,* trans. Elizabeth Fraser [London: Macmillan, 1970], p. 264; from the *Confessions*).

since much more than an illness is involved!). Never should we desire it.[8]

As we have already seen, the drama begins with the inability to distinguish clearly between folly and reason or wisdom. Although they are absolutely contradictory, the dividing line between them is invisible and slippery. Furthermore, on the existential level, no difference exists between the wise person and the fool! They have the same life, the same fate, the same end.

Qohelet returns continually to the trite observation that everyone's life ends in death. Of course, on the purely utilitarian and practical plane,

> There is more profit for wisdom than for folly, just as light is more profitable than darkness [the purely useful and practical character of this wisdom]. The wise person has his eyes open and the fool walks in darkness.[9] But *I also know* [Qohelet's vantage point is situated above both the wise person and the fool] that an identical destiny will fall to both of them. And I said in my heart: A destiny like that of the fool will fall to me also: why have I been wiser, then? And I declared in my heart that this also is vanity. For there is no permanent memory of the wise person, any more than of the fool, because *everything is forgotten* in the days to come. How can it be that the wise person dies as well as the fool? (2:13-16)

8. I set aside the following text without understanding it, and the commentaries all failed to satisfy me on it, especially Podechard (pp. 426-27), and Steinmann (p. 102): "The heart of the wise person is on the right, the heart of the fool is on the left" (10:2, JE). When I read Maillot, his interpretation seemed to shine with obvious clarity: "Wise people are as rare as those who have their heart on the right side. In other words, all people, or almost all, are imbeciles and mad people. However (v. 3), although they may be imbeciles, they still have a heart; that is, intelligence, even though it may be perverted. But they lose this totally when they begin to call others fools" (p. 174). Here is Maillot's translation of 10:3: "Furthermore, he acts like a fool and has no heart at all when he says of everyone else: 'What a fool!' " (p. 168).

9. Triumphant madness in our society takes the form of drugs.

In the final analysis, no existential difference exists. Each resembles the other, even in the realm of usefulness, where the wise person seems to be right. What is the use of being wise? Furthermore, in connection with the observation concerning the death of all people, we note an essential fact: not only does the wise person disappear, but wisdom itself dies also.

We must remember, as we examine this indictment, that the individual being of the wise person is not forgotten, but rather everything he was able to contribute. Remembering this is essential in our world, in which great works, creations, and thoughts are numberless, yet disappear into total oblivion. Do not make the objection that books survive, such as Qohelet's! His book is drowned, disappearing in a cataclysm of hundreds of thousands of books. Each is hailed as a work of genius, as the key for understanding our world, only to be forgotten within ten years.

Before long, we will have a civilization based on images, so that even books will disappear, crowded out by immediately visible replacements. At that point, since the images on television or even in films are designed to be consumed rapidly and then to disappear (in spite of the video recorder), no kind of recourse or return to the sources of wisdom will be left. In any case, wisdom matures slowly—how could anyone transmit it by television?

The triumph of madness in the sublime expression of art as "happening" represents the most extreme manifestation of this involuntary, spontaneous objection. Such manifestations have become typical, along with the current craze for meaningless "festivals." In them we do not have the traditional "feast of fools," but rather fools who take to "performing" at so-called festivities.

Such "folly" is not the only way we see the vanity of wisdom as we note its disappearance in our society of technique, which is characterized by quantity and instantaneousness. We also note that wisdom cannot be communicated from one generation to another. Our text suggests that the wise person is forgotten, and his wisdom as well. We will see that wisdom is inseparable from the wise person. It is not some objective system or separable greatness. When the wise person has been forgotten, nothing remains of what he thought, said, or demonstrated.

This issue concerns our era more concretely than any other, since we live in an age of incessant change, constant innovation, and proliferation of fascinating objects one after another. How can we transmit from one generation to the next the wisdom acquired by the kind of experience Qohelet talks about? This problem has always existed. Nevertheless, how many times have we heard it said that in traditional societies people listened to the elderly, took them seriously because they had lived and remembered so much?

Today we live in the opposite situation. No one asks anymore: "Would you like to hear the advice of wisdom as seen in the experience of the elderly?" Our constant question is rather: "Do you understand young people? Are you 'with it'?" Here we have the opposite of "wisdom." Only the young are in touch with the latest machines.

Imbeciles try to plunge us into the fake culture called "technological culture." In it the only people with something "useful" to offer will be those who can pilot a plane, use a VCR, or run a computer. The elderly, with their utterly useless experience, will have to learn all over again.

Some are foolish enough to believe that the only experience that counts these days is experience in handling objects. But it just so happens that experience in human relations, in the building of a family, or in politics, has changed less than we usually admit! I find it a truly tragic experience to watch the young reproduce exactly the mistakes we made fifty years ago—things we analyzed and from which we drew certain lessons. But it is useless to mention these lessons, offer warnings, or explain to the young what is going to happen. The wisdom we gained at such great cost means nothing. The wise person has been forgotten, and his wisdom is vain. Nothing can be passed on from one generation to the next anymore.

The follies of 1930 reoccur in 1960 and 1980. But with two differences: first, things now move so fast that we no longer have time to arrive at any wisdom based on our experience. Second, our means have become so much more powerful that today such follies have incomparably greater consequences than the errors we committed in a previous generation. So the distance between the wise person and the fool is minuscule. Qohelet told us so, but we live so intensely we have forgotten his warning.

Wisdom is very useful, whereas folly is evil. But the difference between them nearly disappears in the complexity of life: "What more does the wise person have than the fool? What more does the miserable person have who knows how to walk before the living?" (6:8). The wise person knows how to conduct himself, but he ends up miserable because of the utter hopelessness of his situation: he can communicate nothing of his wisdom.

In any case, his wisdom cannot change his destiny, so what does it benefit him? "Everything is the same for everybody: an identical destiny awaits the just person and the wicked, the good person [and the evil one]. . . . The good person is like the sinner. . . . This is an evil in everything done under the sun: that there should be the same destiny for everyone. For this reason the human heart is filled with malice, madness is in their hearts throughout their life" (9:2-3). So we observe a remarkable kind of feedback: we are continually told that wisdom is truly useful. But in the final analysis, it is of no use, changing nothing in our lives. *For this reason* the human heart is filled with evil and folly.

Under such conditions, what good is the exhausting quest of wisdom? The only advice one can give in the light of such vanity is "Let us eat and drink, for tomorrow we die" (1 Cor. 15:32, RSV). The quest for wisdom turns into a kind of self-destruction; there is no point in looking for a way out, since none exists (Eccl. 7:15-16).

Fragility and Impossibility

We have not finished with devastating irony in Qohelet, who tells us that wisdom is both fragile and impossible. We see its fragility in the ability of a gift to turn the wise person's head: "Oppression drives a sage mad, and a gift ruins the heart" (7:7).[10]

_____

10. Another image of this fragility appears if we accept Lys's translation of 2:13: "I observe that there is profit in philosophy compared with confusion, similar to the profit in light compared with darkness" (p. 238). Lys shows that

We must not separate these words from the text that follows, in which wisdom is praised as good and profitable, but then we see it reduced to a means of profiting financially from circumstances! A crueler fate would be hard to imagine. How do we see the wise person, the philosopher, or the scholar, then? As a person who uses his knowledge to live well and acquire this world's goods. These observations cast a strange light on "Wisdom is good!" (7:11): good for making profit! When you come down to it, it is better to have wisdom of this kind than to receive an inheritance. What an amazingly modern point of view we find in Qohelet!

We pride ourselves these days on having made tremendous progress: whereas in earlier centuries people banked everything on receiving an inherited fortune, we now depend on our individual competence for earning a good living. And we view this as just, as tending toward meritocracy. But Qohelet already said the same thing, and he also humiliates our vanity: all the wisdom and knowledge you have acquired boils down to nothing more than a good paycheck? Clearly this is human progress, don't you think? What have we gained from this "progress"? We know perfectly well the answer is "Nothing."

Wisdom is also fragile in that it does not take much to corrupt it. Errors in judgment threaten it constantly: "Dead flies spoil and infect all the perfume of the perfumer; a bit of folly outweighs wisdom and glory—the heart of the wise person is on the right; the heart of the fool is on the left [let us not look for any political allusions here!]. And when the fool walks on the road, his heart fails him [i.e., according to the exegetes, he lacks intelligence], so that he says of each one: 'There's an imbecile'" (10:1-3, JE). The wise person says he has applied himself to the discernment of wisdom and folly, to the distinction between science and stupidity. Yet his own judgment condemns him, since when he points out the person he considers an imbecile, he shows himself a fool, lacking in intelligence.

"darkness" designates death, and that just as light struggles in vain against darkness, the struggle of wisdom against death is vain. There may be some advantage in wisdom, but in any case, we cannot profit from it, because it does not keep us from dying (v. 14; Lys, pp. 240-41).

No mistake about it, Qohelet means to leave us no escape. He warns us that something very small (a dead fly) will suffice to ruin a jar of perfume or scholarly wisdom. I cannot help but think of certain more or less great philosophers of modern times whose entire system appears ruined by their support of a political error: the great G. W. F. Hegel, for instance, whom I cannot take seriously because he sees the culmination of History, Idea, and Spirit in the State! Everything he says is truly wonderful, but when I come up against this dead fly that corrupted and killed Western society in the nineteenth and twentieth centuries, I cannot continue to take anything seriously in his preceding discourse on so many other problems.

The great Martin Heidegger, in whose work everything is so profound, enticing, and innovative, failed to display any lucidity at all in discerning the real nature of national socialism. Those few months of his support for Nazism suffice for me to consider the rest of his work null and void. How can anyone expect me to follow such a guide in his *Holzwege,* when he was unable to make the right choice in that one simple matter in his life? The dead fly — misplaced loyalty — may appear for just an instant! And I fully realize that by blackballing certain thinkers, I in turn deserve Qohelet's other judgment in the same passage!

Wisdom is fragile—it can vanish when we change a single line. Even worse, wisdom is impossible. Anyone who thinks he has reached it has grasped only wind. Who knows anything? Who can pride himself on "knowing"? "Who knows what is good for a person during life, during the number of days of his vain life, which he passes like a shadow?" (6:12). Wisdom is as fragile as the person himself. After all, why should wisdom be surer and truer than those who create it? It is like a shadow. We can measure, situate, and weigh everything, but not a shadow. It has no existence in itself, since it depends both on the object that projects it and on light, which changes constantly.

Under such conditions, who can claim to be wise? Wisdom seems ultimately impossible: "I saw . . . that a person *cannot* discover the work that is done under the sun, since he tires in the search and fails to find anything. And even if the sage *says* he knows, he cannot find" (8:17). As for us moderns, we have discovered a great many things. But, as we have already seen, the horizon continually moves farther from us. In this connection, Qohelet seems to posit a kind of absolute: no matter what he does, he cannot find the ultimate secret, the key that would enable him to understand everything. As little as I know, what strikes me most is that the further we advance, the more everything we know becomes complex and elusive (Morin's enormous effort to synthesize things accounts for this admirably).

As for history, about which I am somewhat less ignorant than other matters, I observe that the more we know, the less we can produce those great historical panoramas that used to seem possible, and which the public still craves. History explodes into the pieces of a puzzle we cannot reconstruct. Each piece has its own particularity and complexity. We can never say the last word; the last insight is never precise enough.

At times we think we have arrived at the outer limit—not of the reality we want to understand, but of our minds' capacity to understand. And here comes the irony: at the very moment a person is obliged to admit how elusive things are (not that he ever stops trying to understand!), Qohelet declares that the sage may *say* he knows. There is nothing more wicked! The wisdom of the wise consists of *saying* "I know," concerning a problem no one has found the answer to.

I believe the ultimate significance of Qohelet's entire book lies in the fact that the activities we examined above in chapter II, all of which turned out to be vanity, all converge toward wisdom. This convergence forms the architectural unity of the book. Finally we see that wisdom itself amounts to the sum of vanities. Each step toward wisdom is a chasing after wind.

This finding brings us back again to "When there are words in abundance, they make vanity abound: how does that profit anyone?" (6:11). We must place this text within the context of wisdom, since it comes almost immediately after "What more does the wise person have than the fool?" (6:8). The texts exhibit a similar structure, obliging us to conclude that for Qohelet, wisdom expresses itself in a flood of words—which is what we often observe. So he identifies wisdom with wordiness.

At this point I put myself out on a limb, since I have no proof, but I feel led to this reflection: do we not find in these texts a gradual movement from an interior wisdom that molds life toward a declared, demonstrated, and spoken wisdom that has been molded into formulas? Disentangling Qohelet's contradictory texts on wisdom is no easy task, but I wonder if most of his critical statements do not apply to a kind of discourse wisdom based on intellectual construction. If this is so, doesn't Qohelet deny the existence of any science of wisdom? But here I am getting carried away with a still riskier hypothesis that may shock the reader: who claimed to be able to talk about wisdom, and who gave us so many words about it? The Greeks!

As we have seen, the influence of Greek philosophy on Qohelet has often been posited, as scholars have looked for relationships between them. I believe I have shown, and I will show even more clearly later, the specific character of Qohelet, and how it belongs to Hebrew thought. This conclusion in no way detracts from the certainty that Qohelet knew Greek philosophy, the love of wisdom. This wisdom was put into words: a constructed and spoken wisdom, developed by means of intelligence. But Qohelet means to remain on the level of what he considers as the only important thing: existence.

Can we not see his book, then, as largely an attack on Greek wisdom, this philosophy that was beginning to make serious inroads into the rather closed world of Hebrew thought? Doesn't Qohelet proclaim the vanity of the Greek treatises on wisdom? However clever, a treatise can never enable a person to escape the vanity of his condition. Nevertheless, Qohelet shows the usefulness of wisdom for earning money and making a place for oneself in society, in order to receive honor. But the true sage is despised and rejected. This observation constitutes a wicked jab at the Greek rhetoricians. I find my hypothesis as valid as some others, and it harmonizes with the polemical, ironic, contradictory tone of this book, which I consider an antiphilosophy.

Science

I am quite taken with this succinct saying from near the beginning of Qohelet: "whoever adds to his knowledge adds to his sorrow" (1:18b, JE). In this basic principle the author places knowledge, or science, opposite wisdom: "abundance of wisdom is abundance of grief" (1:18a). What we have seen about wisdom so far enables us to understand his distinction: the more wisdom you acquire, the further you step into vanity. Consequently, contrary to what has often been proclaimed, wisdom holds no consolation for us, no strength to go on living.

The wiser you are, the more you realize that all is vanity and a chasing after wind. So wisdom increases your problem. But here comes science. Here again Qohelet seems incredibly prophetic to me. In his day science had not yet become so exact, and there were no technological applications drawn from science. Yet we see how he judges it. Should we label this an accident? Just a phrase? It seems to me that Qohelet's judgment of science involves such important consequences that we cannot dismiss it in this way.

How does this issue apply to our time?[11] We cannot label Qohelet's idea a mere psychological matter, where the scholar reverts to humility, recognizing increasingly that the more he knows, the less he knows. No, Qohelet's saying can be interpreted more objectively: "the more knowledge, the more sorrow." We experience this objective situation in our scientific century, when we face certain realities for the first time in history.

11. It is, of course, entirely legitimate to question the extrapolation I make here of the word "science" (knowledge, etc.) to modern science. Let me just say that I feel the extraordinary flexibility, uncertainty, and variability of the word justify my procedure. After all, exact science and social science differ. The criteria of "science," an utterly vague term, vary from one era to another. What people called "science" in the eighteenth century has nothing in common with what people called "science" in 1880. Between 1920 and 1980, the word's meaning changed just as radically. And, of course, all this has nothing whatever to do with what people called *sciencia* in the thirteenth century, etc. All these meanings have something basic in common, however: knowing, accumulating knowledge, coordinating this knowledge, and working out a system that seems to explain it. We find this is Qohelet's precise target!

For the first time, science dominates everything, takes over everything, uses everything. It is our Great Goddess. No one is allowed to say anything against her. Even if we sometimes admit that science is badly applied, that it can be improperly used, we believe it is not responsible for such problems. Sometimes we recognize serious scientific errors have been made, that science forces us to make terrible choices, or that scientists have overturned theories that were accepted for decades. But we turn these admissions around so they become a tribute to science: "See how science advances—to its credit, it acknowledges its own errors."

Today we speak of the crisis in science, but this also adds to its glory. This crisis amounts to nothing more than a momentary transition from lesser to greater knowledge. We harbor no doubts concerning the outcome of the crisis: it will cause science to progress. So science is invincible. And in the final analysis, an appraisal of science becomes completely impossible.

In the nineteenth century, the explosion of scientific knowledge caused it to triumph in unbeatable fashion. Belief in science progressed accordingly, arriving at what we now refer to scathingly as "scientism." These days we believe we have rejected scientism, since we acknowledge that science may involve some negative aspects. But as soon as any such negative ideas surface, science itself co-opts them, integrating them into its method and evaluation. Thus science produces an incessant refinement of understanding and knowledge.

Nothing escapes science—not even its own errors. No longer just quantitative, it has begun to take charge of qualitative matters as well. Science has ceased to be fragmentary, mechanistic, reductionist, disjunctive, and mutilating, as it breaks objects down into separate parts. No, it does just the opposite: it incorporates flexible, complex, unstable elements, like whirlwinds and smoke. But it remains "science." Nothing stops it.

From the inside we will never manage to judge science, then! But if you place yourself outside it, it immediately challenges you, saying that anyone on the outside lacks the competence necessary for making a judgment. Consequently, it is useless to try to talk about science. In any case, we do not intend to make a case against

science here, however you define it. We simply want to hear
Qohelet, with his double warning: what has been is what will be
(1:9). But he also says the reverse: what will be has already been.
Making such a statement requires tremendous pride, unless its
author is expressing a message from the One who knows everything, because he is outside everything—the One whom time does
not limit. Humanly speaking, no possible assessment of science
exists.

In other works, I have tried to show the ambivalence of all
progress in technique (which is completely different from science).
Not only does technique produce as much bad as good (they are
indissolubly connected), but furthermore the problems that technique creates are increasingly large and complicated. We are continually overwhelmed by new inventions, but also continually
thrown off balance by the creation of new and unexpected situations.

Science is something else again, although certainly none of
technique's progress could take place without it. Science retains all
its prestige, no matter how much we admit that it is not neutral or
blameless, or that scientists no longer have pure hands and a clear
conscience. Our confidence in scientific research abounds, so that
we place all our economic and social hopes in "Research and
Development." Nothing reduces for a moment our modern trust in
the great goddess: research centers and laboratories multiply,
methods are continually sharpened, and science has nearly
measureless access to the infinitely large and the infinitely small.

Now we see that the warning about all this came 2,500 years
ago. Just the warning, nothing else. But Qohelet had no way of
knowing science through experience. He could not pronounce a
judgment based on full knowledge. It would be too easy for us to
write this off as the reaction of a disgruntled, reactionary mind that
believed in the past (he does *not* believe in the past, as he takes pains
to tell us: "Do not say, 'How is it that the old days were better than
these?'" 7:10, JE).

It would be too easy for us to say that Qohelet attacks false
science here, or that in his day he could not know what was
involved. For me, his warning has basic importance precisely

because he could not know. He does not say that science lies, or that science fails to reveal truth. He does not pit knowledge acquired through reflection against knowledge revealed by God. He does not say science takes us away from God, or that we would be better off without science. Nor does he say "all things considered," since he considers nothing!

We can lump all the above together in the widely accepted and widespread modern idea that the Christian religion based on the Bible has been hostile to science. Often this notion is buttressed by a quotation from Genesis regarding the prohibition against touching the tree of knowledge. But those who argue this way forget that it was the tree of the knowledge *of good and evil* (Gen. 2:17). This means that it is impossible for human beings to distinguish between good and evil. This has nothing to do with knowing reality or truth. Genesis in no way prohibits such knowledge.

What matters most to Qohelet is not truth, or God, but *the existence of humanity.* He addresses a warning to this humanity, and that is all. Humanity finds itself faced with a choice between two possibilities. We can decide to choose in favor of science, but in that case we must know that it will increase our grief; it may even increase the grief of the world. How? Why? He does not say; he only confronts us with our responsibility.

We can only guess the answer to these questions, using hindsight. A person hearing Qohelet's warning as a word from God can decide to renounce the fabulous pursuit of science, hoping to avoid the increase of sorrow. Such a response was possible. Am I suggesting humanity should have remained in a state of nature, instead of developing its capacities and having an effect on the world? No, since it is clearly said, on the contrary, that Adam and Eve must cultivate the garden, taking the responsibility of administering what is given to them. An individual displays God's image, so that he is inventive, filled with imagination and projects, and has access to memory as well as to the future. But science is something else again: infinite conquest of infinite knowledge. Its limitlessness makes it unacceptable to God and the source of all the evils in the world.

In "moral" terms, we call this limitlessness "covetousness," in the absolute sense of the term. It does not mean coveting an object or a pleasure, but coveting equality with God: coveting everything that can be possessed by knowledge. This way a person tries to rise indefinitely by means of what he has (naturally, this all takes place on an unconscious and *innocent* level!). This is the source of all the grief in the world, bar none. Such is the great passion of science, the only thing that can satisfy absolute covetousness.

Because science responds to absolute covetousness, it becomes the supreme authority. We must never forget this unique position of science. No one can question it, from any point of view. It is the supreme authority from which we cannot escape. The minute you get involved with the machinery of science, with the way it thinks and conceives and presents things, with its reasoning, it immediately becomes absolute.

It is infinitely more absolute and ultimate than nature or God. For a long time, humanity considered nature as its ultimate reference point and deified it in consequence. We now know how to manipulate, use, and destroy nature. We can escape from it in a thousand ways (perhaps at deadly cost!). As for God, contrary to the tenets of simplistic theology, the Bible shows him so respectful of his creation and creature, of his image in us, that he avoids acting all-powerfully. He holds this attribute in check, allowing us our freedom, autonomy, and independence.

Even more, God is the liberator, so that he is exactly the opposite of an all-powerful, blind being who only crushes and refuses to be questioned. God accepts our challenges and questionings, allowing us to get outside his sphere of reference. In the end he accepted submission to humanity, in his son Jesus Christ. Instead of being the tyrant, he became the servant.

God did this because he is love, and love and omnipotence cannot be reconciled. Both the "all" and the "power" of "all-powerful" contradict love. No power can serve love, since love can use all paths except just that one: power. Omnipotence cannot serve love because it results in a contradiction in terms. If "all" serves love, love is superior to it, so that omnipotence is no longer all-power. If we say that the all-powerful One causes this power to serve his love, we return to my earlier hypothesis: God allows us to elude him.

In science, however, there is no love (I do not say "among scientists," since they can of course work with great love for the good of humanity). Science cannot be challenged (by its very definition!); it is supreme. It can never impose any limitations on itself.

Every time someone has thought he could elude science, inventing a "domain" outside it, science has absorbed it, whether it was called the irrational, the qualitative, chance, disorder, the subject, the surreal, etc. Each time the domain indeed appeared outside science initially, but just because it was outside, science's bulimia took it as a subject for research.

We see the conquest take place every time. For the last twenty years people have happily and triumphantly noted that science has "changed," by incorporating chance, randomness, feedback, disorder, and the irrational. Yes, it changes, but it remains the same, beyond challenge. Without being reduced to the status of object (as was done half a century ago), the subject was made an integral part of the scientific system. Progress for humanity, you say? Not at all—progress for science! This absolute supremacy makes science the source of human trouble. We now have a supreme authority, above anything we have ever known, and from which we cannot escape.

The repeated practice of conjuring up ancient myths in connection with science in order to reassure ourselves proves a mockery. Prometheus, Pandora, Faust, the sorcerer's apprentice—they all pale in scope compared with what we presently see. There is no point in saying "See, things have always been the same!," because these comparisons do not deal with the same thing. For the first time, we are faced with this supreme authority that denies its authority.

Science's failings and bad applications do not increase human grief. On the contrary, the problem resides in its very perfection, its capacity for absorbing everything, its veracity, and its effectiveness. Instead of making us slaves, it blots out the very idea that we might be slaves to this benevolent goddess that does so much to augment our "power" and autonomy! In actuality, this is the true pain that science brings about. Rather than the sort of pain the dentist inflicts, this is painful in our deepest being, in the unconscious, where it takes the place of the death instinct, and perhaps of eros.

Ecology exposes external disaster, but much more terrible is the internal ruin of indestructible subjection. This pain, affecting all of humanity (to different degrees, of course, depending on the extent to which a people has been integrated into the scientific process), expresses itself in anguish and unreasonable obsessions.

This pain doubles for individuals, in terms of destructive grief for what has been left undone. The pain stems from the combination of covetousness and science's potential. Science never furnishes us with an ultimate answer, and covetousness demands that it always go farther, advancing more and more. Science does not advance on the basis of its own logic alone, but through the combination of its logic and human covetousness. And human beings suffer endlessly from their insatiability: "You want something but don't get it" (Jas. 4:2, NIV). In reality the very evidence of covetousness is that one never says "this is enough."

Writers have considered covetousness in connection with money and power. But now it is approaching its perfection through science, which seems to place everything, even the unlimited, at our disposal. But at what a price! The whole series of biblical texts telling us about covetousness shows it not just as the root of sin, but also as the root of all the evils that can afflict humanity. Furthermore, these texts show covetousness as the root of human pain in the form of our suffering for what has been left undone. This is precisely what characterizes science: omnipotence and perpetual incompletion. For this reason, rather than referring to so many complicated, ambiguous myths, I prefer to recall this unique phrase that holds a world within it: "whoever adds to his knowledge adds to his sorrow."

At this point, vanity and wisdom have come full circle. We cannot answer the problem of the vanity of life by means of our knowledge, wisdom, philosophy, or science. On the contrary, each forward step, however triumphant it may appear, is marked by vanity looming up. Furthermore, we learn each day, perhaps especially in these tragic times we live in, that we are truly mist on the surface of a mirror (see Jas. 4:14). All our efforts to find ourselves end up as a grasping for wind that no one can catch.

How can I possibly resist the pleasure of quoting Kierkegaard at this point?

If a man proposes to himself . . . to hold fast what the clergyman says on Sunday, understanding this as the earnestness of life, and therewith again understanding all his ability and inability as a jest: does this mean that he will undertake nothing at all, because everything is empty and vain? Ah, no, for then precisely he will have no occasion to appreciate the jest, since the contradiction will not arise which brings it into juxtaposition with the earnestness of life: there is no contradiction in the thought that everything is vanity in the eyes of a creature of vanity. Sloth, inactivity, the affectation of superiority over against the finite—this is poor jesting, or rather is no jest at all. But to shorten one's hours of sleep and buy up the hours of the day and not to spare oneself, and then to understand that the whole is a jest: aye, that is earnestness. And religiously the positive is always recognizable by the negative: the earnestness by the jest that it is a religious earnestness, not the immediate earnestness, the stupid official importance of a counsellor, the stupid self-importance of a journalist with reference to the age, an "awakened" individual's stupid importance before God, as if God could not create a million men of genius if He were in any way embarrassed. To hold the fate of many human beings in one's hand, to transform the world, and then constantly to understand that this is a jest: aye, that is earnestness indeed! But in order that this should be possible all finite passions must be atrophied, all selfishness outrooted, both the selfishness which wants to have everything, and the selfishness which proudly turns its back on everything.[12]

3. The Wisdom of Small Things

Has all this negative reflection brought us to no conclusion? I do not believe we have said the last word yet. But the first step in wisdom consists of recognizing wisdom's vanity, acknowledging

12. Kierkegaard, *Concluding Unscientific Postscript,* trans. David F. Swenson and Walter Lowrie (Princeton: Princeton University Press, 1941), p. 235.

its limitations. We must live, work, and find joy within this under-standing to which Qohelet invites us: no wisdom can enlighten us, or enable us to organize things so as to understand the world and history. No wisdom can establish a scale of moral values; wisdom says, "all the same. . . ." True, no wisdom or meaning exists; *all the same,* we will live; all the same, we will act; all the same, we will be capable of happiness and hope. The only true wisdom we can aspire to consists of the perception that no wisdom is possible. On that basis we must construct our lives, beginning at that negative point.

It would be useless for us to call to our aid the great philoso-phers and the principle of positivity and negativity. Qohelet shows us this principle in action with remarkable effectiveness. All of wisdom boils down to recognizing vanity. Everything amounts to nothing. But once we no longer aspire to understanding everything, to deciphering the universe in order to organize it, we find ourselves faced with a series of small things: small facts of life, small, unpretentious truths. Realizing that all is vanity brings us back to the importance of these little things! We must take them extremely seriously, since we can grasp nothing else. And they make up the salt and truth of our lives.

Such wisdom comes from life's experiences and applies to them. Life in general, in absolute terms, is certainly a useless object for wisdom. What has been will be; do not expect to do a lot better. But this fact does not negate the joy of an encounter, or the happiness that comes from some achievement (even if lowly and unimportant). As Romain Gary said, "that does not keep the night-ingale from singing." A distinguished modern person may say the obvious: "Such third-rate ideas do not go very far." True, we would never have reached the moon by thinking small, or managed to solve certain sensational political or health problems. But what do these grand accomplishments offer us in the end, except for another set of vanities?

Wisdom exists. But it deals with nothing but existence—not with fantasies or the illusion of intelligence and absolute domina-tion. Wisdom involves first of all recognizing our finiteness. Imme-diately following that, it involves this contrapuntal notion: we must choose this finiteness, looking at ourselves in our truth and our reality, and have a reason for living. But it is not enough to speak of finiteness in general terms. Qohelet proposes neither a philosophical abstraction nor a truism. He is much too precise and demanding in everything he expresses and demonstrates! So he speaks to us of our two great areas of finiteness: the future and death.

Finiteness and the Future

We must evoke finiteness with respect to the future very forcefully to our time, which thinks it can take possession of the future. Qohelet presents this obstacle primarily in two texts: "A person does not know what will be; and who will let him know what will be after him?" (10:14). Qohelet relates this thought to the attitude of the fool who "multiplies words," whereas it is pointless to talk so much (10:12-14). He talks and talks to fill up the void left by the great uncertainty: what will tomorrow bring? But it is stupid to replace knowledge with talk. We find ourselves up against a wall, and we must recognize that fact, both for ourselves as individuals and for the community. We must not claim to do better than those who came before us.

This obstacle proves intolerable to us. It is one of the frontiers we cannot put up with, so we gnash our teeth over the uncertainty of the next hour. From the beginning of our species' existence, people have tried to unveil the secret of the future. Qohelet answers that this is always the work of an imbecile: "Who knows what is good for a person during life, during the number of days of his vain life, which he passes like a shadow? For who will let a person know what will be after him under the sun?" (6:12).

In this passage, Qohelet draws a different consequence from the same obstacle: since we do not know what tomorrow will bring, how could we know beyond any doubt what is good today? Qohelet's logic is rigorous: What I do today has consequences for tomorrow. But how will these consequences fit into the overall context of tomorrow? Not just: "How can I prepare the future today, or how can I do well today so that tomorrow will still be good?"

No. Tomorrow an enormous number of factors, over which I have absolutely no control, will have changed. The consequences of what I do today will take their place in that set of facts. I do not know how things will fit together or what the effects will be. Thus, as far as the situation I am acquainted with today goes, I can play my role and make an excellent decision, but when everything has changed tomorrow, my actions today may prove catastrophic.

Since I cannot know what tomorrow will bring, I cannot draw from it the data I need to decide what to do today. Therefore I cannot really know what is truly good in the final analysis for a person in his lifetime. This applies to the material level as well as to the moral level. And I must watch out for all this. Qohelet's very simple statement proves ruinous for morality!

You claim you can tell a person what is good for him by means of morality? What an illusion: you do not even know if what you say will still be good for him tomorrow. (Furthermore, I believe this truth still challenges our moralists and philosophers, since it follows the other one we have mentioned: when words abound, they produce an abundance of vanity!) We cannot tell what is good. Such definitive judgment must be suspended in view of tomorrow's uncertainty. Only with hindsight will we be able to say: "Yes, that is what should have been done after all."

Does this observation merely echo the idea of the "judgment of history"? Absolutely not! For us to believe that, Qohelet would have to have a given philosophy of history, attributing a dimension to it that he objects to radically. No, he always keeps his feet on the ground. History does not judge us; in fact, there is no judgment. All we have is the recognition that today we cannot know. So we have no business telling anyone "Here is what you should do." Rather, we can offer such advice only as our opinion, in solidarity—surely not as another's duty, or as a transcendent command or a way of controlling the future! All we can say at our human level, considering our limitation, is: "I do not know, but perhaps this is better than that."

Above all, we must not create a philosophical, political, or ethical system from which a person would draw consequences labeled as "the good." Based on our acknowledgment of finiteness, we must refuse any such systematization. Nothing is "good" "whatever happens." What happens takes care of proving to us that a given thing was not good!

By maintaining that the future is impenetrable,[13] Qohelet challenges first of all the seers, magicians, sorcerers, fortune-tellers, astrologers, etc., of his day. But I believe his insight harmonizes with the overall tendency of Hebrew revelation. In order to be able to foresee what would come later, one would have to conceive of the future as something already written, established, or fixed, for individuals and for peoples. There would have to be a book of destiny where the future could be found, so that it would be necessary to use any and all means to decipher it.

But the whole tenor of biblical thought goes in the opposite direction! Not because of human incapacity do we fail to "lift the corner of the veil" so as to read the mysterious book. No, the future is not decided in advance. It is not programmed. God has not even established a plan.

But neither does the future consist of a second-by-second divine decision. The hour that is coming is not drawn up by the arbitrary decision of a God who is both all-powerful and self-sufficient. The Bible excludes both conceptions. There is neither a book written in advance that we must learn to read nor a will of God that we must penetrate. Unfortunately, everything the Bible

13. Writers have often emphasized that Qohelet breaks with many of the strongest points of revelation in Israel. But I do not believe anyone has noticed this contradiction concerning the future: "Israel discovered the future, but from the angle of the relationship between judgment and salvation, promise and fulfilment. For this reason Israel's eschatology is the doctrine of coming salvation. . . . [Israel] introduces eschatological thought to the world, and this thought crushes the cyclical conception of history. Israel discovered historical consciousness in this way" (Mussner). Qohelet seems to challenge this fundamental knowledge, but I believe on the contrary that he radically refuses the possibility of this knowledge because he rejects all knowledge of the future that would be *other* than this relationship between judgment and salvation, promise and fulfilment. Qohelet does not reject that future; on the contrary, we will find it again at the end. But we must avoid confusion: one should not claim to know the earthly future beyond what God has promised. This is the radicalism of our text.

describes for us is more complex than that! God is free, so he is not tied to a program, not even to a plan he has established himself beforehand.

Since he is a God free to love, he continually takes into account everyone and everything he loves: his creation, and his creatures who bear his image. Since he takes us into account, he does not make machines of us, causing us to enter some destiny he has prepared, as if it were an iron cage. Rather than making us lie on a Procrustean bed, forcing our conformity, he takes his creatures' actions into account. Using whatever is offered by his creation at any given moment, he brings about the best possible result—just as a father tries to arrive at the best possible result, considering his children's qualities and faults.

God creates new conditions, offering new possibilities to his creation and his creatures. When we come to a dead end, he avoids the deadlock and opens a way to adventure. We find no predetermination here, no mold for the future, no destiny or mechanization of time.

At several points in this book, I insist on the fact that for Qohelet there is no fatality or destiny. I found the contrary sustained, however, by Pedersen, who equates time with fate.[14] Not "only is there a time fixed for everything that happens, but" furthermore "everything has its special condition and its own destiny; everything is dominated by its destiny." "Nothing can escape fatality" (p. 358). The only possible relationship with God is his sending of one's fate, since he writes the destiny of everything. This leads Pedersen to conclude that "blind fate strikes a person." Furthermore, Pedersen finds three terms related to destiny: *miqrah* (2:15; 3:19; 9:2), *ḥalaq* (2:21; 3:22; etc.), and *pagaʿ* (9:11; see Pedersen, p. 358 n. 27). The first of these words, usually translated as "fate," becomes "adventure" in Chouraqui (pp. 125, 129, 144). The second is always "lot" or "share." The third is translated as "luck" (Lys, p. 25), "time and accident" (Chouraqui, p. 145), or "good and bad fortune" (Maillot, p. 162).

14. Johannes Pedersen, "Scepticisme israélite," *Revue d'Histoire et de Philosophie Religieuses* 10/4-5 (July-Oct. 1930) 319, 351-56.

I feel it necessary to go into some detail on this matter. Pedersen's interpretation of fatality stems from the intellectual movement that transforms an existential observation into an element of a philosophical system. This same process led earlier theologians to develop the statement that God has mercy on whom he has mercy (see Rom. 9:15) into a theology of predestination. What authorizes Pedersen to translate "This is the fate of a person" (to be mortal), by "There is a destiny"? Or "This is the lot of a person" (to take pleasure), by "This is fatality"? Qohelet recognizes that human beings are limited and mortal, that we live lives composed of time and mishaps, but nowhere does he signify that we are the plaything of a blind force, caught in a kind of mechanism and subject to absolute determinism. These two kinds of thinking differ from each other. In reality, Pedersen's interpretation, which I believe to be unfaithful to Qohelet, expresses the scientific thought of an era that judged everything by inserting it into a closed system of causes and effects. But this is not what Qohelet teaches!

Considering all this, we conclude that Qohelet was right to say "Who will let a person know what will be after him under the sun?" (6:12b). I can hear the reader reacting: "But, after all, what about prophecy?" We must quickly move to avoid a misunderstanding at this point. Prophets are not soothsayers, "foretelling the future," contrary to what many think. A prophet is a sentry who sees an event coming (these days every politician thinks he can foresee events!). He announces what will happen *if:* if people fail to change their ways, if they do not repent, if they continue down "the wrong path," here is what will happen. Prophets foretell such things by means of their clear perception of the current situation, not through miraculous divination.

Mere political calculation differs from prophecy at two points: (1) the prophet draws his perception from God's revelation: "he assesses the contingencies of a given moment's history in the light of God's permanence." (2) Then, he announces that people should look on the catastrophes they are preparing for themselves and take them as God's punishment. They should then hear God's call and change their ways. God decides to punish, all right, but *in order to punish, all he has to do is let people go on with what they are doing;*

if they continue, the result will indeed express God's anger. God has no need to *add* to the evil people do to each other. Human beings are nearly always the ones who express his anger.

If people change, however, the event does not take place, and we can say that God's anger subsides (for he is slow to anger and quick to pardon). In other words, the prophet does not announce coming disasters as expressions of God's justice or power, for example. Instead, he utters a threat designed to make people change. This approach leads us to modify our view of prophecies. So many historians have written in utterly infantile fashion that since a prophecy did not come true, the prophet erred. But the opposite view should prevail: since the predicted event did not take place, the prophecy succeeded—its intent was to announce to people what they must *avoid,* and what they must do to avoid it!

Jonah provides us with a paradigm of this principle, as well as with its best example. When the disaster he warns of does not take place, we should say not that God changed his mind, but that since people's behavior changed, God moved everything back to square one. He sent the prophet in order to bring about just that change!

In view of these facts, we must not conceive of God as determining everything absolutely, but as the one constantly teaching us. He acts on the basis of his dialogue with us, through his Word, not on the basis of "the laws of nature." We must not think of him as destiny or as an especially powerful form of determinism added to all the determinisms that already weigh us down. The Bible shows us that, on the contrary, God intervenes to change what seems determined. He teaches us that we can escape determinism, inserting some play into the web of causes that surround us: this is one of the ways we can define miracles!

In the light of these insights, Qohelet warns us of the utter vanity of trying to lay hold of the future in order to influence the present: you cannot devise a morality because you know nothing about tomorrow. This means you have no idea what is good. You cannot say it is useful to accumulate money, because you have no way of knowing who will profit from your money tomorrow. You cannot derive the meaning of your life from work, because you have no way of knowing who will make use of what you have done, tomorrow. "Tomorrow" marks the absolute limit of your possibilities.

I find this warning essential for our day, when we experience both the expectation and the necessity of "foreseeing the future." Knowing the future obsesses us. In reality, no other dimension continues to elude our grasp. In our present technical and economic climate, knowing the future has become indispensable. No longer a matter of mere curiosity, or the response to a permanent source of human anguish, foreseeing the future is now necessary for everything we do in society.

Since ancient times people have tried to guess what was coming, since the future seemed a riddle. But in our day technical progress, the population explosion, and economic expansion have placed all of humanity in a situation comparable to that of a great general of an earlier age as he faced a battle only hours away. What does my adversary intend to do? What maneuvers will he carry out? What reserves will he be able to mobilize? What reinforcements can he count on during the battle, etc.? But such problems involved a single army, and lasted only a day or two, whereas our issues concerning the future involve a whole nation and constitute a permanent aspect of our lives.

This bind we are in does not stem from a particular economic or political system, but from the overall structure. We must decide constantly about a given alliance, certain investments, or our choice of adversaries. All such decisions (even when the most powerful make them) depend on the decisions made by all our other partners, as well as by scientific and technical discoveries we *must foresee,* etc. We can no longer imagine a world in which a few politicians and military figures played chess among themselves. We have to anticipate everything. Any time we fail to do so, disaster follows. I maintain that at the very point where it has become urgent to do so, we find it increasingly impossible to foresee the future.[15] The kinds of data we deal with have changed so that the future eludes us much

15. See Jacques Ellul, "Unpredictability," part I, chapter 2, in *The Technological Bluff,* trans. Geoffrey W. Bromiley (Grand Rapids: Eerdmans, 1990). The text above summarizes this chapter.

more than it escaped any prehistoric individual. Prehistoric people did not have enough information to foresee things, whereas we have too much.

We can take one of two possible attitudes. (1) For some, it will suffice to practice futurology; that is, to calculate and evaluate what is actually going to take place. Futurologists are scientists who bring no value judgment to their predictions. They limit themselves to offering the most probable explanation of the future to those who must make decisions. They constantly perfect their extremely diverse methods. (2) For others, who concentrate on future *possibilities,* we should choose a given future and intervene in order to prepare for it and bring it about. This effort involves two parts: evaluating objectively and exerting influence. We should move so as to reinforce or counteract certain tendencies, modifying the direction of others, nullifying any forces we recognize as harmful, etc. We may draw up a plan to show how we might do this. Planning, whatever its object, aims at programming the future (usually economic, but sometimes political or administrative). It tries to shape a future chosen on the basis of existing material givens and their probable evolution.

What impresses me is the bankruptcy of *all* predictions, and I mean *all* of them.[16] No plan has ever been carried out, in any country in the world—not in the Soviet Union, or China, or Cuba, or France. Worse yet, every predictive scientific study has proved inaccurate in practice. Naturally, the early methods, consisting of merely extrapolating a previous trend, were looked on as weak when they failed to predict accurately. When something had progressed by three percent between one date and another, that meant it would arrive at a given figure twenty years later, following the same curve.

16. Pierre Simon Laplace, whose triumphant astronomical prediction is well-known, said something like "If you give me all the factors of the current situation, I can calculate so as to predict the future history of the world." The entire science of prediction was based on this notion. Unfortunately, it appears increasingly certain that no one will ever be able to know all the factors of the current situation, no matter how much we multiply the capacity of our computers. "There are more things in heaven and earth . . ." (Shakespeare's *Hamlet,* act 1, sc. 5).

Today's futurologists no longer support such conclusions. They feel only scorn for such oversimplifications! Unfortunately, we find precisely such reasoning applied in concrete situations today. For instance, EDF (French Electricity) established the need for nuclear reactors by basing the consumption of electricity in France in the year 2000 on a simple extrapolation of the consumption from 1950 to 1960. Similarly, the MIACA (Inter-ministerial Mission for the Development of the Aquitanian Coast) based the need for development of tourist facilities, beds, etc., in Aquitaine by 1985 on the growth of tourism by five percent each year from 1950 to 1965.

Today EDF's and MIACA's predictions have proven totally inaccurate. EDF produces and will continue to produce far more electricity than France's needs merit, with the result that in 1984 we were subjected to a frantic advertising campaign intended to make us use more electricity. But error is consistently denied. Administratively, however, such extrapolations continue to be used, so that the future of an entire country is gambled on the basis of figures that administrators know will never be reached!

Unfortunately, more is at stake here than a deficient method, since other predictions based on very advanced methods prove just as inaccurate. Alfred Sauvy's predictions concerning population figures and J.-J. Fourastié's with regard to the economy have been refuted. Even Herman Kahn's "scenario" method has proved disappointing: none of the predictions for the political future of the world in 1980 based on this method have worked out. No prediction regarding technique has been accurate. The futurologists failed utterly to predict the most important economic, political, and technical events: only two economists foresaw the oil crisis of 1974, for example. No one foresaw the possibility of the birth of a movement like Solidarity in Poland. In 1960, no one had imagined the development of computer science and all its by-products. I could give dozens of examples of decisive events that modified society *entirely* but were not foreseen. These facts should, of course, lead us to denounce as energetically as possible current policies regarding large construction projects and intermediate-term planning, since they are all based on inaccurate predictions.

I will not enter here into an analysis of the reasons for our inability to predict the future in advanced societies. Rather than dedicating a whole chapter to this matter, I will limit myself to two summary observations: (1) the more we find it indispensable today to predict things, the more impossible it is for us to do so (this dilemma is no accident: I believe this impossibility is intrinsically connected with our system). (2) We are no more enlightened with respect to the future than the people who lived five centuries before Christ. Qohelet is just as right today as he was when he wrote, and I believe he will continue to be right. The future is blocked.

At this point we find ourselves faced with another ambiguity: "What has been is what will be, and what has been done is what will be done. . . . If there is something of which it is said: 'Look at this, it's new!' this thing already existed in the centuries that preceded us" (1:9-10, JE). Qohelet denies progress, as we have seen. Some move quickly from this fact to the conclusion that Qohelet holds to a "cyclical concept of history," a circular philosophy of time. They find all sorts of correlations with different philosophies to explain this concept. Or else they show how this book stems from the traditional, archaic concepts of Qohelet's time. This misinterpretation does not stand up to a reading of the entire book; it can stand only if one takes a passage out of context.

Qohelet's statements quoted above teach us three principles: (1) we cannot foresee the future, primarily *because the future does not exist.* A simple reading of these verses would seem to indicate, on the contrary, that we can easily foresee the future, since it amounts to a repetition of the past. But as I read the entirety of Qohelet (including his "pessimism"!), I learn above all that nothing is decided in advance, or written, or foreseen. The "foreknowledge" of God does not exist. Neither does Diderot's "Big Book" (in *Jacques le Fataliste*). There is no destiny. Before us we see absence and whiteness. It is up to us to color in the white, to write on the blank page, and fill up what is empty, bringing it to life.

Qohelet carefully avoids giving the appearance of a dictum. We can see nothing in the future simply because nothing is there. Divination is impossible because there is nothing there to divine! Things are not decided in advance. Qohelet repeats this idea in his great poem "There is a time for everything" (3:1-8), which I consider a radical text.

The future is made—by us. God intervenes in its creation, but he does not make it up, any more than he wrote it all down at the beginning. Nothing is inevitable. We see this in the life of Jesus, which shows the conflict between his obedience to the God of love and freedom, and the legalism of submitting to something already written. Qohelet is the denial of "it is written." Nothing is written.

(2) Contrary to a simplistic, superficial reading of Qohelet's statements quoted above, he continually repeats that time enables us to create new things. Never is it a repetition of the past. This conclusion seems to fly in the face of the obvious meaning of the passage we have quoted! Yet it represents the true judgment of our author. The future amounts to an amazing tangle of potentiality and actuality, of the past, the present, and the unknown. Qohelet's book offers us a skillful model of just such a complicated network!

If my interpretation is correct, why does Qohelet write so clearly "What has been is what will be," etc.? I believe he writes these words to *oppose* those who not only claim they can "read" the future but maintain they can produce or accomplish something completely original! In other words, Qohelet engages in irony in the above passage: "Do not be so sure of yourselves, thinking you can dream up and do something exceptional, more important than your ancestors did! You are filled with your own importance and impressed by your creativity, but you are not as significant as you think. If you knew the past, it would bowl you over!" Rather than teaching that the past and the future are exactly equivalent, I believe our texts deflate people's idea of their own importance.

I take the above passage not as a prophecy but as a foreshadowing of Jesus' saying: "tomorrow will take care of itself" (Matt. 6:34, NJB). We must take his maxim seriously: like Qohelet, Jesus teaches that there is no tomorrow already written, and that tomorrow will create itself. Jesus does not say "God will take care of your tomorrow," or "You must create your tomorrow." Instead of either of these, he says "tomorrow will take care of itself." These words come at the end of his teaching on not fretting about the future: "do not worry about your tomorrow" (Matt. 6:34, JE). What will come will come: *"Qué será será,"* as they sang in 1945. Furthermore, I believe we need to read the entire Sermon on the Mount (Matt. 5–7) in the light of Qohelet, where we find its roots.

We can count on moralists and the virtuous to protest indignantly: "We cannot live as Qohelet suggests; it would amount to laziness and irresponsibility" ("remember the ant and the grasshopper," they will cry!). These days (as we have observed) we must organize the future. They should take the matter up with Jesus Christ, if this is how they feel. We will come back to the theme of time in Qohelet, but for now we have seen the certain meaning of his profound meditation on the subject. The basic elements of the history of people and nations have not varied. We depend not on nature, but on someone more profound than nature.

(3) As we shall see, Qohelet refers us to a different "newness" as a possibility: God's newness. Only God can create something new. He can introduce a radically new factor, both within our hearts and within history. "There is nothing new under the sun" (1:9). This means that in reality what a person is and does is nothing new. Have no illusions in the matter. We discover the truth of this observation not in a negative way, by means of a disillusioned meditation, but when we compare our idea of something new with God's newness. This is Qohelet's secret argument; his discovery constitutes one of the pillars of wisdom.

Finiteness and Death

The other great pillar of wisdom, seeing death in everything, depends on this first pillar of being conscious of human finiteness. When I call these "pillars of wisdom," I do not mean to identify them with its *content,* its ultimate truth. We will discover this positive reality of wisdom at the very end of Qohelet. No, the pillars of wisdom are its supports, the things that hold it up and enable it to function. No wisdom is possible without these negative under-

standings. We would only be chasing after wind if we talked about
wisdom without beginning in this way. Our aim is to keep our
actions and words from being a chasing after wind, or mist that
evaporates from a mirror. The only way to achieve this is to begin
by crashing headlong into a reality that is anything but wind! A
reality we "cannot get around," to use popular terminology: just as
a motorcyclist cannot bypass the wall he crashes into.

Our "wall" consists of an empty future and a radical death. This
death is continually present in life, "emptying the present of all
presence." Death is everywhere, and we must look at it that way.
After we have seen its presence absolutely everywhere we can say
what wisdom may be. Once we have reached this extreme, the rest
is permitted, but not before, and in no other way.

We must keep in mind that the gravity of discerning death's
presence is never eliminated or even reduced by the possibility of
our having access to wisdom and truth. The awfulness of Christ's
cross and his "why have you forsaken me?" (Matt. 27:46) must
never be watered down and made acceptable by the resurrection.
Understanding the cross in the light of the resurrection can lead to
docetism only when gross misbelief is involved. On the contrary,
understanding the cross in the light of the resurrection should only
teach me that God is the one who truly died that day. This involves
an absolute incomprehensibility but also an astounding revelation.
Since God died there, because he did not choose to vanquish and
condemn me, then I am . . . I *am*.

In this way, Qohelet shows us a path that leads to wisdom as a
possibility. But we have to go down that path, recognizing that death
makes wisdom possible.[17] This is so because death eliminates

---

17. Remarkably, a work I often cite as one of the rare important works of
our time follows this same line of thought, although its author probably fails
to realize its relationship with Qohelet: the trilogy by B. Ronze, *L'Homme de
quantité* (Paris: Gallimard, 1977); *L'Homme de foi* (Paris: Desclée de
Brouwer, 1979); and *L'Homme de Dieu* (Paris: Desclée de Brouwer, 1980).
Ronze ends *L'Homme de quantité* with a long discussion of death as the only
thing possible in the light of human annihilation as we see it in human beings
oriented toward quantity (pp. 163-263). He is right that only beginning with
that understanding can we speak of an orientation toward faith, the subject of

everything that calls itself wisdom and philosophy. Death is the very measure of wisdom's quality; it makes wisdom fragile (1:13).[18] But for Qohelet, unlike Job, death also makes wisdom possible because it turns the quality of life into an absurdity (for Job, death signifies rather the lack of immanent justice). Only this insight can serve as a foundation for wisdom and philosophy.

Just as we explored the relationship of finiteness to the future, we must clarify how discerning death relates to our time. Throughout Qohelet, the understanding of death bears no relation to the two tendencies I observe in our era: (1) the obsession with suicide and nihilism; and (2) the naturalization of death.

(1) Obsession. What a strange spectacle: in intellectual and aesthetic circles we continually hear the praises of works that celebrate death. In the music and films of the 1980s death is always bombastic and glorified. Every so often another astounding vindication of Mishima appears, whereas we would react more appropriately with compassion or horror (*Le Monde* praises him enthusiastically again several times as I write this in June 1983). Such praise is misplaced, since Mishima represents the equivalent of World War II's kamikaze pilots and the best of the Nazis. They scorned death to the point where they gave it and sought for it with the same amount of pride.

For the Nazis and Mishima, taking the taste of death to an extreme was a reality. But today people hold forth on the subject out of snobbishness; it amounts to nothing but a spectacle, as I suggested above, or aestheticism, in the worst sense of the word. Such talk demonstrates that the "death instinct" has not been sublimated, but, on the contrary, exalted. This attitude has nothing in common with Qohelet's harsh, supremely ironic observation.

(2) In the same manner, Qohelet challenges our present temp-

---

his second book. Of course, Ronze's work has been utterly ignored by critics and the public, as I believe they ignore anything that has existential value.

18. Edmond Rostand concluded his poem "L'Heure charmante" with these lines: "Adding to so many rare charms the charm / Of all that the barbarians already threaten, / Of all that will soon be completely gone!" (*Les Musardises,* new ed., 1887-1893 [Paris: Eugène Fasquelle, 1911], p. 165).

tation to naturalize death. We tend to look at death as a simple biological phenomenon, which should neither frighten nor outrage us—as something natural (which of course it is, except for the fact that we are conscious of death!). So now we have the tame death of funeral parlors: a decent, proper death, momentarily accompanied by life. As if nothing had happened—only this "nothing" we call "death."

Another way to naturalize death involves considering it a condition for life. Of course! How could life reproduce itself without death to nourish it? Even more importantly, death enables life to recreate itself as youth and beauty. Taken to extremes, this view leads to creams that nourish beautiful skin, made from the placenta. Perhaps soon we will make them from fetuses! It is certain that dead fetuses are going to be very useful. We continually hear such reassuring lessons on death.

Reassurance is what we seek, since we no longer have any other recourse or hope. Some seek their reassurance in the exaltation of death, others in its naturalization. Qohelet has no other hope either, but he hangs tough, leading us over this obstacle by the halter. We must recognize the issue of death as an obstacle—a fatal one. Until we look it in the face, no wisdom is possible, no faith can exist. If we could find any guarantees, we would not come back to this point. Qohelet continues down the difficult path: death has the last word in every way.

You find this idea lacking in originality? Just listen to how he expresses it: "Better to go to a house of mourning than to a banquet house, because it is every person's end; and the one who lives will consider this in his heart" (7:2). Do you try to escape death by going to parties, banquets, and other means? But banquets soon come to an end. *Carpe diem*, but the day is short and death has no end. You crave enjoyment, but so few people find it, whereas death is everyone's destiny. Death is our end: not just the conclusion but also the goal, the unknown objective that is deeply hidden and disguised. If you want to be a brave person, go to a house of mourning. There you will begin to learn the one really necessary thing.

Qohelet adds: "Better grief than laughter" (7:3). He is often

considered disillusioned at this point. But we want to concentrate
on one of the words he chooses. The passage is always translated
"Sorrow is better than laughter" (RSV, NIV, NASB, KJV) or
"Vexation is better than laughter." But the word used here,
missehoq, clearly does not have the same meaning as Isaac's name
(yishaq): joyous laughter, laughter stemming from fulness, peace,
gratitude, or rejoicing. Qohelet's word designates mocking or
scornful laughter, or the nervous laughter that accompanies conflict
and confrontation. Hazan calls it the laughter of nihilism (p. 101;
see also pp. 98-100).

The laughter of the fool (7:6) confirms this understanding of
the word "laughter." The entire passage comes clear on this basis:
rather than opposing joy and death, Qohelet shows that our only
choice is between orgies or confrontational mockery on the one
hand, and death on the other. The wise person will prefer death to
this "house of joy" (7:4b), which is worse than death. For this reason
"the heart of the wise is in the house of mourning" (7:4a).[19]

Qohelet continues with several generalizations: "Better the end
of a matter than its beginning; it is better to be longsuffering than
proud in spirit" (7:8, JE). For if death is the measure of everything,
but also the first measure suggested by wisdom, we should start at
that point, from that truth.[20] Yet when Qohelet speaks to us of death,

---

19. At this point I follow Maillot's very remarkable interpretation: "Death
is superior to birth. Why? Because in it we find nothing unexpected. Qohelet
feels a holy horror for the unexpected . . . , especially if it consists of misfortune, illness, oppression, or ruin. The dead person knows nothing of these
problems, and no longer suffers anguish: in particular, the anguish of death.
Only death delivers me from death. Furthermore, the day of my death is the
day of truth: the day that enables us to judge all the other days. The day that
gives birth to my 'name,' my existence in all its truth. Death strips away all
appearances. . . . It was not up to us to be born, but it is up to us to die well"
(p. 105).

20. Here as well I want to underline the strength of Maillot's interpretation
(pp. 111-13): he emphasizes the opposition between Western thought, which
looks mainly for causes, mechanically deducing effects from them, and Hebrew thought, which considers the end more important than the beginning. We
look for the data of the hypothesis, whereas the Israelite is oriented toward the
solution. "The Westerner asks 'Why?,' whereas the Israelite asks 'For what

he never yields to the morbid temptation to exalt it. He does not indulge in any death's-head delirium, or inspire any dance of death. In no way does he revel in the spectacle of death or in annihilation.[21]

Qohelet speaks of death with firm and tranquil assurance; he encloses awareness of death within a process connected with life and designed to make us even more alive. We must note this approach. Death is the common measure of everything that lives. It reminds us that we are animals: death is the carnal part of our being. "For human beings and animals have an identical destiny: the death of the one is the same as the death of the other, and both have an identical breath. Human superiority over animals amounts to nothing, for all is vanity. Everything goes toward the same place: everything comes from dust, and everything returns to it. Who knows if human beings' breath rises upward and animals' breath descends toward the earth?" (3:19-21).

Death humbles our human pride, power, idealism, and spiritualism. Learning we are just like the animals as far as death is concerned is the condition for attaining wisdom. Certainly Qohelet has no notion of the immortality of the human soul. But the introduction to the passage quoted above is utterly remarkable: learning our similarity to the animals is a test God imposes on us: "It is in order for God to test them and *in order for them* to see that they are themselves animals" (3:18). Death is imposed on every-

---

purpose?' " [French *Pourquoi?* and *Pour quoi?*—TRANS.]. In this manner the Israelite progresses in hope, as we see in the following verses (e.g., 7:9). Israelite thought is humble, submissive to God's plan and to facts, whereas Western thought is proud, taking God's place by positing causes. Israelite thought is slow and patient, filled with detours; Western thought is impatient, hyperactive, and lacks understanding. I agree fully with these ideas of Maillot's, including his attack on impatient people in the Church (pp. 113-15).

21. For this reason, according to Lys, Qohelet speaks of death as the "place," or "dwelling place": "All go to the same place; all come into being from dust, and all return to dust" (3:20). Lys comments: "We have a goal, then, an outcome, but a ridiculous one: the moment when we could finally find rest coincides with the moment we no longer exist. In order to have a dwelling place at last, one must die. Death is the only place where human beings can lay their head. . . . This unique 'dwelling place' is *the same* for all, like the destiny and breath of 3:19" (p. 393).

thing; it constitutes the common denominator. But there is *one* decisive difference: "that they may see themselves." No animal can do that. Our *only* superiority (and the source of wisdom!) is that we know our condition.

This observation moves us much farther along. Scholars have shown decisively the relationship between vanity and death (*hebel, riq, behalah, tohu,* etc.; see Chopineau, pp. 39-43). Death is an expression of vanity. Vanity dominates wisdom, which is subject to it. Death is the concrete fact that manifests the ruin of wisdom. Working with all one's intelligence without seeing the success of one's effort, witnessing the death of one's children—this amounts to working for death's benefit. Human effort achieves nothing. This wisdom also serves death, since we can neither build work that will last on it, nor pass it on to our children as it stands.

Have we reached Qohelet's final conclusion? We misunderstand him if we think so! In a verse we examined above (7:2) we failed to take a small phrase into account. After saying it is better to go to a house of mourning, Qohelet adds: "the one who lives will consider this in his heart." This is a decisive act. Later he adds "the living at least know that they will die" (9:5, JE). Pascal was not the first to say so. Human beings resemble animals in that both die; people differ from animals not in having a soul (breath, spirit) but in knowing they will die. Wisdom consists of realizing this. This reversal is what makes us human. Our awareness—of what ruins both us and wisdom—is precisely what makes possible both wisdom and our orientation toward the thing that will give us life.

These days we are used to such thinking. Marx gave strong expression to this "dialectic": as long as a person does not realize he is alienated, there is no way he can be liberated from his alienation. Emancipation begins when a person realizes he is alienated. The deeper one's alienation, the more decisive his liberation.

Bernard Charbonneau has centered his entire work on this dialectic that states freedom can begin only on the basis of the discovery of necessity. We must remember that such a realization is not some kind of release. Charbonneau would never say that when I become aware, I place myself outside necessity, or that necessity ceases to exist. Not at all. Necessity remains, and we remain subject to it. But the awareness of a *given* necessity shows that a person is free of it: one must be free in order to realize that he is.

Similarly, Qohelet tells us that death remains death: it is useless to deny it or tone it down (we will return to this matter). But my awareness of this death shows that I have situated myself outside and beyond it. Otherwise I could not be aware of what it *is*. But we must go all the way to the end of this reality and not shrink back at any point. We must hold on to both sides of the dialectic: I am mortal *and* conscious of it. The constant temptation has been to replace the *and* with an *or else:* I am either conditioned or else free.

All the "spiritual" people made this mistake. Since they believed in Christian liberation through the Holy Spirit, they thought they were free from their human condition and already in heaven. This spiritualism, as we see it in Augustine and Luther, is the source of all ethical deviations. But, on another level, Eduard Bernstein makes the same mistake when he considers that humanity *ceases* to be subject to necessity and conditioning at the moment it comes to understand the fatality of history and the fact of human conditioning through economics. At this point humanity becomes complete master of economic activity. Marx never said so! The economic reality still remains as a constraint, but people can at the same time be free of it, through their consciousness of it.

We have seen that we must not try to soften or tone down the reality of death in any way if we expect our consciousness of it to serve as a pillar of wisdom. Qohelet can teach us a great deal along these lines: we must know death as absolute, unlimited; it has no solution. It leaves us no human hope: "The living know indeed that they will die, but the dead know nothing at all, and there is no more reward for them, because their memory is forgotten. Their love, their hatred, and their jealousy have already perished, and they have no more share ever again in anything that is done under the sun" (9:5-6). Here we have Qohelet's final word on death. For him no afterlife is conceivable. As we have seen, he allows for no immortality of the soul; neither do we find the idea of resurrection in his book. Consequently, we cannot place our hope "somewhere else." *Everything* takes place here.

We need to avoid two misunderstandings, however. Let us

begin by reminding ourselves again that Qohelet speaks of what happens *under the sun.* He makes no claim to go beyond that sphere. Even more important, the second possible misunderstanding consists of making a philosophical judgment at this point. We must not conclude from the prime importance Qohelet attaches to death the "idea" (which would be nothing but an idea) that he puts forward a philosophical doctrine. He does not take a position on the debates of his era concerning the question of the resurrection, or against Platonism. Qohelet gives us neither a philosophy of revelation nor the entire revelation. He is not a doctrinarian or a professor.

Qohelet meditates on death. On that basis, some have said that his view of death as radical flies in the face of the usual teaching of the Bible that life is a supreme value, an absolute, that God is the Living One, that life is necessarily victorious, etc. Qohelet does not expressly say the contrary. But he says that life on this earth is infinitely fragile, and that its meaning stems not from life but from death.

We cannot fairly say that Qohelet does not attach much importance to life.[22] After all, he wrote this scandalous phrase: "Even a live dog is better than a dead lion" (9:4b, JE). When we reflect on the way a dog was regarded in Israel, we understand Qohelet's meaning: that even the most vile, contemptible life utterly devoid of interest is better than death. "For the one who is united to all the living, there is hope" (9:4a), as he says in introducing the phrase on the live dog.

We cannot consider Qohelet our ally, then, when we are sorely tempted to think "life is not worth living if we are not free, or rich,

---

22. I found this same interpretation in Lys, but with an unusual emphasis: "Precisely because life is what matters, a person rebels when it becomes clear that life is not enough, in quality more than quanity, to have meaning. Paradoxically, death becomes attractive" (p. 258)—out of spite, perhaps? Lys continues, quoting Neher: death " 'is the only certain aspect of life. . . . The attraction of death increases as one's attachments to life cool down' " (Lys, pp. 258-59; Neher, p. 26). Lys continues: "I am not sure Qohelet is blasé and tired of living here. He does not end up recommending suicide or the convent. . . . He is distressed . . . by the lack of meaning in life, to which he is utterly attached. . . . Paradoxically, Qohelet detests life because he loves it" (p. 259).

or if there is no justice," etc. "Yes it is," answers Qohelet with
cynicism and realism: a live dog is better off than a dead hero.
Because where there is life there is hope? Such simplistic popular
wisdom! Too bad for heroes.

Nor can we accuse Qohelet of meaning that we must sacrifice
life for certain values. On the contrary! He has shown the vanity of
all "values," and we place the highest value on life. But Qohelet
approaches everything with relativism, so that we find also the
opposite: he says yes to life, yet death is better than life lived under
conditions of oppression, violence, injustice, and evil: "Furthermore, I have seen all the oppression that is done under the sun:
behold the tears of the oppressed, and they have no comforter. On
the side of their oppressors there is violence, and they have no
comforter. And I praised the dead who are already dead more than
the living who are still alive; and happier than both of them [I say]
is the one who has not yet been, because he has not seen the evil
work that is done under the sun" (4:1-3). You accuse Qohelet of
contradicting himself? No: life as an utterly relative reality is
something good we must receive and accept. But the power of evil
and its domination make this good as vain as the rest.

Qohelet's two affirmations complement each other. Everything
is subject to vanity. We see this expressed in different ways, but
wisdom consists of knowing it is true. We must not claim to hold
the key to the meaning of life (of history!), not make an absolute of
it, but not refuse it, either. Like the rest, life is subject to vanity: to
nothingness and idolatry.

Life is not without content or direction. Error and trickery begin
at this point, so we must keep in mind its radical finiteness. With
that foundation, we can begin reconstructing life with all the activities we engage in. We have seen, indirectly, how Qohelet does just
that, taking the point of view of death with respect to our activities:
money, work, pleasure, art, etc. This is the "beginning of wisdom."
But on the basis of precisely this knowledge, life becomes possible
again.

Qohelet does not present life as tedious, however. Disgust
overcomes only those who hoped for too much from life and power,
who gave it their heart, their strength, and their love. They experi-

ence a terrible reaction. But not Qohelet. After trying everything, he comes to his conclusion. And he knows the knowledge of death takes the place of all possible disappointments. Life is humbly possible in spite of injustice.

Now we come up against a new obstacle: Qohelet presents the mechanism of retribution that Job criticized so much and rejected: "Although I know that there will be happiness for those who fear God, because they fear before him. And there will be no happiness for the wicked person; like a shadow, he will not prolong his days, because he does not fear before God" (8:12b-13). This is absolutely staggering! This man who questions everything, this antiestablishment person who goes to the bottom of things, now comes up with a platitude that flies in the face of reality. Qohelet must have known how Job protested, yet he offers precisely the arguments of Job's friends. This statement of Qohelet's is so hard to believe that some exegetes have claimed to see in it the hand of a pious interpolator— someone who added this comment in order to salvage God's honor in the final edition of the book. I believe we can find a much more consistent explanation if we just take time to look at the context.

Let us begin with two important comments. (1) The quotation above involves a kind of declaration or confession of faith: "But *myself,* I know . . . ," begins Qohelet. Again he calls himself into question, and in an act typical of faith, he proclaims the opposite of what the evidence seems to show. Our experience indicates that the unjust person reigns and lives on, and that the good person fails to be recognized. Faith rears up in the face of this evidence and declares: "True, that is how things are, *but I know . . . ,*" making its appeal to another dimension—something qualitative and not observable. As I have often emphasized, faith like this, that stands in the face of all the evidence to the contrary, is the very essence of hope.[23]

We find an additional dimension in our text, however: harsh social and political criticism. Qohelet began this chapter recalling the happiness of evil people, and then went on to attack power: "It

23. See Jacques Ellul, *Hope in Time of Abandonment,* trans. C. Edward Hopkin (New York: Seabury, 1973).

is because the sentence pronounced against an evil work is not rapidly executed that human hearts are filled with the intention to do evil, because the sinner does evil a hundred times, and prolongs [his days]" (8:11-12a). Then, following our quotation above, we read: "There is a vanity that is done on the earth: there are just people treated according to the work of the wicked . . ." (8:14a).

In other words, because the authorities do not intervene to punish the unjust person when he does evil, he finds happiness on earth. Judgment may be pronounced, but not applied; a criminal may be condemned to death, but he continues to live as if he had not been so condemned. Still worse, the authorities punish the just and reward evil people. Qohelet emphasizes that the unhappiness of the just and the happiness of evil people do not come from chance, circumstances, or God, but from other people: they "are treated as" others deserve. People and power are responsible for this situation. Facing it would normally lead a person to despair of life, but Qohelet affirms his faith in God's justice.

We must interpret his statement as a confession of faith; otherwise we will make the mistake of identifying Qohelet's words with traditional doctrine. Nothing in the text indicates that God will intervene to reestablish justice in this life, on this earth. The text implies a future, something unfulfilled, but specifies nothing. The clear element is the opposition between the injustice of political power and the justice of God. When we can no longer trust those who should administer justice, God is our last resort (and our first!). Qohelet has already alluded to the fear of God, which we will rediscover at the end of the book.

This way of understanding the text gives us good reason, I believe, to modify the "traditional theory" of retribution. I can hear the skeptic say: "Here we have proof that religion is the opium of the people; it provides a refuge for those who have no desire to change anything on earth." I have no response to this, except to say that faith has nothing to do with this kind of calculation. Qohelet has been careful to say that he is talking about *his faith* rather than some universal and objective verity. Who would dare say to this all-out protester of everything that he has no desire to change anything?

In any case, Qohelet deals in this passage with the possibility of living. He affirms that his faith in God's justice, presence, and care, and in his relationship with him, enables him to go on living in spite of everything, in a universe of wickedness and cruelty. But he always reminds us of the fragility of this possibility. Yes, life remains possible, but the whole pyramid rests on this tiny point: "I know. . . ."

(2) Consequently we must remain thoroughly humble in life. Everything is subject to death in the end—even the statement: "I know." Our humility should show in the way we place limits on our own actions. Since everything is finite, subject to relativity, the wise person will limit himself. This is where all Qohelet's advice on being cautious, silent, etc., fits in. Those who fail to make the connection at this point readily accuse him of petty bourgeois morality. "Do not be excessive in your wisdom. Your wisdom is subject to vanity. If you are too radically wise, you will learn that all is indeed vanity. You will know it so well that you will stop doing anything at all, and will stop living. Do not be too foolish, because your folly would lead you to attempt things beyond your human limits, so that you would take yourself for God or the Devil. When you enter excess, you move into *nothingness*. Cover your mouth with your hand and weigh your words—not from respect toward others or political caution, but because (as we shall see) words are the only reality that commits a person. When you say words rashly, you devalue what gives meaning: the 'But I know. . . .'"

"Don't necessarily listen to everything that is said around you, because you will hear even your servant speak evil of you" (7:21, JE). Limit your curiosity (these days we might say: "limit your thirst for information").[24] Is the servant wrong here? Of course! But reflect on "all the times when you yourself have spoken evil of others" (7:22, JE). So "information" in itself is not at all a good

24. This advice has nothing in common with second-rate bourgeois caution, but constitutes the realization of the decisive importance of limits— establishing them and voluntarily choosing them. See Jacques Ellul, *Les Combats de la liberté* (Geneva: Labor et Fides, 1984); partial Eng. trans. in *The Ethics of Freedom*, trans. G. W. Bromiley (Grand Rapids: Eerdmans, 1976).

thing. We realize this daily: life is certainly more livable when it is not deluged with information! This is true not only because it robs us of the only quality life has to offer, but also because such information necessarily reminds us of what we have done or not done. In this way it always makes us feel falsely guilty, causing us to lose sight of the fact that the only life possible is one that is relative and limited in character.

So do not try to become too well-informed (at the time, of course, such advice had to do with espionage on the king's behalf, which sometimes took place even at court; but we should not forget that in a democracy we are all kings—the people are sovereign). Since life is fragile and finite, marked by death, respect it all the more by adopting modest and humble rules of behavior. "The one who observes the precept knows nothing evil, and the heart of the sage knows time and judgment" (8:5). Accept that there are rules to follow, and when you obey God's commands, you will keep from committing *any* evil deed.

Qohelet does not refer to the Torah here, but I believe he has precepts based on it in mind. To live your life well, you need to observe certain times (we will examine Qohelet's meditation on the subject at length), and make certain necessary judgments and assessments. These things make life possible. Qohelet goes no farther; for example, he does not say that life is marvelous. On the contrary, everything he teaches us points to the opposite! But he states that if we observe the Law, the times for things, and make certain judgments, we can live, and life is not so bad. But we must never claim to go beyond this humble possibility. We must always remember: "a live dog is better than a dead lion!" (9:4b).

Perhaps I amount to no more than a dog, and perhaps we lead a dog's life, but it is still life—to be saved and protected, even when it suffers scorn or indignity. Do not consider yourself better than a dog; this will give you a good idea of life's humility. Consider how necessary it is to teach and witness to this, if we are to counter our society's hubris. Society aims to conquer galaxies and stuffs itself insatiably with all the riches of the earth. It behaves like a wild, mad dog, not realizing that its greed shows it has stooped to an animal level. This fact should show society its true value, and bring it face to face with its impending end. Such madness comes before the end, just as Qohelet shows us that moderation can ensure that life will last.

We have examined Qohelet's two pillars of wisdom: acknowledgment of our finiteness as we face the future, and recognition of death. These two principles, constantly linked with wisdom, make it possible and enable it to function. If they are eliminated, wisdom becomes vain. They are neither the content nor the truth of wisdom, however. They make philosophy possible, but do not make it true.

To end this section I would like to cite Jean Sulivan's quotation of Emil Cioran, since it fits perfectly with Qohelet: "It makes no sense, writes Cioran, to say that death is the goal and end of life. But what else can we say? That life is the goal of death."[25]

4. Tests for Wisdom: Applications and Examples

As we have seen, awareness of our finiteness and the discernment of death in everything constitute the two pillars of wisdom. But where does this awareness of finiteness apply? Qohelet shows us three primary areas: the word, possessions, and women and the couple.

Before looking at them, we need to remember that for Qohelet, wisdom is fragile but essential. He was disappointed in his quest based on wisdom, and found nothing valuable or certain, but that will not stop him. On the contrary: the more bitterness and limitations we find, the more important it is to be wise—wise, knowledgeable, philosophical, skillful, self-critical, and exacting.

"I experienced all this by wisdom. I said: 'I will be wise!' And it is far from me. Far off is what was, and deep, very deep; who will discover it? I began again, with my heart, to learn, examine, and pursue wisdom and reason, to know that wickedness is insanity and folly is madness" (7:23-25). Here we have an admirable text. Wisdom is subject to vanity, to nothingness. It leads me to the

25. Jean Sulivan, *L'Ecart et l'Alliance* (Paris: Gallimard, 1981), p. 19.

discovery that everything is nothing. It lets me down in my efforts to be wise, since just at the moment I decide to be wise (in myself!), I realize that I am not.

Wisdom shows me the worst: how evil rules, how out of reach things are. Wisdom teaches me that the past is far off; and I have already seen that what has been is what will be. I find myself caught between an unknowable past and a future that does not exist. These are precisely the situations where I must proclaim that, having lived all this, I will gather up my courage and set out again in pursuit of wisdom and reason.

The Word

This "and yet" reaction parallels the one we examined earlier: I observe injustice as universal, *and yet* I affirm God's justice. Just so, my quest for wisdom has produced nothing but piled-up rubble, *and yet* I choose to search for nothing but wisdom! I choose to recognize that wisdom differs from folly. Perhaps wisdom expresses itself only in words, but words amount to something!

Remarkably, the only human reality Qohelet does not declare vain is the word. Indeed, as we have seen, everything labeled "vanity" relates to the world of action. The word is infinitely more serious; we gather this from the beginning of the book, which places everything under the title: "Words of Qohelet" (1:1). So after concluding that everything is vanity, Qohelet begins his words. The word is not vanity, then; otherwise he would have remained silent.

After all his action, having noted the vanity of everything, the most important thing that remains for Qohelet is to *speak* this vanity. His words begin with the proclamation that "All is vanity," but they end with promise and hope, as he declares that God is God. We must not separate the beginning from the end. We will return to this matter. For now, we must consider that if the word was also subject to vanity, why would Qohelet use words to tell us about it? Why take the trouble to set out again on a road that leads nowhere?

Qohelet speaks because only the word escapes vanity.[26] The word constitutes our similarity with God, in spite of the infinite difference involved. This word is constantly threatened, however, with being captured by vanity. We see this throughout the book, as Qohelet repeats his harsh warnings against multiplying our words. Too many words constitute an evil, a scourge: "The foolish word comes from the abundance of words" (5:3b). In the excess of words and the superabundance of discourse, the word inevitably becomes folly. It goes beyond the speaker's intention and will, beyond his meaning, and produces the same effect as the fool.

The passage above (5:3) and a later verse posit a strange relationship between words and dreams. Dreams here must certainly stand for illusion: the trap of the unreal, the fictitious. We have already noted several times that Qohelet is an unrelenting realist. He finds dreams dangerous and harmful because they prevent us from seeing the reality he wants to reveal.

By "dreams," however, Qohelet means not only what we dream in our sleep (which he probably envisages in v. 2), but also our idealism, aestheticism, ideology, millenarianism, and utopianism. These are the butt of his attack, I believe, in verse 7: "In the abundance of dreams are vanities and words in abundance. But fear God." Such dreams turn us away from God, moving us to believe in something else. And dreams characteristically get us to take them for reality.

Qohelet attacks not only seers and interpreters of dreams in these passages, although he surely has them in mind, along with the whole science of dreams. But I believe his attack is more extensive: as if *all* vanities and *all* superfluous words stemmed from the abundance of dreams. This interpretation, if correct, would confirm what I said above, which might seem extreme: ideologies, idealisms, and utopias turn us from God by offering other objects for our faith. At the same time, they produce the vanities denounced by Qohelet (money, work, politics, etc.), and give rise to endless

26. This observation inevitably reminds me of Poor Tom's words in Shakespeare's *King Lear:* "the worst is not / So long as we can say 'This is the worst'" (act 4, sc. 1).

discourses. Qohelet attacks these causes and disparages the word when it is reduced to mere parroting or wild delirium. In both cases, the word becomes insignificant.

Abundance of words should serve as an utterly radical sign for us, enabling us to spot illusion and vanity. *Abundance* of words stands out in this way because of the infinite seriousness of the word. The more one goes on speaking, the less he exists. Qohelet has still more to say in condemning excess words: "When there are words in abundance, they make vanity abound [as we have seen]: how does that profit anyone?" (6:11). A cascade of words produces a lessening of our being. Thus the only grave matter is thoughtlessness or excess in connection with the word.

Finally, "a fool multiplies words" (10:14). This is important, too. Since the word is very important, it cannot be said any way we choose. The person who has nothing to say launches into an endless tirade; his excessive words reveal and compensate for the emptiness of his life. But this is true because of the power of the word.

As we have traced Qohelet's view of the word, have we not seen outlined a whole aspect of the world in our day? In the overabundance of information, political discourse, books (including mine, of course!), newspapers, and philosophical theories, we see the vanity *of our whole culture and civilization,* in their present state. The multiplication of words of all kinds, whatever their source, causes us to take one thing for another, so we end up thinking the moon is made of green cheese.

This relevance for our day makes me regard Qohelet as a critical focus for our reflection—for our bending back, as the word's etymology suggests: giving a critical glance back over our shoulder. The word is too serious a venture to leave it to be produced by fools. It should not be squandered. For this reason, Qohelet recommends caution in speech, even when we speak with God! "Don't let your mouth be hasty or your heart hurry to utter a word before God" (5:2a), and "When you make a vow to God, hasten to fulfill it. . . . It is better not to make a vow than to make one and not fulfill it" (5:4-5, JE).

Qohelet's justification for such caution may astonish us: "For God is in the heavens and you are on the earth: therefore let your words be few in number" (5:2b). We may also be surprised at the possible consequences of too much talk: "Do not let your mouth make your flesh sin" (5:6a). Qohelet immediately connects the word with God. Every use of the word reflects God's way of acting: the word reflects the fact that God's revelation comes to us through the word. But God is unknowable, so we must exercise caution when we enter a relationship with him. We may do this through a vow, or even a word we do not think of as a prayer. A word addressed to our neighbor still brings God into play, because we have used his astonishing creation: the word, the gift of God. Thus the word "sin" appears in this connection. Everything else is vanity, folly, or nothingness. Qohelet calls only one thing "sin": abuse of the word!

How could we fail to notice that Jesus gives the same advice, apparently inspired by Qohelet: "When you pray, do not multiply vain repetitions, useless words, like the pagans who imagine they will be answered because of their many words" (Matt. 6:7, JE). Jesus always gives evidence of the greatest restraint in everything he says.[27] Conversely, he warns us that merely saying a word implicates our whole being: "It suffices to say 'Raca!' to one's brother to merit being punished by the Sanhedrin. And it suffices to say 'Fool!' to merit being passed through the fire of hell" (Matt. 5:22, JE). The word is as decisive for Jesus as for Qohelet. Decisive and definitive: for in the long run the word is more effective than action. It involves extensive consequences.

We must remember that "the words of the wise spoken calmly are more listened to than the shouts of a leader in the midst of mad people" (9:17). Even in war and politics, the word is sovereign. For this reason Qohelet continually emphasizes the importance of being circumspect and controlling our tongue. We will be judged according to our words (contrary to what we usually think: that it will be according to our acts!). On the basis of this word, God can destroy what you do, if you speak carelessly: "Why would God blame your word and destroy the work of your hands?" (5:6b).

In the final analysis, the word always relates to truth. It takes

27. To my mind, this is one of the criteria distinguishing Jesus' words from gnostic discourse.

its place not in the area of Sartre's "practical inertia" but in that of
"truth and falsehood." There are no halfway points: the word either
speaks the truth or it is falsehood, and leads our whole being into
falsehood.[28] So the word is wisdom's best agent. And Qohelet
shows us just how this works: through denunciation of vanity and
recognition of our finiteness.

Possessions

The second test of the practice of wisdom offered to us by Qohelet
deals with possessions. Naturally, at this point I will not take up
the overworked theme (which remains valid) of the contrast
between being and having. Qohelet is more provocative than that:
"Cast your bread on the face of the waters, for after a time you
will find it again. Give a portion to seven or even to eight, for you
do not know what evil may occur on the earth" (11:1-2, JE). On
the surface, this command seems clearly absurd.[29] (Can we consider Qohelet's words less than a commandment? Why would we
refuse to consider the "imperatives" of a book of wisdom as
commandments of God, just as much as those of other books?)
Qohelet's words do not constitute merely a version of the well-
known order to stop economizing and planning ahead (as Jesus
said: "Look at the birds of the air. . . . the lilies of the field," Matt.
6:26, 28, RSV). Our text goes much farther: Qohelet openly
recommends squandering for no reason—an incomprehensible
and scandalous act.

We should note at the outset, considering Qohelet's thought as

28. I have examined this matter at length in *The Humiliation of the Word*.
29. I find utterly stupid the rather common explanation that says "Cast
your bread on the water" means "Trust your provisions [why provisions?] to
the sea; that is, to commercial ships, because one must risk his wealth to
augment it"! In view of his overall perspective, why would Qohelet give advice
to make business practices more profitable? If anything is foreign to him, surely
it is this! The only source of wealth he accepts is agriculture. But the idea of
"maritime commerce" has been exploited to the extreme by Podechard
(p. 442).

a whole, that his words here cannot condone the irresponsible attitude of someone who squanders foolishly or for ostentation. Nor does he refer to the person who wastes things unconsciously, because he does not know any better, who is attracted by everything and does whatever he feels like. Our author's "cast your bread" implies, on the contrary, utter awareness of one's act, and a deliberate intention to desacralize and to detach oneself.

We cannot, therefore, use this text to legitimatize the appalling wastefulness of our society: throwing away things others could use and squandering the unrenewable resources of our planet! Qohelet is not talking about squandering by wasteful, lazy, or weak individuals. He has no intention of justifying an absurdly extravagant approach to life as over against an approach involving exaggerated planning for the future. He does not advocate a kind of "duty to abandon foresight." He never decrees a duty. He proclaims a word of God addressed to a wise and reasonable person who naturally wants to economize and plan ahead, but who comes up against a rock: "Cast your bread. Learn to do things in the present (as we have seen, the wise person consistently recommends this), and gratuitously."

The gratuitousness of the act is decisive in this passage. Alone among all the actions we have seen, the gratuitous act eludes vanity's grasp. Qohelet's recommendation is all the more remarkable in that it counters conventional wisdom. "Do this without counting the cost," he says, "fearlessly, not worrying about it. Learn to separate yourself from what is most essential—bread!—and at the same time learn to do the things the world judges most severely. An act of this nature necessarily provokes a scandal. In a world where everything must serve a purpose (at least in appearance, according to our society's criteria of efficiency), learn to make a useless gesture. 'That is pointless!,' they will say. Of course!"

I cannot help thinking of the enormous number of useful actions that push us closer and closer to disaster. Then I remember those other gestures (made by hippies and nonpolitical pacifists, for example) which are considered futile: prayers and "useless" solitary self-sacrifice. These acts enable our world to survive. I think of

Ignazio Silone's novel, *The Seed beneath the Snow.*[30] After all, why does everything have to serve a purpose? Qohelet encourages us to learn to do things without motivation, just because God tells us to! In this case, the meaning, strength, and efficacy of our act are immeasurable, since they come from God.

We must emphasize, however, that the advice of our text carries no promise—not the slightest guarantee. Qohelet does not say "You will save your soul." But he does make a remark I attribute to his irony: "after a time [or, a long time after, in a number of days] you will find it again" (11:1, JE). Of course you will find your lost, cast-off bread that you saw carried off by the current—one day or another. Qohelet does not say "it is not lost for everybody," or "you will get it back when it has multiplied," due to some mathematical kind of justice. But he says "after all, in the years to come, you will still have bread—that same bread, or other bread."

At this point Qohelet intersects the Sermon on the Mount again. The bread you save today cannot help you in the years to come, any more than Israel's manna could be preserved for the next day. If only our stockbrokers and investors could understand this lesson! You may squander your bread today, but in a few years you will no longer remember it! The main thing is, "do not worry, do not be concerned" (Matt. 6:25, JE). In any case, you follow the same path as the bread cast on the face of the waters, and in the years to come, you will necessarily join it!

Qohelet takes us a step farther, however. First he says: "Learn to squander, don't look ahead, stop holding back and worrying." Then he adds: "Learn to give and share." At this point he reassures us. We know this terrain, and as Christians we find it solid: giving, helping, caring for the poor. But in reality, these take second place to learning to free ourselves. Then we can give.

Qohelet's approach is amazing; he does not advise useful or carefully calculated charity. "Give a portion to seven or even to eight," he says (11:2). After all, you have enough to help or even take care of seven or eight people. We are not dealing here with the

30. Ignazio Silone, *The Seed beneath the Snow,* trans. H. Fergusson (New York: Atheneum, 1965).

five thousand Jesus fed, but with our five loaves and two fishes. Qohelet speaks on our level, although we may find his recommendations impossible. Considered rationally, what I have is not enough for seven or eight people, but Qohelet is not speaking to us on the level of reason!

"Be generous," he says, "have a generous heart, welcoming the person who asks of you" (see Jas. 2:15-16). "There are riches enough in God's storehouses."[31] If Qohelet added this, we could feel comfortable with a logic we know well: "Who gives to the poor lends to God."[32] "Give and you will get one hundred times as much back." But Qohelet does not say this! He suggests an astonishing motive for giving: "for you do not know what evil may occur on the earth" (Eccl. 11:2). At this point our human wisdom wants to retort: "All the more reason to plan ahead, take precautions, and economize." But God's reason (only the wisdom of God would dare proclaim such a thing to us!) tells us the opposite: "give today and share now, since tomorrow misfortune may strike you."

"So what?," you ask? God answers: "Tomorrow you may no longer be able to give; you may not have anything to share." Someone may come to ask you for something, and you will not be able to help. Not only that, but you will no longer be able to obey God's command. You will simply not be able to love your neighbor anymore. For if you cannot do anything for the other person, love is an empty word. Paul tells us that when willingness is present, it is acceptable according to what one has, not according to what one does not have (2 Cor. 8:12). Today, then, while you can cast your bread and share with seven or eight people, hurry and do it, without keeping count and without measuring. Do not be stingy! That is how a different wisdom calls possessions into question.

The verses that follow, which we have already encountered in connection with the subject of work, remind us that our author by no means intends to encourage negligence. On the contrary, if you

31. See Louis Simon, *Une éthique de la sagesse: Commentaire de l'Epître de Jacques* (Geneva: Labor et Fides, 1961).

32. Victor Hugo, "Dieu est toujours là," l. 226, in *Oeuvres poétiques complètes,* ed. Francis Bouvet (Paris: Jean-Jacques Pauvert, 1961), p. 216.

are to give something, first you must have something to give. Work may be vain, but we must do it—without harboring any illusions. Here lies Qohelet's main point: without grandiose words and vain talk. Everything is subject to the uncertainty of what may happen: "When the clouds are full, the downpour falls" (Eccl. 11:3a, JE; there is no use calling on the gods for rain; Qohelet demythologizes again!). "When a tree is cut down, it will be there where it was cut down" (11:3b, JE). And whether it is in the north or south, what difference does it make?[33] If you wait until circumstances favor you, you will never do anything (see 11:4; you cannot foresee the future, you cannot prevent the tree from falling the way it does). You know nothing; in particular, you do not know the work of God (see 11:5).

So do what you have to do (11:6). But certainly not with a view to the goals people aim for, since no prediction or farsightedness is possible. Do what is at hand, without thinking ahead, since you do not know what will succeed! Do not try to figure things out for tomorrow: today is when you must act. Remember that God makes the final decision about what will succeed, in everything you do.

In our time, we can pride ourselves on being much more advanced than Qohelet! We know how to keep the rain away, even making it fall where we want it (not without difficulty). We can decide where a given tree will fall, or we can enable it to remain standing. We know precisely when an embryo's life begins, how its bones are formed in the womb (see 11:5), and what the breath of life entails.[34] In other words, we have much more skill than Qohelet, whose examples have lost their validity.

33. Following his usual bias, Lauha (along with many others) thinks these verses mean everything is "determined" (p. 201).

34. I have purposely followed the usual translation of 11:5, but the following may be more accurate: "As you do not know the way of the breath of life in the bones, in a pregnant woman. . . ." With this translation we are faced with our modern ignorance: we do not know any more about this subject than Qohelet's contemporaries knew! We may know how the bones are formed, but we do not know the *way* of the breath of life; that is, its essence and its origin. "Just so [and the comparison still remains valid] you do not know the work of God who makes everything" (11:5b, JE).

All we need to do is modernize his examples, however. When the circumstances of a worldwide conflagration or economic crisis come together, the crisis bursts open. If cancer begins in a lung or uterus, it remains there, in that same spot. No matter how long you watch economic trends, if you fail to act, everything will go to the dogs. Transposed for our day, Qohelet's ideas can be seen as principles such as "you know nothing of the ultimate reality of matter" (which is veiled reality), "you do not know the reason for the infinite variety of the forms of life," etc. Just as we fail to know these things, we "do not know the work of God, who makes everything" (11:5, JE).

Like Qohelet's first readers, we are stretched to our limit. Whatever our knowledge may amount to, we cannot understand God's work (assuming we part company with the amazingly ignorant, cocksure unbelievers who exclaimed, the first few times someone traveled in space: "See, God is not in heaven; no one met up with him." Now, with the first space probe to leave our galaxy, they have begun again—including some intellectuals, I regret to say!).

So we are as bound up in our ignorance as Qohelet's contemporaries, as far as what will be successful is concerned, and what will happen in the end. Do whatever you have to do, because something just might finally work. Will some pacifist movement bring about peace? Will our economic methods have some effect on the third world's poverty? Will an ill-conceived charity meet real needs? Will a better administration provide more justice? You do not know. Whatever your hand finds to do, do it, and surely, of all the things you do, something will end up successful. But which one? Your success will remain relative, offering no advantage, except for your ability to give to others and cast your bread on the water. This is all possessions amount to—nothing more.

Women and Men

Qohelet's final application of wisdom concerns men and women. Here I will boldly part company with most scholarly exegetes and refer to a text that seems irrelevant to this theme: the "better two than one alone" passage (4:9-12). I use this passage for two reasons: (1) Many agree, as we have seen, that Qohelet writes with the text of Genesis in front of him. Several of Qohelet's texts refer explicitly to Genesis passages, including these verses in chapter 4, which inevitably call to mind the following passages: "It is not good for the man to be alone. I will make a helper suitable for him" (Gen. 2:18, NIV); "The man said, 'Behold, this time one who is bone of my bones and flesh of my flesh'" (2:23, JE); and "the man will leave his father and mother and will cling to his wife, and they will become one flesh" (2:24, JE). The unity of the man and the woman makes them together the image of God.

(2) All of us surely recall the famous passage on the abomination of women (Eccl. 7:26-29). It has been used against womem, and it has marked Qohelet as a terrible phallocrat, obsessed with contempt for women. But this interpretation seems to me to contradict flatly the very structure of his thought as we see it revealed, in terms of contrast, irony, and constant paradox.

Standing over against this awful text against women, there *must* be an opposing passage—not merely a counterbalance or something to provide equilibrium, but the other side of the coin. There must be a yes opposed to this no, to form the paradox that constitutes wisdom. So, although the reference is not explicit, the "two" of 4:9 must of necessity refer to woman and man (but then what is truly *explicit* in this book? Is it not filled, on the contrary, with ironical statements?). I cannot prove this philologically! Qohelet's book does not reveal its message when a single method of interpretation is used. It presupposes biases, and invites the reader to have them, too!

The first side of this question, then, which is inseparable from the second, is: "Happier are those who are two than the one who is alone, because they have a good reward for their work. For if they fall, one raises the other up again; but woe to the one who is alone and falls and has no one to raise him up again. Furthermore, if they sleep together they keep warm; but how can the one who is alone get warm? And although someone may get the better of the one who is alone, two can resist: a threefold cord is not quickly broken"

(4:9-12). Let us dismiss right away a possible misunderstanding of the last image: the threefold cord does not suggest it is better to be three than two.[35] A cord can have one strand or three, but a two-strand cord cannot be made. A threefold cord, then, refers to a cord with several strands.

Apart from the image of the threefold cord, everything in the above passage involves two people: a couple. Not necessarily a man and a woman, of course: two friends, two fellow workers, or a homosexual couple could fit the text. Obviously there is nothing impossible about any of these suggestions. But in any case the text involves a stable, durable couple. The "cord," which is fashioned and entwined, suggests more than a simple work relationship, however.

To appreciate the strength of the relationship involved, we should note the progression in the passage: (1) working together; (2) helping when one or the other falls ill; (3) sharing the same bed; (4) withstanding an outside danger. I think we can see here the description of the various "uses" of the couple. We need not stumble over any objection concerning shared work, since women frequently worked, and not only at home: in agriculture, in artisans' shops (e.g., weavers), but also in higher occupations (commerce, banking, etc.). We could add the arts, music, and dance. Everywhere it is better for two to work than one person alone.

These days we understand this principle especially well, since a second salary is often essential in a household. The other advantages of the couple are obvious: caring for the sick person, mutual encouragement, the possibility of standing up to danger. Doesn't "a suitable helper" (Gen. 2:18) encompass all these aspects?

We do not want to force our text, but we should consider the passage that precedes it, which mentions the "child" that one does

35. But I find Maillot's observation interesting: he thinks the number three in this passage suggests the family, and alludes to the miracle of the third bond. A child knits his parents inextricably together, and gives them a strength they lacked previously. In a play on words, Maillot translates this third bond by the word "son" (p. 73).

not have (Eccl. 4:8). Perhaps the absurdity of working with no child (or brother, admittedly) suggests the need for marriage, to be a couple, in order to have a child. I do not claim any certainty for this interpretation—it is just my reading. In any case, the triple judgment is certain: it is *absurd, vain,* and *unhappy* to be alone (working for no one is vanity!).

Two are happier than a person alone; God himself makes this judgment in Genesis. Conversely, the solitary individual is unhappy. Our text does not contemplate a group or collectivity, in which one would still be alone, but rather a couple: a woman and a man, it seems to me, who constitute a force to be reckoned with, and who make happiness possible for each other. On this rare occasion, Qohelet envisages the possibility of happiness, without calling it vanity. What joy to read such a thing, in such a dismal world and in such a harsh context!

When we consider the reality of the couple today, however, how it contradicts our text! How few couples (I do not care whether they are officially married) are committed for life, for better or for worse, each always giving the other what he needs, especially human warmth and presence. How rarely do we see the one helping the other in his work and struggle in life, without reserve or bitterness, in utter faithfulness (for a couple is two people and not three!). Now one-third of marriages end in divorce, and 90 percent of married men and women commit adultery. Marriage is considered a partnership, and this most serious of life's relationships no longer involves promises or gravity. Observing the reality of today's couples sends us back to Ecclesiastes, and that is also vanity and a chasing after wind! So we must harbor no illusions.

Having examined Qohelet's "better two than one alone," we must now examine the other side of the coin, following Qohelet as he strips away all illusions and leads us to a difficult learning experience. Couples are marvelous, but unfortunately there are infinitely few possibilities they will work out. In his continued quest for wisdom and his pursuit of folly, Qohelet encounters women. Here we come up against a wall (7:26-29):

I find woman more bitter than death, because she is a trap, because her heart is a snare and her arms are bonds. The one who is upright before God will escape from her, but the sinner will be seized by her. See what I found, said Qohelet, as I considered them one by one in order to find a reason. My soul has searched for a reason until now, and I have not found it. I found a man in a thousand, but no woman did I find among them all. Just see what I have found: that God made man upright, but they have sought to reason a great deal. (Guillaumont)

Here is what I have found: more bitter than death is a woman who is a snare, when her heart is a trap and her arms chains. The one who pleases God escapes from this, but the one who is a failure will get caught by it. Look at what I found, says the Assembler, one by one, in order to find the reason that I still seek but have not found! I found a man out of a thousand, but no woman did I find among them all. Just look at what I found: that God made man honest, but they seek to reason too much. (Lys)[36]

I give both these translations because the reader can grasp their radical opposition immediately. The Hebrew text obligates us to make choices and interpretations. In the first translation, woman in herself is evil (a trap, a net, a bond holding the sinful man). In the

36. Maillot interprets this text on women as related to the preceding passage regarding the impossibility of finding wisdom: "Wisdom is inaccessible, and as versatile as a woman. . . . But wisdom is not found with women. . . . As long as there are women, a man can never be wise. . . . Women compel wise men to err . . . ; they make them . . . lose their heads. . . . For this reason women can be a snare, even for the most resolute of wise men. . . . This is a delightful confession for Qohelet to make: I have always been taken in, I have always let myself be duped!' . . . Furthermore, this entire passage is a direct tribute to love and its power. Qohelet discovers for himself that 'the heart has reasons that reason does not know.' . . . Qohelet puts Don Juan on trial here rather than women. . . . This passage amounts to indirect and unconscious (?) praise of exclusive, monogamous love" (pp. 131, 133, 135). I find Maillot's meditation quite remarkable.

second translation, the worst thing of all is a woman *when* she is a trap, etc. In other words, woman's essence, destination, and truth are not like this, but she *can* be so.

How can we choose between the two understandings of the text? It seems to me that the text itself (rather than the grammar) reveals its meaning: when Qohelet claims he has not found a woman among all of them, he cannot have in mind "the" woman, according to his description of her. Consequently, "woman" is not a snare, etc., in herself; otherwise, obviously, he would have found her, has found her! Necessarily, then, we must adopt the translation describing a woman as terrible *when she becomes a snare,* etc. Qohelet means, then, that he has never encountered a true woman (not meaning by this merely a woman who is not a sinful snare); that is, a woman as God created her, fulfilling her true woman's essence.

We can consider God as in favor of woman in verse 28, since Qohelet shows him in favor of man in verse 29. But what about the meaning of this series of verses (beginning with 7:25), seemingly incoherent, and labeled "obscure" by Edouard Dhorme?[37] It seems to me they display a certain coherence: Qohelet declares again that he is pursuing wisdom and reason. After some bad experiences, he begins again. He wants to prove, he says, that wickedness is folly (or, according to Lys, p. 22, that folly is madness—the madness of wickedness; this is the most satisfying approach, but it strays from the text). And he wants to prove that folly is madness (or that confusion is illumination? Or the stupidity of folly? Translations vary widely, and it is difficult to decide among them).

In any case, the overall meaning is easy to grasp: wickedness, madness, and folly go together. Qohelet discovers these in his quest for wisdom, which leads him to women: a new experience. Why does he relate women to wickedness, madness, and folly? Women seem to represent in his mind a sort of pinnacle of perversion. He declares them more bitter than death (the consequences of which we have explored).

Why is a bad woman (*when* she is a trap and a chain) worse

37. Edouard Dhorme, ed., *La Bible: L'Ancien Testament,* vol. II (Paris: Gallimard, 1959), p. 1520, note to 7:27-28.

than a bad man? I believe we can see the same logic at work concerning the word: it is the highest good, but precisely because of that, when it is perverted, it becomes a worse evil: sin. Similarly, in the case of woman: she should be what Qohelet expects her to be: wisdom, and, even more remarkably, reason. She should embody these characteristics better than man. She should be the marvel that dazzled Adam, the one who imparts strength and brings man to his highest point and his completion. She is the height of creation,[38] and should epitomize everything good, beautiful, and wise. Instead, she becomes the trap that incites man to fall, the bonds that imprison him; this is much worse than all the rest!

Furthermore, the woman who completes the unfinished man forms with him the image of God through their love for each other. But when she replaces love with seduction, and love's freedom with manipulation and the shackles of sexuality, she is more bitter than death. This brings us to the Song of Songs, which tells us that love is stronger than death, prophesying that in the end, love (God's love!) will vanquish death. True, but when the earthly repre-sentation of divine love turns into degradation and indecency, the one who effects this transformation is not just vanquished by death but becomes herself more bitter than death. When the best goes bad, that is the worst thing possible. This is why Qohelet becomes so violent when he speaks of women.

Following this passage we find an enigmatic phrase, which can be read: "I examined women one by one in order to find a reason," or "I examined [things or reasons] in order to find the reason" (7:27). In any case, after his experiences with men, Qohelet notes that his experiences with women are even more disappointing. Solomon exemplifies this when he multiplies his relationships with women, having 700 princesses as wives and 300 concubines (he

38. I develop this theme at length in my forthcoming *The Ethics of Holiness*. In a nutshell, the argument that women are inferior to men because woman was created after man is stupid. In that case, men would be inferior to animals! On the contrary, her creation at the end shows woman to be the culmination, the final perfection, of creation. [For a fuller exposition on this theme, see Ellul's *Les Combats de la liberté*, pp. 328-29.—TRANS.]

almost reaches Don Juan's 1003! See 1 K. 11:3). His "foreign" wives led to his downfall. Not only did he fail to find satisfaction and fulfillment with them, in terms of wisdom and reason, but even more, these women turned his heart toward other gods (1 K. 11:4). He began to worship idols: Ishtar and Milcom, which brings us back to *hebel:* idol, vanity! This result stemmed from his wives' acts, but Solomon chose his path. Qohelet also betrays a trace of anger because of this leading astray. Idolatry is more bitter than death.

Now that we have nearly arrived at the end of vanity's long groping toward wisdom, we should perhaps return to King Solomon (in more depth than we did in chapter I), since Qohelet seems to allude clearly to him in his treatment of women as a peril. Scholars have stated that Qohelet wrote while meditating on Genesis; it seems clear that the book is also a reflection on Solomon's reign. Solomon represented the height of the Hebrew monarchy: the wise, glorious king, the builder, the prince who opened the door to relations with other countries, the possessor of the knowledge of God (think of the cabalists!), a type of Messiah's royalty.

Since I respect historical convictions, I have granted that Qohelet uses Solomon's name partly to follow the above tradition. But Qohelet mentions Solomon mainly to challenge him. His awe-inspiring reign? Vanity, mist, a chasing after wind. The wise king pursued wisdom, but even he found nothing. When he fell into the female trap, he proved he had found nothing. This whole passage represents what Solomon might have said if he had been truly wise. But precisely because he could not say these things, we say them in his place. This thought is at the bottom of Qohelet's words.

In this light Qohelet appears as even more of an iconoclast than we thought. He questions not only traditions, theologies, ideas, and sermons, but a man: Israel's hero and model, the person the whole nation looked on with veneration, longing for monarchy like his to be reestablished. Solomon himself is reduced to nothing by Qohelet (who showed considerable boldness in assuming Solomon's name in the first place!). Qohelet provokes a much greater scandal at this point than he would in a theological debate. God alone escapes vanity. Not even Solomon can serve as our example, mediator, or as a promise for the future! Again in this passage, Qohelet doubt-lessly prepares us for Jesus' words: "even Solomon in all his glory" (Matt. 6:29, RSV). How brash, to compare Solomon to a wild-flower about to disappear. Qohelet had already foreshadowed this shocking analogy.

"The most I could find," continues Qohelet, "was one man in a thousand" (a man in his fulness, in his completeness), "but I found not a single woman among them all" (see 7:28). Does this mean that men are better than women? Only an overly direct, simplistic reading would lead us to such a conclusion. Qohelet's meaning is that Adam's vocation (to work, care for, and worship) was a relatively simple task—something a man can accomplish. But the woman's vocation was infinitely more complex, elevated, subtle, and difficult. For this reason it may be possible to find, at length, a man after God's own heart. But a woman never manages to achieve the fulness of her kind. Furthermore, her vocation is contradictory in itself.

Qohelet's conclusion on this matter comes as a surprise. God made this being (in the fullest sense: a being consisting of a man and a woman, the image of God, in two different persons)[39] just and upright. The adventure of the couple as the image of God was possible, "but they began to reason a lot" (7:29, JE; cf. Guillaumont above). This is utterly extraordinary: Qohelet says he seeks after reason, but then he deplores the fact that people have begun to reason much too much. Their efforts at reason complete and explain their perversion; in the final analysis reason has to do with the relationship between men and women and women's actions (as snare, etc.). Usually writers refuse to concede that women reason too much!

On the contrary, I find this point of view utterly consistent: God created a couple with a direct relationship. Their love transcended

39. My words in no way describe an androgyne, the ideal Greek being comprising both sexes! The androgyne is the opposite of the biblical concept, which emphasizes neither the division of the sexes nor their unity, but love. And love presupposes *two different beings.* The androgyne loves itself; ho-mosexual love involves love of two similar beings for each other. In both cases, death results.

their differences and also implied the recognition of the other's immediacy ("This is . . . flesh of my flesh," Gen. 2:23), and of his freedom (by faith). The break in the couple's relationship with God entailed a break in their relationship with each other. Following this event, the man tried to reestablish the relationship between things, and their meaning, through reasoning.

This reasoning, however, is not the same as the "reason" sought by Qohelet. "Reasoning" (in excess) is neither science nor philosophy: it is a detour that gives the impression of a straight and serious road. It amounts to getting somewhere by the longest possible route, and entails the continual risk of going astray. It is a fracturing, since in order to reason, you must break down into little pieces a whole that could be understood otherwise. It involves dividing repeatedly into separate steps what could have been a flowing process. Reasoning gives a sense of false security, because it reduces the problem in such a way that only one path seems necessary and good for solving it. It excludes immediacy, always assuming everything to be mediated.

Because of these characteristics, when excessive reasoning is applied to everything, it destroys human relationships, which are the only relationships we can have. Thus it constitutes an alienation. Haven't we all known people who were prisoners of their opinionated reasoning, unable either to establish a nonrationalized relationship with others or to live in a different way from the one their reasoning caused them to take for the truth? Obviously, far from guaranteeing us a straight path, reasoning (which gave us rationalism in the 19th century) turns us away from others and from any other truth. Searching for a woman to fulfill God's given model, Qohelet finds only the desert of reasoning, which fills up in its own way the emptiness of perfection.

Conclusion

We still have one possible observation to make, although nothing makes it obligatory. We have noted three applications of wisdom in the making: the word, possessions, and couples. These themes, as we observed beforehand, are not treated in dogmatic fashion but flexibly, and not presented as a whole but found here and there, like the skillfully scattered fragments of a complex puzzle. It seems significant to me that each of these themes ends, each time it appears, with a perspective on God. In the case of the word, after he denounces the overabundance of words, Qohelet the Wise concludes: "But fear God" (Eccl. 5:7). The fear of God constitutes the true limit of the word; our fear of him should restrain us from abusing this gift. Each time we speak, we are thus called to remember that God is the Word: "In the beginning was the Word" (John 1:1, RSV). He is the source and the limit of our word, and Qohelet's last word on the subject!

As for possessions, everything boils down to "the work of God, who makes everything" (Eccl. 11:5; we will return to this matter). We are to bring what we have and what we do back to this ultimate truth: that finally (scholars would say "in the last instance"), God is the real overseer of the work, and the true possessor of the wealth we are to give liberally. Concerning woman and man, we have just seen the last word: God made humanity upright (just and honest). Thus every road brings us back to this decisive point: what God does.

Above we challenged the idea that Qohelet's invocations of God were added by a pious copyist to make the book less scandalous and facilitate its acceptance into the canon. The importance of what God does shows the utter vanity of such a notion, which takes its root in vain reasonings. Qohelet's remarks direct us to God and suggest our last main theme, for chapter IV: God himself. Who is God, according to Qohelet?[40]

---

40. We can appreciate again in this context the extent to which the presence of *Elohim* rescues Qohelet from being trite, especially when we compare him with Cioran's mediocre nihilism or Pierre Bettencourt's artificiality. In *Le Bal des ardents*, Coll. Nouvelle Gnose (Paris: Lettres Vives, 1983), Bettencourt denounces the vain ambition involved in explaining the universe. He states Qohelet's ideas, but not so well! Like so many others, he emphasizes the contradictions of life, finally noting that we are on earth, not to work or suffer, but for no reason—for pleasure, in order to "dance with this fire that burns in our feathers, with this death that eats into our lives, and hounds

Most certainly, I could conclude this reflection on wisdom by relating it to Jesus Christ. As Maillot says, "There is no intellectual, conceptual answer to existential problems. . . . God has not given us a system or wisdom to resolve the enigmas of our existence, but Jesus Christ. Only Existence responds to our existence. Wisdom is not a thought or concepts, but a person: Jesus Christ" (p. 149). This is true according to our faith, since "Jesus Christ was made *for us wisdom*, justice, sanctification, and redemption" (1 Cor. 1:30, JE).

Such a conclusion would involve a leap over the abyss, however. And since I am trying to listen to Qohelet, I will not take that leap at this point. Instead, after considering the possibility of wisdom and its points of application, I cannot help remembering the meditation Thornton Wilder creates for Caesar: "I shall probably die by the dagger of a madman. The Gods hide themselves even in their choice of instrument. We are all at the mercy of a falling tile. We are left with the picture of Jupiter going about dislodging tiles which fall upon a lemonade vendor or upon Caesar. The jury that condemned Socrates to death were not august instruments; nor were the eagle and the tortoise that slew Aeschylus. It is probable that my last moment of consciousness will be filled with the last of many confirmations that the affairs of the world proceed with that sense-lessness with which a stream carries leaves upon its tide."[41] I could just as well have chosen a text from Albert Camus. Wisdom is

---

us. Still, we are to dance with a smile and with the trembling, slightly crazy lucidity of the young stars in our eyes" (p. 27). But unlike Qohelet, Bettencourt regards God as nothing. He is nothing, a nothing that dwells in us and leads us to destroy as well as to create; he is a ballet master. For this reason, says Bettencourt, we should not serve God but be served by him: make the best possible use of him: "amuse him, . . . disarm him, and keep him busy with peaceable creations which will win over his appetite for fire and blood" (p. 31; see also pp. 30, 46-47, 53-55, 58). At this point we have returned to platitudes and trite ideas. Making use of God! How innovative, how worthy of the genius Bettencourt takes himself for. He fails to realize that humanity has made God its factotum in precisely this way, for about 200,000 years! Qohelet's radical challenge to just such constant diversion is what makes him so deep and true!

41. Thornton Wilder, *The Ides of March* (New York: Harper and Brothers, 1948), pp. 217-18.

neither vain nor impossible, but it cannot answer the question vanity asks us: Are the world and life *decisively absurd?*[42]

5. Epilogue

If we use contemporary vocabulary, we could say Qohelet brings a "crisis" to light: a crisis of morality and philosophy, of human customs and grandeur, of the foundations of our collective life—a political crisis. It is a crisis of both the individual and society, a crisis of both the immediate and the chronic. This revelation of our crisis is utterly essential, since it suddenly makes us aware of the presence, the strength, and the form of something that normally remains hidden and invisible. Qohelet proposes an idea that is more than modern: he does not consider disorder, nonsense, incoherence, and contradiction as accidents, like an evil we must eliminate, some secondary or chance event. Instead, he treats these elements as inherent in human social life. He integrates disorder and contradiction into humanity's "normal" being. This is simply extraordinary.

Because of this view, Qohelet has been rejected and left out, or interpreted in a moralizing, normalizing sense, to make him conform to the "norm." The norm of human life was order, peace, noncontradiction, reconciliation, and all sorts of laws (moral, natural, political, and later scientific). It was regularity, consistency, and harmony. So perturbation and disorder seemed abnormal: "accidents" to be eliminated at all costs. Fortuitous tendencies had to be reduced and clarified.

But now modern thought has brought us to just Qohelet's point of view. Physics and biology, sociology and philosophy lead us to consider disorder, accidents, and "noise" (in communication), not as bothersome and paradoxical, but as existential, fundamental, and revealing. Qohelet had already seen this: that what exists is not the normal, the reasonable, or the good, but the absurd, the paradoxical, and the contradictory.

42. Decisively: that is, no matter what decision is made.

Qohelet shows us these characteristics not just in his content, but in his very manner of organizing his material and proclaiming the contradictions of being. He makes visible all the blanks and gaps: the gap in our knowledge, the gap in social reality, and the gap of existence. The Greek ideal of a reasonable, sound mind in a sound body implied the exclusion of disorder, of broken equilibrium, and of what we are tempted to call evil. In order to go beyond the Greek ideal, we must conceive of individuals and society as systems subject to crises; they constitute a complex system composed of antagonistic forces. Unless we adopt this explanation, our theory of society and our understanding of human beings prove insufficient, and the concept of crisis becomes inconceivable.[43]

Qohelet describes this system for us, bringing to light all kinds of disturbances. His strength lies in his ability to reveal these disturbances to us in such a way that we are obliged to consider them as an integral part of the human event. By thus revealing the crisis in its totality and complexity, Qohelet forces us to accept the existence of a revealer of reality and of a revelatory "agent" (for this reason reading him proves so painful!). The crisis Qohelet presents to us reveals what is hidden (and the things psychoanalysis tries to bring back to light).

Qohelet reveals the crisis, and, as he intends, the crisis reveals the "deep, deep" things (7:24). But the crisis is also an agent or catalyst: when we become aware of reality, the need to bring about change appears! The crisis sets the agents of change, transformation, and evolution in motion. Qohelet's apparently incomprehensible intention becomes clear at this point. He says to us, "The situation is absurd and all efforts are vain. But that is no reason to become discouraged; on the contrary, do whatever your hand finds to do." In reality, then, Qohelet leaves behind simple, direct thinking, whether from Jewish wisdom or Greek philosophy, and leads us to *complex knowledge* (see Morin).

Crisis thinking: I find the term "crisis" especially well suited for Qohelet. The Greek word *krisis* has three meanings: (1) sorting, division, or separation. The king of Jerusalem does precisely that:

43. See E. Morin, *Sociologie* (Paris: Fayard, 1984).

he sorts out all values and certainties, believing that until a person has carried out this chasing after wind, he has done nothing, and thus cannot begin anything or claim the right to speak.

(2) Judgment or sentence. Qohelet accumulates "sentences,"[44] of which he is a specialist: exemplary judgments of the type that made Solomon the model of perfect equity. But we need to understand that Solomon was the great enunciator of sentences or maxims because he was a just judge. He based his general verities on the specific cases in which he had arrived at good judgments. His maxims communicate truth only because they stem from the judgment handed down at the end of a long process. And we have seen that Qohelet develops his meditation as if it were a long trial—primarily against himself.

(3) Decision, or the decisive moment, the turning point. As we have said, a crisis is not an accident in a society or a morality that *in other respects* worked so well! On the contrary, a crisis constitutes the moment of decision, the decisive moment when we must commit ourselves. This is Qohelet's view. At the moment of crisis, at the turning point, we find the thing that makes a diagnosis possible. For many years doctors were taught they must wait for a crisis before they could diagnose. Just so, a crisis is always the factor enabling us to diagnose society or the life of an individual. Death, the final crisis, means we can pronounce a final diagnosis.

Bringing a crisis to light, then, is no deplorable, negative, or harmful act; on the contrary. Rather than marking the discovery of an uncertain, blocked future, the discovery of a crisis brings into view the possibility of a correct diagnosis and the necessity to progress toward change. Morin has said a crisis "corresponds to a regression of the determinism peculiar to the system under consideration." In this light, we see that the discovery of a crisis permits freedom to advance. In the midst of a crisis, a person finds himself undetermined in such a way that his freedom can function. We find this message throughout Qohelet.

44. The French word *sentence* means both "judicial sentence or decision" and "maxim." Ellul combines the two meanings here.—Trans.

At this crossroads we find ourselves faced with a threatening question. We have said that the revelation of a crisis shows it to be an agent. But do we not risk coming up with arbitrary or artificial solutions, or, worse yet, systematic ones? Does the process work as we have outlined, or does Qohelet have a solution in his pocket while he *pretends* to disclose the crisis to us? In other words, is Qohelet not indulging in a trite form of Christian fraud? "See, the world has no value; neither do people or philosophy." Then, when he has wiped the slate clean, he pulls out his trump card: "God! God is the solution, the stopgap, the simple explanation. With God, there is no more crisis; in him, we find all the answers. . . ."

We are unfortunately well acquainted with this apologetic. It was all the rage for centuries, contrasting the unhappy life of people without God with the happiness of those who were on his side. At other times it preached sin to move people to accept grace. After all, when I spoke of three threads making up Qohelet's cloth—vanity, wisdom, and God—did I not show that we find the same method in his book?

We need to exercise precision here, and to avoid moving quickly without reflection. Nowhere in Qohelet can we find this approach of "producing" God, based on the experience of vanity, as a magician might. Qohelet offers us neither a demonstration nor an argument. He establishes no cause-and-effect connection. Nor does he ever bring God in as the answer to a question he asks or implies, since in the final analysis he never asks questions! Qohelet advances on the basis of brutal observation of reality. God proves in no way useful in this process. He is not even an adequate consolation for Qohelet's discoveries, as we shall see.

Instead, we find in Qohelet's structure, as he advances step by step, an opposition and confrontation between "That is how things are" and "But I say." Far from being a coherent series of propositions, God is contradiction. He does not soften the harsh and radical facets of our observations. God does not prove useful in making problems like the scandal of death or injustice seem acceptable or tolerable.

Qohelet never says "from God's point of view" there is a higher order, or a way of seeing things as less tragic, or some possible meaning. Our author leaves us with a lack of meaning. God must not be used, lest we make him into the missing piece of the philosophical puzzle, or into the idealist's guarantee of consolation in the face of vanity. Qohelet's God is never "usable." But he is constantly present as contradiction. He even adds to the gravity of our situation, since, although inaccessible, he remains present! But he is not at our disposition. "God is in the heavens and you are on the earth" (5:2). This situation lies at the bottom of the incompatibility, and keeps us from accusing Qohelet of producing a deus ex machina or a solution.

We need to return to the difference in Qohelet's attitude when he observes and when he affirms. When he proclaims repeatedly, with respect to God, "But I say" or "But I know," he places himself on the level of proclamation and decision. At this point he is involved in witness rather than apologetic. Faced with such a proclamation, one either believes or one does not; one trusts or does not. Qohelet's only option lies in this realm of decision; he invites his listener to make a decision, too. He does not lead us by the hand down a reasonable path toward the easy acceptance of a consoling God. Rather, he leads us to the abyss of vanity, where we have to make a decision.

The decision we make does not enable us to fill up the chasm or to jump over it. The chasm remains a chasm even if we receive and believe God. To use Kierkegaard's vocabulary, this situation is unconditioned. God is unconditioned. The believer must accept this and make his decision on an unconditioned basis; that is, without cause and without reason. (Furthermore, this fundamentally "theological" exposition led naive exegetes to believe that Qohelet's texts on God were later additions.)

Thus Qohelet means neither to convince us nor to resolve anything by his proclamation of God. Once again, he says a thing is because it is, and that is all. But in conclusion, to show that Qohelet's approach does not constitute weakness, we should remember the contrast formulated by Bertrand de Jouvenel, to which

I have often referred: the distinction between a problem and an existential situation.[45] For there to be a problem, the particulars of the problem must all be known, so that we can compose a statement and conclude with a precise question. In this case, all we need is correct reasoning using all the particulars, to arrive at a QED, or a *solution* to the problem. But an existential situation can never be posed as a problem. We never have all the particulars, and there is no coherence of the various factors. There can never be a "statement" of the situation, so that, no matter how much we may try to reason, we will never arrive at *a solution!*

In every existential situation, whether political or individual, we can only make a decision. We must *resolve,* cut the Gordian knot, with all the uncertainty and unknown factors that involves. Faced with an ultimate existential situation, then, no solution is possible; all we can do is make a decision. For this reason, Qohelet does not try to convince us through reason of the existence or reality of God. He is utterly faithful to revelation as a whole. The Wholly Other is the Wholly Other. I can only tell you that he is, and that he is waiting for you.

45. Bertrand de Jouvenel, *Arcadie, essais sur le mieux vivre,* Futuribles 9 (Paris: S.E.D.E.I.S., 1968).

CHAPTER IV

God

I would like to begin this chapter with two texts that I believe follow Qohelet's thought closely:

> I don't know Who—or What—put the question. I don't know when it was put. I don't even remember answering. But at some moment I did answer *Yes* to Someone—or Something—and from that hour I was certain that existence is meaningful and that, therefore, my life, in self-surrender, had a goal.[1]

The second text complements the first:

> I know that this world exists.
> That I am placed in it like my eye is in its visual field.
> That something about it is *problematic*, which we call its meaning.
> That this meaning does not lie in it but outside it.
> . . . .
> To believe in a God means to see that the facts of the world are not the end of the matter.
> To believe in God means to see that life has a meaning.[2]

1. Dag Hammarskjöld, *Markings*, trans. Leif Sjöberg and W. H. Auden (New York: Knopf, 1964), p. 205.
2. Ludwig Wittgenstein, *Notebooks: 1914-1916*, 2nd ed., trans. G. E. M. Anscombe, ed. G. H. von Wright and G. E. M. Anscombe (Chicago: Univer-

1. Elohim

I have found over thirty significant references to God in Qohelet.[3]
I think this number signifies something in itself, in such a short
book. Clearly, if you remove everything about God in this book,
thinking to produce a text on secular wisdom, you utterly dismember it. I am not speaking apologetically when I say this! I base my
statement on a simple, straight, reasoned reading of the text, as
critical as anyone's, and as wary as anyone of my a prioris.

Consider an initial observation that I think is decisive: Qohelet
always calls God *Elohim*,[4] never using the name God used to reveal
himself to his people, the holy Tetragrammaton *(YHWH)*. Such
usage clearly betrays some purpose on the author's part. *Elohim*, as
we all know, designates God "in general." Some say it means "the
divinity," but I prefer to avoid this definition, since it involves us in
the field of other religions.

Elohim is the God who created: the subject of the cosmogony
(Gen. 1). With two exceptions, we have no need to emphasize the
many differences between this God and the peoples surrounding
Israel: (1) *Elohim* is a plural word, whereas the verbs used with it

---

sity of Chicago Press, 1979), pp. 72e-73e, 74e. I cannot claim the credit for
choosing this text or the preceding one. I found them in the very beautiful
meditation of H. Zahrnt, *A l'ouest de l'Eden: Douze Propos aux adeptes et aux
détracteurs de la religion chrétienne,* trans. J.-P. Bagot (Paris: Cerf, 1983), p. 7.
Italics added.

3. Lys counts 40 texts related to God, in a total of 222 verses. He claims
this amounts to twice as many references as we find to vanity (p. 78)! On the
subject of God in Qohelet see L. Gorsen, *La Notion de Dieu dans l'Ecclésiaste*
(Louvain: Ephemerides Theologicae Lovanienses, 1970); H. P. Müller, "Wie
sprach Qohälet von Gott," *Vetus Testamentum* 18 (1968) 507-21; André
Dumas, *Nommer Dieu* (Paris: Cerf, 1982). See also G. Scholem, *Le Nom et les
symboles de Dieu,* already cited.

4. Lys emphasizes that Qohelet uses this word in the absolute sense, in
itself, rather than related to other words. *Elohim* usually occurs with the article,
which "depersonalizes it still further" (32 times out of 40). Qohelet never says
"my God." Also, *Elohim* in Qohelet is always in the singular, in spite of its
plural form. This can be seen by means of the verb of which *Elohim* is the
subject, or by the use of a possessive with *Elohim* as antecedent (pp. 77-78).

are usually singular. In other words, he is a multiple God who is One. We might go so far as to say he encompasses all the possible forms of divinity, but remains the Unique God; his action is always decided in himself.[5] Nevertheless, he is situated at the beginning, like the gods of the various religions, so that we can contemplate him in his works. (2) We see another special quality of *Elohim* in his creation of man and woman, since he establishes a specific relationship with them.

No point in insisting, however: in spite of these differences, if we had only *Elohim* in the Bible, we might be tempted to place this God in the pantheon, readily assigning him a role in the history of religion. Then we could translate *Elohim* by the usual word, "God," which means anything and everything. Thus we can perfectly well accept that when someone says *Elohim,* he means the same thing the Muslim means when he says *Allah.*

But such an attitude, too restrictive on the one hand and too broad on the other, cannot be adopted with respect to the biblical God, since *Elohim* revealed himself as *YHWH.* He communicated his name: *YHWH Elohim.* He is not *a* god, he is this particular God, and the history involving *YHWH* has nothing in common with the myths, legends, cosmogonies, and epics concerning the gods. In this sense, when we read *Elohim,* we must remember that he is This One, and not identical to a god or divinity. *Elohim* may signify a distant absolute god with no point of reference. But when we add *YHWH,* we have the God who reveals himself, who enters our history, and who participates in human existence. These qualities describe him *also* as *Elohim,* so that the name of the God of Israel has nothing to do with *Allah.*

Thus it is very significant that Qohelet uses only the name

5. The formidable presence of God, which remains constant in the midst of all Qohelet's complex thought, prevents us from agreeing with Maurice Gilbert (and many others), when he writes that belief in God is of no "help for Qohelet in the night: he merely fails . . . to deny God, just as he fails to renounce the morality that seems to him to have no meaning" ("Comment lire les écrits sapientiaux de l'Ancien Testament," in Maurice Gilbert, Jean L'Hour, and Joseph Scharbert, *Morale et Ancien Testament* [Louvain: Centre Cerfaux-Lefort, 1976], p. 152).

Elohim, by itself. By it he means, however, a personal God rather than an unqualified divinity. From the outset, we need to understand the author's position, which seems obvious to me. He no doubt uses the name *Elohim* in order to eliminate any Hebrew particularity. He says simply "god," or "the divinity." But when he does this, is he using Paul's tactic in the Athens discourse: beginning with the unknown god with whom the Athenians feel at home, in order to lead them by the hand to Jesus Christ, the unknown God? Does Qohelet use common religious language in order to get his message through and make it understood? This tactic seems obvious, but it takes for granted the question of Qohelet's intended reader!

To whom does Qohelet speak? Does he design his book for Greek readers, for non-Jews? Does he mean it to be spread all over the Eastern Mediterranean, like a kind of tract? Is this an apologetic work? But an apology of what? Of Jewish religion? Obviously not! Of the revelation received by Israel? We have emphasized the contradiction implicit in precisely this view. Is the book a new philosophy destined for presentation to a philosophers' convention? Certainly not! A single fact proves this view impossible: the book is issued under Solomon's name. No, this text is clearly intended for the Jews. It takes for granted throughout that the reader knows the Torah (e.g., Gen. 1 and 3), and will understand the allusions to Jerusalem. What possible hope could Qohelet have had of penetrating the Greek world using such names?

If we have here a Hebrew (or Aramaic?) text addressed to Qohelet's fellow citizens, why does he systematically exclude the name God used to reveal himself, or rather, the synonyms of that name? I have wondered if Qohelet's usage might constitute a protest *against* the synonyms (*Adonai*, etc.). Just as he sifts through customs, proverbs, and common wisdom, does he also question the very formal manner of respecting the third commandment that consisted of refusing to pronounce God's name at all? Did he mean us to understand that in his opinion this pseudo-respect of the Name was just a cover for hypocrisy? Not taking God's name in vain cannot mean replacing it with another name! How childish! If you really want to avoid pronouncing God's name, let us be consistent and go all the way: we will eliminate his name altogether and speak just of *Elohim,* thus doing away with anything specific about the Jewish God!

This explanation seems insufficient to me. It is sufficiently caustic to fit, but I feel Qohelet's reason for using *Elohim* goes deeper. I also reject the simplistic explanation that he was influenced by the practice of his day, by the way people spoke, so that he unconsciously put himself on the same cultural level as all the surrounding nations—in other words, that the pagan way of looking at the divinity carried weight in Israel. I find this impossible for a man as clear-minded and self-critical as Qohelet. He reviews continually what he has done or not done and the influences he has known. He cannot have imitated others unknowingly! This is especially true since he maintains the specificity of *Elohim* in the face of all other religions, as we shall see.

What, then, is the point of his use of the name *Elohim?* I believe I distinguish two reasons for it: (1) the first relates to one of the objectives of his book: the struggle against the influence of Greek philosophy in Israel. Qohelet wants to lay before us the weaknesses and vanity of this philosophy. He wants to reveal that it, too, is subject to God, even if it claims to be utterly independent and rational. He continually relativizes Greek philosophy. For this purpose he must not allude to *YHWH,* since that would suggest claiming that Greek philosophy is judged by the standard of the God of Israel—and he might be challenged at this point. Instead, he refers to the God everyone can recognize. But he draws amazing and disconcerting inferences from the existence of this God, showing his true identity as *YHWH!*

(2) The other reason goes farther: in my opinion, Qohelet wants to show that the things he describes, his experiences, his criticism, and his failures, are not specifically tied to the Hebrew people or a Jewish sage. He means to be universal. He shows us everyone's reality, true for Greeks and Persians, Bedouins and Egyptians. Life's failure and limitation, the absence of wisdom, absurd behavior— these typify humanity (and, we might add, this is true today just as it was three centuries before Christ!). Qohelet must avoid the objection that these problems stem from the specificity of *YHWH,* enabling readers to dismiss his analysis as that of a soured Jewish mind.

Qohelet avoids this problem by making *Elohim* his standard: a god with all the characteristics of the pagan deities.[6] Readers can accept him, since they have their own gods. But, as I said, Qohelet addresses his own people first. For them, the revelation is that wisdom from *Elohim* is universal wisdom they can offer to others. Qohelet's words constitute the reality of every person in the world. Jewish people can thus speak of this reality as a universal experience, referring to God, who is in the final analysis the God of the gentiles as well as of Israel.

For this *Elohim,* whether a person likes it or not, is also *YHWH!* And we are aware that we know nothing about him: *The* God, *One* God, and a Unique God for Qohelet. This was a commonplace truth in Israel, but it referred to an insurmountable obstacle: "For the Unique One, even more than infinity, eludes our grasp. We cannot apply the experimental method to him. Logic cannot arrive at him deductively from any point, nor can he be arrived at inductively from anything."[7] Our minds cannot conceive of something unique: as soon as we posit it, our minds inevitably present us with two. In the case of God, however, there are not two, but One. For this reason Qohelet seems so radically non-Egyptian and non-Greek. Qohelet speaks constantly of the one God, whose presence we will shortly trace throughout the book.

At the outset, we must establish a first sure principle: we can say nothing about this God in himself. He is different from all the

6. This corresponds to the use of *Elohim* with the definite article and to the translation we find at times: "the divinity" (see Lys, e.g., on 5:1, p. 17). But I have already mentioned that this translation bothers me, because the concept is too hazy and lacks consistency. I have heard an ingenious hypothesis concerning this Hebrew expression: on the one hand, it might indicate Egyptian influence. Wisdom texts in the Egyptian literature do not speak of a given god, but over against polytheism, they mention "the god." This affirmation of monotheism occurs in the framework of a philosophical current of thought rather than a theological one, and suggests god in relation to humanity. But on the other hand, this same Hebrew expression could signify an affirmation of monotheism (*the* god: there is only One!), over against Canaanite polytheism, still present and active in the 3rd century.

7. Paul Nothomb, *L'Homme immortel: Nouveau Regard sur l'Eden,* Bibliothéque de l'Hermétisme (Paris: Albin Michel, 1984), p. 141.

other gods of all religions. Everything was known about those gods, but we cannot grasp, analyze, know, or encounter this *Elohim*. All we know about him is his relationship with us.

He is an unknown God. Solomon himself declares, at the beginning of his great prayer for the dedication of the temple, that "the Eternal wants to dwell in darkness" (1 K. 8:12, JE). Solomon acts in obedience as he constructs the temple. He does not act to appropriate or localize this God, a God who dwells in obscurity. How could we fail to contrast Qohelet's proclamation that all is vanity "under the sun"? Everything lit by the sun's light belongs to the order of vanity, and is useless and sterile. But the God who can give meaning is beyond the sun, in a darkness we human beings cannot fathom. For us he is truly unknowable: "And even if the sage says he knows, he cannot find" (8:17b). God may appear arbitrary to us, as his decisions seemingly run counter to what we call "justice" or "the good." But we must accept from the beginning that we have no qualifications, no capacity for judging the matter.

Qohelet leaves us without recourse: "There is an evil I have seen under the sun and it is a great evil for humanity: here is someone to whom God gives riches, resources, and glory, who lacks nothing for himself of all he desires. But God does not give him the power to enjoy it, for some stranger enjoys it. This is vanity and grievous suffering" (6:1-2). God has done this, as he did to Job, based on an incomprehensible decision. As we see God before us he seems arbitrary. But what do we know? What is his purpose? We must not separate God's decisions from each other, since he is the one who gives everything abundantly, but also the one who makes us upright.

Paul's response, "But you—who do you think you, a human being, are, to answer back to God?" (Rom. 9:20, NJB), echoes Qohelet: "In the day of good fortune, be happy, and in the day of misfortune, *understand:* God made this day as well as the other one. So a person can perceive nothing of what will be after him" (Eccl. 7:14, JE). Furthermore, however you may judge things, you can in no way change this reality: "See the work of God: who will be able to straighten what he has bent?" (7:13). As far as we are concerned,

God is arbitrary, absolute, unknown, and unexplainable.[8] Once he has shown the vanity of natural explanations for what occurs, Qohelet rigorously obligates us to recognize the impossibility of using God as explanation, system, final cause, etc.

For me, it seems essential to show here that in this process, rather than speaking about God, Qohelet forbids us to speak of him! By no means does he say: God is like this or like that. On the contrary, if we are to understand everything that follows, we must grasp that as human beings, we have no right to use God for our satisfaction: in philosophy, science, theology, moral self-satisfaction, justification, etc. God absolutely cannot be used; we cannot insert him into our concepts, systems, or knowledge. He is always other, and always somewhere other than the place I try to pin him down. All I know is that I stumble onto him, and that he is the one behind the absurdity I can discern and partly define. Qohelet tried to express this situation through paradox and irony: God as my obstacle.[9]

What has been called "negative theology" becomes a temptation at this point. But that will not do either, since it constitutes a *theology*—still another discourse about God, and therefore a means of forcing him into our categories. But Qohelet remains utterly convinced of the reality of this hidden, obscure God, who approaches human beings, remains with us, penetrating our lives so we find it impossible to eliminate him. The more we try to exclude God from our action, experiences, wisdom, and knowledge, the more enormous he looms, a crushing presence.

8. Lauha sums this up perfectly by saying that Qohelet affirms the sovereignty and the transcendence of God, thus establishing a radical opposition with regard to all immanent religiosity and all pantheist prayer (see pp. 14-17).

9. For Lys, this means one can only live in expectation of the free grace of God. This wisdom, stemming from experience rather than revelation, rejects theodicy and reassuring pagan counterfeits. The problem of humanity's relationship with God is a mystery. We can see only the limitations of our search for answers. We must "recognize that there is meaning but that only God knows what it is. . . . [Qohelet's] 'respect for God's sovereign freedom is so great that it is impossible for him to try to make use of God as you would a figure or a function in calculation, or to try to prove God's existence or to justify his rule' " (Lys, p. 75; p. 76, quoting Vischer, *Valeur de l'Ancien Testament,* p. 118).

He appears arbitrary precisely when I have a preconceived notion of his role.[10] When I have a definition of justice and an established morality, he seems unjust . . . but near us! This constitutes our only certainty: the same one Solomon alluded to in his temple dedication prayer. This *Elohim*, God of all nations, is in any case never enclosed within any of their religions. And above all, he is never the God of the philosophers and sages, not a watchmaker or mechanical God!

Having understood all this, we must not remain silent about this God. We must not turn away, saying that if this is how things are, we do better not to be concerned about the issue. For if you do not concern yourself with God, he will concern himself with you. We experience his concern in a strange way in this world. We proclaim God's absence (or his death!), and it turns into an overwhelming presence: the presence of human power, which has us all terrified.[11]

This arbitrary God seems even more scandalous when Qohelet identifies human beings with animals. He speaks of overpowering injustice among human beings, and then: "As regards human beings, I said in my heart: it is in order for God to test them and in order for them to *see* that they are themselves [or in themselves, for themselves] animals. For human beings and animals have an iden-

10. Qohelet shows us that God seems arbitrary to us, in his choices and decisions, when we have a preconceived idea of what he should be like. We have a clear example of this in Pedersen, when he identifies God with fate or destiny (2:14, 21; 9:11). "Blind fate strikes a person"; God is bound by no law, he is purely arbitrary! This remarkable assertion fails to consider whether God would still be God if he were bound by a law (as the Greek gods were bound by Destiny or Time). Then something would be "above him." Pedersen adds to the confusion when he introduces chance: "God offers his gifts at random." So he is nothing but a "despot," and the king, a human despot, merely reflects him (see 8:2; Pedersen, pp. 355-59, 361, 364). I find Lys much closer to the mark when he emphasizes that all these texts in Qohelet involve grace rather than arbitrariness. They show God's *good* pleasure (understood not as despotism but as pleasure that is good). God "gives when and as and to whom he wills, without having to give account to anyone or to any principle" (Lys, p. 293, quoting Vischer, *Valeur de l'Ancien Testament*, p. 113).

11. This point reminds me of G. K. Chesterton's extraordinary parable: *The Man Who Was Thursday* (Bath: Chivers Press, repr. 1987; 1st ed. 1908).

tical destiny: the death of the one is the same as the death of the other, and both have an identical breath. Human superiority over animals amounts to nothing, for all is vanity. Everything goes toward the same place: everything comes from dust, and everything returns to it. Who knows if human beings' breath rises upward and animals' breath descends toward the earth?" (3:18-21).

This basic text establishes first of all the extreme distance between human beings and God, and the identification of humanity with the animals (which squares well with Gen. 1 and 2). The breath of life vivifies animal and human being alike. But the word here is *ruaḥ*, well-known as an ambiguous term. Qohelet says nothing here about spirituality, human beings bearing God's image, etc. Therefore, unquestionably, we are animals.[12] After all, this conclusion does not strike me as so out of the ordinary: since humanity does not behave like the image of God, it is nothing more than an animal.

Our identity with the animals is indicated by our common lot: death. A human being may have *ruaḥ*, but he can in no way claim to be God's equal. He knows nothing of an afterlife, and this indicates his distance from God. Human beings wanted and established this distance, pretending to be equal with God! One wonders why Christians have been so scandalized by scientific hypotheses, including Charles Darwin's, considering they had Qohelet. Human beings and animals are subject to the same fate, just like the wise

12. Nothomb is very hostile toward this text of Qohelet's, which he finds false with respect to creation (p. 169 n. 19; see also p. 44). In Gen. 2:19 the animals are made of earth, whereas Adam is made from dust. Nothomb concludes that whereas animals belong to "heaviness," human beings were formed as "lightness," not bound to the earth and heaviness. Nothomb may be right, but both are equally subject to death. In other words, there may be an important difference in their origin, but in their earthly destiny, animals and human beings arrive at the same defeat. And they have received the same breath of life, the same *ruaḥ*. In Gen. 2:7 and 19, this word does not mean God's Spirit, but "only" what makes animals and human persons into living beings. Nothomb's theory stumbles on the Hebrew expression for "breath of life" in Gen. 2:7: *nishmat ḥayyim* (see Nothomb, pp. 37-59). We will return to this problem. [This note has been somewhat revised in accordance with Ellul's statements in a July 1988 interview.—TRANS.]

person and the fool (2:14), the righteous and the wicked, and the pure and the impure . . . (9:2). Their lot is identical: death. But this has nothing to do with destiny or fate.

Since we cannot fail to come up against death, we must question our identity with animals, who have the same lot, as we have already seen. But we cannot offer a definitive answer; we can only ask: "Who knows?" (3:21). You cannot maintain that your spirit will experience a different fate (rising upward) from the life-breath of an animal (which will go downward). We can state nothing in this regard. The unquestionable difference between human beings and animals does not allow us to infer an absolute qualitative difference. Qohelet obliges us to limit ourselves to the question: "Who knows?" No revelation can simplify this issue for us. All we have is God's work, this blockage, and this insoluble question.

Qohelet can help us understand, however. We find ourselves faced with this problem because human beings are unjust, because where justice should be proclaimed, injustice reigns, because humanity in no way reflects God's justice. When a human being behaves wickedly toward another, choosing to obliterate his function and his relationship with God, he must recognize that he is nothing but an animal, behaving like any animal would. The judgment on his injustice produces this result.

All human pretensions are abolished. Since the breath of life serves to permit a person's wickedness, why would he claim to expect a lot any better than an animal's, thinking he will "rise upward"? In this case as well, God's work manifests his power, distance, and unknowableness. In short, since human beings do not behave like the image of God, they are no more than animals. The proof lies in their common lot and a common end, indicated by death. Thus a human being can in no way claim to be God's equal. He knows nothing about a possible afterlife that has nothing to do with him. Because of evil, everything establishes our distance from God.[13]

13. According to von Rad, in a very important observation on this theme, evil and injustice constitute a test sent by God (pp. 200-201). But rather than drawing a moral lesson here, as in the other biblical writings, Qohelet offers a

"God . . . makes everything" (11:5). Qohelet affirms this truth in several passages, but with different emphases. Everything is accomplished for all time, so that there is nothing to add or take away (3:14). God brings about the beginning and the end: of the universe, of each life, of each event. He makes it possible for reality to exist. God always acts in the same way. You cannot claim to add or subtract anything ("By your worries, can you add a cubit to your life?" Matt. 6:27, JE). And throughout the infinite future, there will be nothing to take away, either. For everything is good.

The world shows us its visible face, in this sense, but in reality it remains impenetrable. Qohelet affirms this constantly. You must *know* that everything is made by God, but you can in no way explain or understand it. You cannot straighten what has been made twisted (1:15a). You cannot change what is (your apparent efficacy not-withstanding!). You cannot call into existence something that does

---

caricature of this idea of a "divine testing" (found in 3:18), an idea common in his day. Qohelet gives a different meaning to God's testing or "sifting" of human beings: it serves to take us back to our feeble condition, showing us our nothingness, since we are no different from animals. Maillot sees rightly that our paradoxical human superiority lies precisely in our ability to discover that we resemble animals. Having said this, Maillot goes on to insist on the demystification of humanism and the eternal soul, emphasizing with J.-P. Sartre and A. Camus that all mythologizing enslaves. The main question for Qohelet is: How can we keep from fooling ourselves when we avoid alienation by means of so-called eternal values? Finally, Maillot emphasizes that the radicalness of death enables us to reach a good understanding of the promise of the gospel concerning eternal life. This promise constitutes neither an evasion nor a negation of our present life, nor an anti-life, but rather the totalization of our present life (pp. 57-59). Lys holds that the central theme in this passage is chance (pp. 388-89). As animals and human beings, we are accidental, born by chance. He reminds us of Herodotus's "a human being is nothing but uncertainty." For Lys, the central theme of v. 21 is "Who knows?" (pp. 395-99, 403). No one can say if there is any difference, or if animals have a soul. Those who affirm the immortality of the human soul must prove it. Philosophy can offer no answer, since it can only recognize the reality of death. Lys shows that Qohelet's "Who knows?" should end all discussion of these issues. "Who knows if" constitutes a question within a question—a model of humility (p. 399).

not exist (1:15b). The world's flaws being what they are, you cannot pretend they do not exist and you cannot really correct them!

Fundamental reality, the relationship between the Creator and the world, remains unknowable and impenetrable. We can only "know" that a given action of God exists—no more. "In the day of good fortune, be happy, and in the day of misfortune, consider. God made the one as well as the other, with the result that human beings can know nothing of their future" (Eccl. 7:14, JE). Reality is as unknowable as the future, because of God's omnipotence. "A person cannot manage to arrive at what God does . . . he seeks and seeks, but he does not understand" (8:17a, JE). These words do not constitute a condemnation of trying and wanting to understand. But first we must realize that if God, the Wholly Other, does things, we cannot expect to fathom them.

Qohelet, far from recommending pessimism, despair, or discouragement, merely offers us a clear response to "God is in the heavens and you are on the earth" (5:2). This concept means distance, incommensurability, otherness. True wisdom means allowing reality to instruct us (and Qohelet continually advises us to do this—just as modern science does!). True wisdom does not consist of proclaiming something straight when it is twisted, but of knowing it, or even learning to use it instead of changing it!

Qohelet does not concern himself with the origin of the world, but how to live in it.[14] He attacks magicians and sorcerers, along with false prophets (today we find their counterparts in a twofold trend: the false "prophecy" of politicians and the hubris of technicians). We must learn that reality cannot be denied or fundamentally changed, because, as Qohelet would say, what God does is done forever. Nothing we can do could reach the bottom of the problem or change his work, unless we annihilated it. Qohelet does not express this last possibility—I have added it. If we annihilate it, we do not act alone: we are helped, even guided, by the power of emptiness.

---

14. Maillot makes the perfect comment on this subject: "God has not given us a system or wisdom to resolve the enigmas of our existence, but Jesus Christ. Only Existence responds to our existence [1 Cor. 1–2]. Wisdom is not a thought or concepts, but a person: Jesus Christ" (p. 149).

Qohelet abruptly states: "God . . . makes everything" (11:5). We have not finished with this theme, since we find these words reassuring, once again. They reflect what we thought about God. But we need to read Qohelet's affirmation in the context of the first six verses of the chapter. On the one hand, cast your bread on the surface of the water, and share (vv. 1-2), but then work. Work at everything: "do not let your hand rest, for you do not know whether this or that will succeed, or if both together are good" (11:6). We find Qohelet's forceful words "God makes everything" between these two ideas. If you do nothing, if you fail to sow, if you keep staring at the clouds, you will not know the work of God who does everything. These words astonish: God does everything, yet I must do something! God will cause one thing or the other to succeed, or both things. But you and I must do them! We cannot fail to act because God does everything. Paul will later repeat this: "Work at your salvation with fear and trembling, *for* it is God who produces in you the willing and the doing" (Phil. 2:12-13, JE; Maillot abridges by saying "God does everything," p. 188).

If you do nothing, you will be unable to perceive the work of God, because there may be no work of his to observe! You do not need to concern yourself with the ways and means of his work, either, any more than you know "the development of the breath [of life] in accordance with the bones in the uterus of a pregnant woman" (Eccl. 11:5a). But this great declaration also relates to verse 2: "Give a portion to seven or even to eight, for you do not know what evil may occur on the earth." Thus we are guided toward this unique and final point of reference: your life is written on the heart of God (we will return to this concept). Let God make provision for you. Do not hinder him. Let God do his work through you (but his action is through *you*, so your action is necessary!).

At this point we have reached the keystone of the whole book: you cannot know in practical detail what is good and what is not, what you should or should not do. You cannot know what will succeed and what will not. This shows how deep the vanity of wisdom goes. But you can know that, overall, God does everything. Here again we find ourselves faced with Qohelet's radicalism. He does not distinguish between the good things as coming from God, on the one hand, and the bad things, assigning them a different origin, on the other. What irony, or what a contradiction! We have surveyed everything that is absurd, vain, and meaningless, and we founder on the statement that God does everything.

We saw in an earlier passage (3:11) that we cannot understand God's secret work. This time Qohelet begins with the same idea: you cannot know what happens in all the mysteries of Creation (even if you knew, it would not get you anywhere!). But this time, almost at the end of his book, Qohelet goes beyond the mysterious work of God, and we come up against this brutal affirmation: God does everything, including all the things we have just criticized.

Qohelet might mean this statement as a kind of barrier: "Stop asking" (this would be in keeping with our passage: do not ask yourself anxiously if you should do this or that. You do not know what will succeed, since God does everything). But we cannot limit Qohelet's statement in this way. His declaration is too abrupt. The limit would be: you will never know the work of God. But our rebellious minds (along with Qohelet's rebellious mind—he does not declare this in vain) inevitably pose the question: "Then God also produces absurd things, folly, evil, and suffering." Now we have arrived. It was inevitable that we come to this point.

Unlike Job, Qohelet does not make evil and suffering the mainspring of his reflection. This does not constitute *the* question for Qohelet. But indirectly it does, since he places us in the contradiction: "Everything lacks consistency. God makes everything." Numberless philosophies and theologies have been constructed to respond to this impossibility. Numberless absurd questions have been asked, such as, "If God makes evil, he is not good. If he is good and does not choose for evil to exist, he is not all-powerful." Or "Either God is universal, in which case evil is in him, or else evil exists outside him, in which case he is not everything!" And finally: "If creation was good, where does evil come from? When you see how bad off the world is, you have to admit God is a poor workman."

We will not try to answer these commonplace objections here, in a few lines. Nor will we pretend to elucidate the "problem" of evil! All the more so because we would be placed in the terribly uncomfortable position of presenting an apologetic, playing the role of "God's advocate." We would be charged with justifying God's action to human reason (this is what Job's friends did, and for doing just that they were condemned!). Nor do we want to try to explain this action of God, since that would run counter to all Qohelet reveals to us.

We can avoid all such foolishness and still make some observations, two of which have to do with method. (1) We must root out the notion of cause that haunts our thinking: that everything has a cause, and God is the cause of these causes. This kind of logic comes to us through Greek philosophy, reinforced by eighteenth-century science, but there is nothing Hebraic or biblical about it. God cannot be considered a cause.

(2) *We* make a *problem* out of evil and suffering, so that they must have a logically satisfying answer. But biblical thought (Job in particular) fundamentally denies the formulation of evil as a problem. Evil is an existential matter rather than an intellectual one. The *existence* of everything—Creation, humanity, and God—is at stake, so that no philosophical or scientific answer to the issue holds any interest for us. Here we have the central theme of the debate of Job (*I* am suffering) and his friends (we resolve the "problem of evil" this way . . .). Thus, we must simply reject all our little questions, in that they stem from intellectual curiosity.

(3) This observation is philosophical: evil constitutes an indispensable element for the functioning of creation. Without death, life cannot exist. Life subsists on death: "all creation is a mighty wheel, / That cannot move without some being crushed."[15] We find this principle widely reflected in modern science: the idea of disorder (necessary for the creation of order), the idea of noise (necessary if we are to have a wealth of information), etc. Evil is necessary, but Qohelet has taken us by the hand, leading us through the twists and turns of the absurdity of the world and humanity. He has shown us that evil, inherent everywhere, transforms everything into vanity, smoke, and a

15. "At Villequier," trans. Dean Carrington, in Victor Hugo, *Selected Poems*, vol. 3 (Philadelphia: George Barrie & Son, 1897), p. 128, line 65.

chasing after wind. "This is an evil," he says, "not the happy condition of the best of all possible worlds!"

(4) Finally, we must eliminate two theological "arguments": original sin,[16] which really explains nothing but has provided entire generations with a pretext for laziness, and evil as God's punishment or warning. The latter idea constitutes one aspect of an interpretation we cannot possibly accept, in view of Jesus' statements (concerning the man born blind, the massacre of the Galileans, the tour of Siloam, etc.). Nothing of this nature can prove satisfying. In the existential drama of evil, we cannot say: "That is enough, we can stop now, we have found the solution!"

Limiting ourselves to Qohelet (who has eliminated any clear distinction between good and evil!), what do we find? Not that God brings about directly every event and circumstance. "Everything" (11:5) does not mean all the accumulated details. Here, as in 3:11, God makes the totality, the whole, the universal, everything created, etc. For this reason, each element can be understood only in connection with this whole, as it is put back into the totality of this whole. Qohelet makes this point continually. We must see everything at the same time, and not make judgments about this God who directs the whole, since we do not know it.

Qohelet's second message emphasizes the word "makes," as in 3:11. In the present passage, the words "God makes everything" form the conclusion to: "You do not know where the tree will fall, you do not know the path of the wind, or how the fetus is formed" (see 11:3-5; we may know these things today, but that does not affect our understanding of Qohelet's thought). Likewise, you do not know the *process* by which God makes everything. Qohelet does not emphasize "many things," but the totality, and the idea of making and doing. In other, simpler words, "My thoughts are not your thoughts, neither are your ways my ways" (Isa. 55:8).

If we consider our text as a whole, however, I believe it also teaches that we do not know how every circumstance relates to the

---

16. See Alphonse Maillot's remarkable analysis of sin, original sin, and death in his commentary: *L'Epître aux Romains: Epître de l'oecuménisme et théologie de l'histoire* (Paris: Centurion, 1984), pp. 144-54, etc.

whole universe (as in modern physicists' principle of nonseparabil-
ity?). How, then, could we possibly judge? At this point we come
back to the problem of distinguishing wisdom from folly.

Thus, by remaining within Qohelet, we have not answered the
"problem" of evil, but we have outlined our limitations and our
impossibilities. As a Christian, I find myself inevitably attracted to
another dimension, which constitutes neither an answer nor a
reassurance. This God who does everything is also the God who
made himself known and who bound himself to humanity. For the
Christian, he is the God who gave himself to us in Jesus Christ. He
did everything in the sense of "It is finished," rather than in the
sense of "the machine is assembled."

Qohelet says nothing of Jesus Christ, of course! But I believe
the God of Jesus is also the God of Qohelet, not just of Abraham
and Moses. If he was the God of Jesus, the relationship goes both
ways. For the God Qohelet describes chose to be Jesus' God. He
did everything in and through Jesus. If this is true, you can cast your
bread on the water, since your future is certain; it is already worked
out in the act accomplished by God in Jesus Christ. God has already
chosen this future for you; it is assured because God gave his only
Son.

This is our future, if we understand that we do not cross the
boundary of death in our own strength or wisdom. You can move
on, then, without fear, anguish, or despair, participating in the
common fate of all humanity, presented so harshly by Qohelet. You
can also move on in the unique story of your own life (which also
concerns Qohelet), freeing yourself daily of "unjust riches," because you have now been placed in this whole made by God. You
have chosen as your lot something no one can take from you.

Now we can understand one of the few rays of light that
penetrates Qohelet's darkness: "He scarcely thinks about the days
of his life, because God fills him with the joy of his heart" (5:20).
True, the person in question has wealth, and joy in his work. But
Qohelet's thought here goes beyond the commonplace notion that
on happy days one thinks neither of death nor of evil to come. The
passage holds a much stronger message: "*God* keeps his heart
occupied with joy." The joy here is not merely human, but the

fulness of the gift of God, who fills a person's heart with joy precisely when he knows that this is God's gift.

2. Contradiction

Here we are again face-to-face with "in spite of everything." For we are to live this joy and confidence in spite of reality. We know that the righteous die, and the wicked are rewarded or praised by other people; we know life is vanity, and yet, as we have already discovered (8:10-13, 17): "Although *I* know. . . ." However much wisdom we may have, we cannot fathom the work of God: "I saw, concerning the work of God, that a person cannot discover the work that is done under the sun, and he tires in the search and fails to find anything" (8:17, JE).

Thus our relationship with God cannot be situated in the domain of knowledge, science, or philosophy. We need something else (inevitably, we will think of faith!), the shape of which we find outlined in Qohelet's entire description, as he progressively eliminates everything we thought we knew and could cling to, everything we thought gave meaning to our lives! Qohelet outlines a different relationship with this God who is different than we thought. This new relationship looks like an astonishing compensation. I deliberately choose the word "compensation," because accusers use it against the faith! They claim "faith" is our search to compensate for what we feel we lack. But faith is not at all what this futile controversy would have us think, and the "compensation" is not a solution, an equilibrium, an answer, or a counterweight. We would like to have all these, but the God Qohelet speaks of is something else! I find the model for this in his great poem on time (3:1-11, JE):

1   There is for everything a moment, and a time for every matter under heaven:
2   A time for giving birth and a time for dying;
    a time for planting and a time for uprooting what has been planted.

3   A time for killing and a time for healing;
    a time for knocking down and a time for building.

4   A time for weeping and a time for laughing;
    a time for mourning and a time for dancing.

5   A time for throwing stones away and a time for gathering stones;
    a time for embracing and a time for refraining from embracing.

6   A time for searching and a time for losing;
    a time for keeping and a time for throwing away.

7   A time for tearing and a time for sewing;
    a time for keeping silent and a time for speaking.

8   A time for loving and a time for hating;
    a time for war and a time for peace.

9-11 What profit has the worker from his toil? I have seen the worry
      that God has given to human beings to keep them busy. He has
      made everything beautiful in its time, and in addition he puts in
      the human heart the desire for eternity without our being able
      to discern the work God has done from the beginning until the
      end.[17]

I believe the above passage in no way constitutes a meditation
on time. Rather, as we often find in Qohelet, it presents a contrast;
in this case, between a basic human reality and something still more
basic: God. Qohelet contrasts the idea of occasion and moment, a
series of moments and times, on the one hand, with the desire for
eternity, which comes from God, on the other. We need to meditate
on this great text, with its extraordinarily valuable lesson.

17. This text has given rise to a great variety of translations. But some
aspects of the passage are indisputable: Qohelet uses three Hebrew words for
"time": the first, found in the beginning of v. 1, is variously interpreted. Some
see it as pointing to a moment (e.g., Dhorme, p. 221 n. 18); others consider it
a duration ("a season"; see Lys, pp. 303-4). The second word (used in 3:1b-8)
designates a moment or occasion (but I prefer "a time," which renders well the
meaning of the word). The third Hebrew term concerns eternity (3:11), but, as
we shall see, we must not understand the term as we usually do. This passage
has moved exegetes to give free rein to their convoluted imaginations; e.g.,
"stones" become a military tactic consisting of gathering stones in order to hurl
them at the enemy's camp! Lauha identifies "time" with fate (pp. 64-65)! He
claims human beings are in no way free, and their possibilities are reduced by
insurmountable walls.

Qohelet begins, then, by asserting that there is a moment for everything. I believe we must understand this statement in two ways. First, as André Bouvier puts it so well, "there is no time for doing nothing."[18] Here again we note that Qohelet is no nihilist; he does not praise nothingness. He does not prefer inactivity to human activities. By no means! He simply declares that there is no place for doing nothing—no place in life or in time. We need not reduce ourselves to nothingness; we are not doomed to negation and self-destruction. All is *hebel,* vanity, smoke—but not nothingness.

Second, when Qohelet says there is a moment for everything, he means time is *always* available for our numberless human activities. As long as action is involved, there is always time; every action, every reality, receives its allotted time.[19] We can make two observations at this point as well: First, whatever the work in question, time can be found for it.[20] So when we undertake one thing or another, we need to know that this time exists. But also, in a

18. André Bouvier, *Un temps pour planter, un temps pour arracher* (Champigny-sur-Marne, France: Service Concordia, 1983), p. 273.

19. Applying this principle to modern times, Maillot finds we need to know how to take time. Christians err when they say continually " 'I have no time,' not realizing that when they say this they transform the time restored and redeemed for them by Christ into lost time. . . . Christ is above all a person who has rediscovered time: time to be a human being among other human beings. . . . A true Christian has all the time necessary. . . . We must not be without enough time" (p. 41). Maillot denounces modern activism, which can no longer find time for anything.

20. As Lys points out, "if there is a good time for each of [our] acts, this means the least significant things are not excluded from the time offered to us; each of them has all the importance (or insignificance) it should. Also, however, our freedom is not complete, since our simple acts require an appropriate moment" (p. 330). Von Rad shows clearly that the term used means "the opportune time, the occasion or possibility" (p. 139). But this thought goes beyond the simple observation that there is a favorable moment for sowing or harvest. There are "evil" times when the word is given no opportunity (Amos 5:13). According to von Rad, this text also teaches us two things: (1) A limitation can become an opportunity (if we know how to discern the proper moment). (2) Although we are called to recognize the times God has fixed, this does not mean we are subject to "deterministic predestination." On the contrary, it means we need to know which things come from God and which ones involve our freedom (pp. 141-43).

personal vein, we need to remember continually that each of us has time. However aged or ill we may be, we need to receive the reassurance offered us by this text: there is time for every occupation under heaven. Tell yourself you have time before you, precisely the amount of time God gives each act.

After all, if you die before you finish something, someone else may finish it, for all you know. In any case (as we have seen), you do not know who will inherit from you. Paul comments indirectly on this passage when he proclaims: "I planted, Apollos brought about growth, and it is God who gave the fruit" (1 Cor. 3:6, JE). The important factor here is neither Paul nor Apollos, but God! Just as Qohelet writes, God is the one who appreciates each work and allots time to it. This constitutes a first bouquet of lessons we need to learn.

Next we come to Qohelet's great series of twenty-eight possible activities, arranged in fourteen pairs. It is tempting to think of twenty-eight as seven times four: a seamless totality with no possible additions, involving everything a human being can do. This may well hold some truth. It is difficult to come up with an action or feeling one could add to Qohelet's list. Our entire life, including all our activities, boils down to precisely these twenty-eight starting points.

We will probably find "throwing stones away" or "gathering stones" irrelevant. And we will want to mention again at this point that our present day boasts many additional activities! What about science (but there is "a time for *searching*," and this word involves all research), technique (but there is "a time for building," one for healing, for sewing, and for killing—all eminently technical activities), and the accumulation of capital? What about economics in general? But this is precisely the meaning of "gathering" stones. Why would this not apply to accumulating (gold, silver, etc.) and setting up capital? "Gather"[21] is the operative word here rather than

---

21. I was very glad to find in Lys's book that my instinct in this connection was correct. The verb for "gathering" *(kanas)* already used in 2:8 and 2:26, normally involves gold and riches, as it does in these contexts of Qohelet. Furthermore, the verb does not mean to gather something from off the ground, but to accumulate, treasure up, desire to possess in quantity (Lys, p. 329). This shows how ridiculous such human actions are, when they involve mere stones!

"stones," and "keeping" (3:6) could very well point to the accumulation of money! Naturally, I do not insist on these applications, but I find them suggestive, in the light of our discussion of "nothing new under the sun."

As far as political activity is concerned, I find it all bound up with war and peace! I believe all feelings and events in human life to be summed up in being born, dying, weeping, laughing, mourning, dancing, embracing, refraining from embracing, keeping silent, speaking, loving, and hating. I think Qohelet has said it all, including all people, societies, and eras within his view.

Here again we need to absorb two lessons: First, we have no moral judgment to pronounce. The sage does not tell us it is good to make peace or love, and bad to make war and hate. He observes that these constitute the entire reality of human life. He finds that there is a time for each of these activities and feelings. He neither judges nor advises. God has given a time for each thing. We may find some activities good or bad, but we must take them into account and not forget them. War exists. It has had, presently has, and will have its time, its occasion, its season. If you want to consider humanity, you must consider *everything*. For God takes everything into account.

Incidentally, I would like to point out that in our day people prefer to exalt or give special consideration to the side of things we may judge negative in Qohelet. Look at our works of art; listen to them: they seem to deal only with death, destruction, disintegration, breakdowns, wounds, hate, and war. Every film and television program involves these things. The answer comes: but that is how the world is. Qohelet knows better: of course, the world is like that, but the opposite also holds true. We should forget neither horse of the team. Otherwise we lie. So the "information" we rely on lies to us. Qohelet's pairs are contradictory. As we have seen, this means there is room for both, and it will always be this way. All these things belong to the order of possibilities.

Thus we find here a challenge to the idea of moral choices, or a denial of the possibility of establishing morality based on the facts as they are. But even more: this passage shuts the door on our claims to choose one action or another based on its own merit. We cannot establish the excellence of an action, whether we consider it on the basis of its own criteria (e.g., science), or situate it within history. Planting has no superiority over uprooting, nor is laughing better than weeping. This text excludes the possibility of an act having its meaning or value within itself. We cannot consider one action as always better than another.

Thus we are forbidden to take any given action or reality seriously in an absolute sense, even if we judge it to be excellent. We prefer healing to killing, but some civilizations have been oriented toward death. We prefer peace to war, but this is peculiar to a given moment in time. Spartans and Nazis preferred war to peace. In this way Qohelet eliminates our eternal, definitive value judgments! Even a morality of the moment or a morality of ambiguity becomes impossible and unfounded when we try to find a natural basis for it, because a series of moments in time does not constitute our entire reality. Qohelet also shuts the door on the secondary intellectual and aesthetic meanings we attach to an action—meanings that go beyond ethics.

However, we need to repeat continually that Qohelet's rigorous affirmation is not that of a skeptic. It leads us neither to indifference ("everything is the same; anything goes") nor to despair ("why bother?"). No, he concludes consistently: God "has made everything beautiful in its time" (3:11). Thus each thing, whatever it may be, is worth living. Yes, even death. We find this scandalous; we cannot accept war, breakdown, tears, and hate. But even death is worth *living* (thus the importance of the question we encounter these days when faced with the insistence on therapy and the virtual confinement of dying patients who are made to lose all awareness of their death).

Nothing is absurd; nothing is unacceptable. However difficult we may find it to say and hear, God made each thing beautiful and good. This defies our judgment and our feelings. When we think of the reality of the modern world, we are obliged to wonder how anyone could ever uphold such folly. We shall return to this problem. But looked at from another angle, this "folly" can offer us extraordinary encouragement, since the things *we* do also matter. Here again, we find this incentive: not only the things God does, but our acts are also made good and beautiful by God. This fact should help us do whatever our hand finds to do (cf. 9:10).

The second lesson we learn from this passage is to welcome each new moment, each new adventure, each new accident, with the certainty that it contains something valid we must learn to discover. Thus we should approach things with an utterly critical mind, but without pessimism! However, Qohelet does mention a remarkable limitation to this principle: everything is made "beautiful *in its time*" (3:11), which ties in with "there is a time for everything" (3:1).

This time is a gift of God, a part of his gift—*a* gift, not any gift whatever. This seems obvious: there is a time to plant, of course, just as it is time to give birth at the end of nine months. But we need to understand another point: there is not only a "naturally" favorable time, but also, mysteriously and miraculously, there is a time to weep and a time to tear, even a time to hate and to make war. I believe that Qohelet speaks not of the proper moment to plant by observing the natural order, but of discerning the time God has bestowed on that action.

I also believe that Qohelet suggests two aspects of this discernment: (1) The time when a thing is beautiful is God's time. In our action we must try to discover how to accomplish, in our time, the work God wants beautiful in his time. This amounts to discerning God's time. We need to learn how can we do a work at just the moment God makes it beautiful, when he will take it up and take it over. How can we express this beauty of God, even at "negative" times? There are deaths that accomplish this.

So we are called to discernment rather than to doing things any time we choose, however we choose. From all the possibilities offered to us, how shall we choose—not the one that enters into God's plan, but the one that he will transform, so that it becomes beautiful and can take part in the Kingdom? Like God's time, this choice is difficult or impossible, since we do not know what it is. But we do not need to bury ourselves in scruples and pangs of conscience. They cannot change the way things are. This possibility of choice remains always open before us, and should fill us with courage rather than paralyzing us. In our relationship with God, we should also avoid behaving like the person who examines the sky and measures the wind, trying to choose the best natural moment (11:4). During all this time, of course, he does nothing!

(2) The last certainty we find in our text is that the only person who can discern this beauty that comes from God "in its time" is the one carrying out the action: the one who lives at that moment and participates totally in it. Never can the beauty be perceived by a person remaining on the outside who merely watches the action, or, even worse, who sees nothing but the televised spectacle of it. Nothing foreign to us can ever seem beautiful. There is no objective beauty accessible to mere curiosity or indifference.

This principle calls to mind the wonderful words of the Pomeyrol liturgy based on the beatitude: "Blessed are the pure in heart, for they shall see God" (Matt. 5:8, RSV): "With their eyes opened, they see God in everything." We must have a pure enough heart to see him and discern his action. But in this time chosen by God to be the time of a particular thing, decided by him, everything has its beauty.[22]

We have tried to show the import of the contradictory, and apparently paralyzing, nature of Qohelet's "pairs." But we need to make an additional observation: each pair contains a positive and a negative element, so that they apparently cancel each other out: tears and laughter, searching and losing, etc. (but healing cannot compensate for killing, so that we do not have complete parallelism). These compensations are sometimes positive and sometimes negative. Among the negative we find planting / uprooting, embracing / refraining from embracing, searching / losing, keeping / throwing away, and loving / hating. Here are the positive compensations: killing / healing, knocking down / building, weeping / laughing, mourning / dancing, tearing / sewing, war / peace. I have omitted several pairs (giving birth / dying, throwing stones away / gathering stones, keeping silent / speaking), for obvious reasons!

---

22. Concerning war, I have mentioned elsewhere how Pierre Maury's view scandalized me as a young man. He told me that it was during World War I he had seen the most admirable acts of devotion, solidarity, pity, friendship, courage, and capacity to go beyond hate—and even war.

Thus Qohelet in no way says that everything we do is destined to failure or nullification. Or if he says that, he also says the opposite: everything we destroy will be rebuilt. Things we judge as bad will turn out well. Our work may be contradictory, but it is still work! As people in my area of the country used to say, "In any case, whether you do or undo, it is still work."

Unfortunately, we can point to no positive or negative balance. In human history and life, everything is compensated. For this reason, we can understand the question Qohelet asks after the above survey: What does a person gain in the long run from going to so much trouble and working so much (3:9)? In any case, so far as humanity, civilization, or history is concerned, nothing remains: nothing positive and nothing negative. There is no gain—not for the person who makes war and not for the one who makes peace. There is no lasting benefit without its opposite. As we have seen, there is not even an eternal, indisputable trace of one's actions left in history: we have forgotten people from the past who have gathered or lost, laughed or cried. We must not lose sight of what Qohelet tells us indirectly, however: there is no time or occasion for doing nothing![23]

At the same time, Qohelet excludes the dialectic we might find tempting. When he presents these fourteen contradictory pairs, Qohelet by no means opens the door to some historical *development* that would produce progress. "There is a time . . . ," and that is how things are. In the succession of moments there is no logic or scheme. For this reason, I believe, we find no consistent order in Qohelet's enumeration (always going from positive to negative or vice versa). Nor is there any third term (a synthesis or a result) or progression in his list. Qohelet gives the impression that he wrote these pairs as they occurred to him. I am impressed by his refusal to make things easier for himself, to "explain" them in some artificial way.

---

23. Obviously, I disagree utterly with Dhorme when he writes that this whole text means that a person "is the plaything of events, and is incapable of grasping the meaning of what God does" (p. 1508, note to 3:1-15). On the contrary, throughout this text, human beings act and live; there are no "events" without us!

As a Christian, of course, I feel tempted to go beyond the passage itself, following Qohelet's strict, honest series of statements with an "understood" announcement of the end of time. Then everything involved in human history will be finally reunited and reinstated in what we call "the heavenly Jerusalem." Since everything has its place in God's memory, *in him* nothing is lost; we have the promise that everything will be summed up by Jesus Christ. At that point he will bring to light the meaning of every work and everything each human being has lived.[24] But at this point I am introducing the proclamation of Christian hope. It is not in our text, which leaves us expectant in the face of *all* we can know and live. But Qohelet does not leave us with this expectation alone. He also points to something else, in the two statements that in my opinion conclude the passage.

God gives us two gifts: worry or concern[25] ("I have seen the worry that God has given to human beings," 3:10), and the desire for eternity (3:11). Human worry—how unbearable we find it! Yet Qohelet clearly affirms, at least twice, that God gives us worry or concern. Often translations encounter difficulty with this word, substituting "preoccupation" or "task," but the word really appears to mean "worry" in two places (1:13 and 3:10).

But Qohelet does not mean any sort of worry whatever. Obviously, it is in no way the worry Jesus told us to rid ourselves of in the Sermon on the Mount: worry connected with the material affairs of life, such as worry about tomorrow, concern with business and economic life. These worries by no means constitute a gift from God. On the contrary! They imprison us, subjecting us to a kind of torture that we err in dreaming up for ourselves, and that our faith should teach us to slough off. We should live without this sort of worry, but not in indifference, lack of awareness, or thoughtlessness! God requires that we be present in the world. And he makes us a gift of a different kind of worry.

24. I have developed this theme at length in *The Meaning of the City* and *The Apocalypse*.

25. Or the "work," "task," etc. But all these words involve a connotation of preoccupation and worry. The phrase that follows has produced a great variety of translations: "to be busy with" (RSV), "to labour at" (NJB), etc.

We encounter it first as reflection, philosophy, or wisdom: "I began to study and examine by wisdom everything that is done under the heavens [here we have the critical and cognitive form]. It is a difficult ["unhappy" in some translations, "evil" in others] worry that God has put in the human heart" (1:13, JE). To prove one is fully human, one must try to look at, understand, examine, and analyze all of reality, and this constitutes a heavy burden. But this comes from God. It is even a *gift* of God, however astonishing we may find that thought.

We must situate this gift, then. I think it stems from Adam's rift with God. If this man, separated from the source of life and truth, had fallen into unawareness or misunderstanding of reality, if he had not taken some critical distance, he would have become an animal. He would have lacked two things that God requires: freedom and love. Far from becoming like a god, he would have regressed by losing his spirit. The gift of God entails the intervention of our intelligence and of our concern to understand. Once we find ourselves with the "understanding of good and evil," this gift enables us to become something other than the expression of the Evil One!

In turn, this knowledge enables us to distinguish the "good" and "evil" that the Evil One might offer us from the true good: communion with God. Here we see again the need for a critical approach. Qohelet declares, however, that such knowledge leads only to observing the existence of vanity. He is perfectly consistent at this point: a person looks into many things, finding that the specific intelligence God has given him is a heavy burden that enables him to examine all these things and to conclude . . . (see 1:14). The meaning of everything that happens escapes us, but we experience the constant concern for understanding these things. Our desire to understand is infinite.

The worst thing that could happen, as Kierkegaard tells us, would be for us to declare "Eureka!" Our suffering, he says, stems less from knowing than from not arriving at knowledge. For this unattainable knowledge (wisdom and erudition) entails both understanding and living. Qohelet says almost the same thing when he repeats: "I have seen the worry that God has given to human beings for them to attend to" (3:10, JE). This burden or worry consists, first, of seeing that all our activities can be legitimate (but is peace not better than war, and loving than hating?). Everything depends on the timing! Second, our worry involves observing that our enormous contradictory effort produces no gain in the end. But knowing these two things has positive value! This knowledge saves us from being thoughtless in what we do. We may find this a hard, bitter "gift," and it may thoroughly unnerve us, but it comes from God.

As for the second gift, it concludes in a burst of light, immediately controlled by harsh wisdom: "God has set the desire for eternity in human hearts,[26] yet human beings cannot succeed in discovering that which God accomplishes from the beginning to the end" (3:11, JE). I find this proclamation, that God puts the desire for eternity into our hearts, both conclusive and recessive. It is conclusive, for Qohelet observes that people devote themselves to a multitude of different and contradictory activities, each of which has a time, but no more than that (so each activity is necessarily temporary). This observation leads us to note that we are never satisfied with what we have accomplished. We start over and over: since planting does not satisfy, we must uproot; since tearing fails to satisfy, we must sew, etc.

Our insatiable activism comes from our desire for something else—something that will finally prove stable. As with our desire

---

26. I retain the traditional translation, in spite of the wide diversity of renderings. Some eliminate the word "desire" or "sense" and read simply: "set *eternity* in people's hearts" (but I believe this inclines our thinking dangerously in the direction of the immortality of the soul, which Qohelet denies). Others interpret the word '*olam* as "world" (Barucq, pp. 81-82, especially n. 42; Neher, *Notes sur Qohélét,* demonstrates the error of this translation). Others, like Maillot, replace "eternity" with "secret" ("he has even placed in people's hearts the secret without which they cannot discover the work God has accomplished," p. 44; this translation goes counter to the contradictory tension in Qohelet, in my opinion). I find all these attempts less consonant with the text as a whole than the traditional translation. Delitzsch (pp. 260-62) retains the "desire for eternity," roundly criticized by Lauha, who considers this expression an "idealist anachronism" (p. 68).

for wisdom, we aspire to something good and true. Once we have observed the changeableness in history and civilizations, how can we help but conclude that the human heart is permanently dissatisfied? We have a desire for eternity.

This statement is also recessive, however, since we measure fleeting things by the standard of our desire for eternity. Each thing that has a time has only that, and cannot satisfy us—not because of its contradictory nature, but because everything slips through our fingers. Because of this thought and desire of eternity, and perhaps because eternity is a hope coming from God, we continually require that love last eternally. We want our life to have meaning—perhaps absolute meaning. And we find it tempting to despise everything relative.

Nonetheless, God gives us relative things for our lives, and calls them "good" (so we should not reject them!). At the same time, and in the same way, he places this "hidden time," this desire for eternity, in our hearts.[27] God's double action seems contradictory, but in reality he is asking us a question. Each of us needs to hear this question as I have heard it, addressed to the contradiction of our being. I find the answer beyond me, however. We cannot find it in wisdom, and everything else is vanity! Only God can give the

27. We might, then, tentatively offer a hypothesis concerning the assertion "What has been is what will be" (1:9) and the circular view of things Qohelet expresses in his first chapter. As we have already pointed out, this does not constitute a cyclical view of time, although it may appear to. Could we not suggest that, instead, these passages express permanence and unchangeableness, based on the desire and eagerness for eternity? We should note that these texts mention aspects of permanence: "A generation comes, a generation goes, *and the earth remains for ever*" (1:4). Water circulates constantly in the rivers, etc., *"and the sea is never filled"* (1:7, JE). These images express the desire for eternity which furnishes the key to understanding "nothing new under the sun." The simplistic idea of a philosophy of cyclical time falls short as an explanation of Qohelet's theme. Nothomb connects this desire for eternity with his interpretation of "dust," which constitutes a promise of eternity. Because human beings are created from dust, they "know they are mortal . . . but feel immortal" (p. 55). Beyond the sexual instinct and the instinct of self-preservation, the instinct of eternity gives us the feeling we are invulnerable: we never expect to die (Nothomb, p. 148).

answer. Since God places the question within us, he also answers within us.

I find that Jesus Christ exemplifies this contradiction: God in a human being. But we must always remember that God's answer is neither metaphysical nor theological. The answer has nothing general, absolute, or abstract about it. Jesus Christ is not the solution to a problem! God's coming in one (only one!) person is a precise event, a reality with a precise location and time. And this event gives order and meaning to time. Our encounter with Jesus Christ is also a precise, localized event: it takes place at a moment in history as well as at a given moment in our personal history. This event takes its place in the middle of the different contradictory things that make up our life. Beginning at the point of this answer that God gives in his Son to our desire, we are to live concretely.

In this way the two themes of our text come together. For in each of these moments, made beautiful by God in its time, we observe both elements at work: in each one the desire for eternity poses its challenge, and in each the presence of the living Christ intervenes. His presence is a living presence in the fluctuations of life, rather than some stupefying and miraculous phenomenon. In the final analysis, this thirst for eternity is nothing but the pursuit of life! "Since death is inescapable, life itself is a contradiction, for life wants to live, not die. The *thirst for living is the thirst for eternity*."[28] The two prove inseparable!

One final note: we must not err concerning the word "eternity." Many translators attenuate at this point in order to avoid leading the reader into error. But I find the remedy worse than the disease, since it robs the text of its force! We must not read our metaphysical concept of the "idea" of eternity into this word. We conceive of a contrast between time and eternity. Qohelet does not present us with the perspective of entering into something unknown, some unknowable dimension that human beings cannot conceive of. His eternity is neither the infinite in the Greek sense nor an "eternal present." Rather, it amounts to indefinite duration. Qohelet does not

---

28. J. Moltmann, *The Trinity and the Kingdom*, trans. Margaret Kohl (San Francisco: Harper & Row, 1981), p. 36; emphasis added.

speak of immobility or a stopping of time[29] accompanied by entry into some immeasurable dimension, nor of an absence of change!

It is very strange that such concepts have been able to infiltrate Christianity. All the visions in John's Apocalypse, for example, imply duration (singing, alternation of acclamations and bows, the existence of flowing rivers, etc.). There is no point in maintaining that such details in a text like John's betray philosophical incapacity or childishness, since Jewish thought is consistent on this point. It deals with reality rather than abstraction, and is lifelike rather than mathematical.

Concepts like the absolute, the infinite, and "eternity" can of course be represented mathematically, but Jewish thought, and the Christian thought that follows it, are *historical*. Entrance into the heavenly Jerusalem does nothing to change that. The history of "God with humanity" continues, but in another vein. Thus the desire God places in our heart does not focus on stopping time, but on a life of indefinite, unlimited duration, on *total time*, which truly has no end—no conceivable end, and no certain end. Our desire for eternity has to do with ourselves, those we love, and our work—living things. This desire amounts to the will to live, contradicting the idea that there is a time for each thing, but that this time is soon over (and that the time for the opposite activity will soon end as well).

The desire for eternity is not limited to Judeo-Christian thought. We need to realize that people belonging to a wide variety of societies and cultures experience it. When Hitler spoke of the Millennium of the Reich, he expressed this desire. So did Marx when he declared that humanity had been living in prehistory and that human history would begin with the founding of communism. In communist society there would be no more dialectical mutation,

29. This relativization of the term "eternity" coincides with the consideration that Hebrew may not have "eschatological" terms. The Hebrew word *'aharon,* often translated into Greek as *eschatos,* means "what comes after." Thus the two occurrences of this term in Qohelet (in the plural form, *ha'aharonim,* 1:11 and 4:16), although translated as *hoi eschatoi* in Greek, become "those who will come after" in French translations (rather than "the last," or "those associated with the end of time"). [Cf. also most English translations, e.g., KJV, RSV, NIV, NASB.—TRANS.]

yet history would not be abolished. We sense the same desire for eternity in the Vietcong's marching song, "May Uncle Ho live ten thousand years," and in the Egyptian practice of embalming bodies so they could take a trip that would last indefinitely. They all desired endless duration rather than some metaphysical eternity. They wanted to vanquish time so it would no longer be their master.

These spontaneous desires do not amount to exactly the same thing we catch sight of in Scripture, however. We have seen that the past and the future do not exist: all we have is the present. And only in this present can we meet God: "Where or when could God be, if not in a given instant? He is absolute beginning. We must see the Gospel as a series of instants. Today. This very instant. Living *sub specie aeternitatis* means living day to day" (Sulivan, p. 57).

The only certainty regarding time that we can find in Qohelet is that of duration as the present, and the present as history. This corresponds to what was promised at the time of creation. For time and space, created in the first two days, are the boundaries of human life rather than its masters. Humanity is master of the creation! So we desire to recover our life as it was created. Instead, we find transience, instability, contradiction, and the disappearance of our work.

Our desire for eternity remains only that. This time with no beginning and no end, this indefinite duration we desire, remains out of reach, so we feel tortured, like Tantalus. This situation produces the utter pessimism we find in Qohelet. On its own, our desire cannot be attained. Realizing this limitation is part of wisdom, as we know. But now we take a further step: realizing this means arriving at certainty concerning God. This contradiction, between what exists and what we long and hope for, testifies that God is there in our silence, absence, and ignorance.

So we do not wait for some nondescript, meaningless eternity that would have value in itself. Our desire does not express our paranoia, or a return to our origins (which are hidden!). Rather, it is the secret call God has placed in our heart. A call to something utterly "other," which we cannot define, grasp, or invent. Thus at the bottom of wisdom, as it bears pitiless witness to reality, we find a way of access to this other world.

If we have to give a name to what results from the rigors of wisdom, we might call it an existential theology. It is not a negative theology—stating that we know nothing of God holds no interest for us. But stating that we have an emptiness within us, a torn or broken place, and that we *are not* mere rotating physiological organisms or collections of neurons—this understanding leads us deep into truth. Nothomb forcefully reminds us that "every desire amounts to a lack, and every lack implies a presence somewhere. A lack corresponds to a fulness rather than an emptiness."[30]

We must not neglect another aspect of the Hebrew word translated "eternity" (*ʿolam*): specialists all connect it with the root *ʿlm*, meaning "to hide," which we will consider later. Eternity, then, represents what is hidden from us: what we are ignorant of. Not just a hidden time or a hidden work, but *what* is hidden, as opposed to everything conceivable and visible, related to our hands and our works.

Consequently, even if we could convince ourselves that we rule over time through mathematics, for example, or that we know the sum total of human history, down to its smallest details, we still would have failed to grasp eternity. Eternity would still elude us because it remains as hidden as the God who put it in our heart and who leads us down the path of wisdom.

So we come to the point of considering the work of God in Qohelet. But first, faced with this question, we will come forward timidly, on tiptoe, as Christians to testify to our faith. God has answered our desire for eternity in Jesus Christ. Only he can gratify our desire, since he is God incarnate, God with us, the Eternal One in a human being. But this response to our desire does not come in some abstract generality or in heaven. The incarnation is a precise, localized event. It took place at a *given* time—at a time in history and at a given time in my history that comes under Qohelet's "there is a time for everything." Only this time it was different, since it was a time for *everything*. This event took its place within the series of opposing events in my life, but had no opposite paired with it.

30. Nothomb, p. 140. See also Petru Dumitriu, *To the Unknown God*, trans. James Kirkup (London: Collins, 1982).

Thus absolute time cuts across our relative times. Absolute love encompasses the specific, circumstantial choices we are given to make, giving them meaning and giving us peace.

In conclusion, we may consider Kierkegaard's words as a kind of counterpoint to our text. The last sentence of the following quotation can even serve as a commentary on Qohelet:

> Marry, and you will regret it. Do not marry, and you will also regret it. Marry or do not marry, you will regret it either way. . . . Laugh at the stupidities of the world, and you will regret it; weep over them, and you will also regret it. Laugh at the stupidities of the world or weep over them, you will regret it either way. Whether you laugh at the stupidities of the world or weep over them, you will regret it either way. Trust a girl, and you will regret it. Do not trust her, and you will also regret it. Trust a girl or do not trust her, you will regret it either way. Whether you trust a girl or do not trust her, you will regret it either way. Hang yourself, and you will regret it. Do not hang yourself, and you will also regret it. Hang yourself or do not hang yourself, you will regret it either way. Whether you hang yourself or do not hang yourself, you will regret it either way. This, gentlemen, is the quintessence of all the wisdom of life. It is not merely at isolated moments that I, as Spinoza says, view everything *aeterno modo* [in the mode of eternity], but I am continually *aeterno modo*. Many believe they, too, are this when after doing one thing or another they unite or mediate these opposites. But this is a misunderstanding, for the *true eternity does not lie behind either/or but before it.* Their eternity will therefore also be a painful temporal sequence, since they will have a double regret on which to live. My wisdom is easy to grasp, for I have only one maxim, and even that is not a point of departure for me. One must differentiate between the subsequent dialectic in either/or and the eternal one suggested here. . . . My eternal starting is my eternal stopping. . . . I do not stop *now,* but I *stopped* when I began.[31]

31. Søren Kierkegaard, *Either/Or,* 1:38-40. Emphasis added.

3. The God Who Gives

We have just spoken of two mysterious gifts that God[32] gives us: the concern to seek after wisdom and the desire for eternity. But "God has put in the human heart the desire for eternity, although [or "in spite of this"] . . . we cannot grasp the work God does, from the beginning until the end" (3:11, JE). Thus the distance between what is, which we can analyze, and what God does, which is *his* work, remains infinite. No science will be able to bridge this gap through an increasingly profound knowledge of reality. This reality constitutes part of God's work (we have seen that God makes all things, 11:5), but only a part. And the profound truth of the whole goes beyond our knowledge: " 'For my thoughts are not your thoughts, neither are your ways my ways,' says the Lord" (Isa. 55:8, RSV). Even angels long to look into the mystery of God's love, but cannot (1 Pet. 1:12). His immeasurable, endless love finally reached its climax and fulfillment in all his work in Jesus Christ. Our desire can neither suspect the existence of this work nor grasp it. Even for the finest of Christians, God's work in Jesus Christ remains elusive.

We do not really know the immensity of God's love, this love that exists at the beginning and that we find at the end. It moved God to create, in order to love and be loved. It gathers up the life and work of each of us. It *forgives everything* and *never dies.* Of course, in writing these lines, I go far beyond what Qohelet said or meant! But he leads me by the hand to this two-pronged discovery of forgiveness and undying love. The reason I do not know the totality of God's work does not lie in its greatness or complexity (this explanation betrays a rationalist perspective). Rather, the reason lies in the qualitative difference between God's work and ours. His is not conceived like our works (such as those we have just examined), which are uncertain, quantitative, and contradictory. Qohelet does not mention love, but I believe it is the

32. I find it extraordinary to note that according to authors who consider Qohelet's references to God to be corrections inserted by a pious commentator, God amounts to almost nothing in this book. See, for example, Lauha, who identifies the God of Qohelet with Destiny (p. 59)!

significant factor in his recognition that we cannot grasp what we desire above all else.

For, in the final analysis, what do we desire any more than, or in addition to, loving and being loved? What do we seek beyond the amazing security and the trembling risk of *being loved;* what do we long for more than the tremendous experience of the expansion and blossoming of everything that comes with loving? This experience, expressed in so many ways, was not invented by the Christian West. We find it everywhere. Sexual love constitutes a concrete sign of this power that moves us. So does political love. Both involve errors, because they do not take the unique love of God as their source. Significantly, generation after generation takes up the platitude that love takes us into eternity (even if only orgasm is meant!). Love makes the lover and the beloved feel they are invincible and immortal. They believe what they are living at this moment to be eternal.

When I establish a relationship between the God of eternity and his incomprehensible work, I am not being completely arbitrary. Qohelet is too radical and profound to be satisfied here with the oversimplification that human work is fragile and God's work eternal! But he tells us what human work consists of, and he remains silent with respect to God's work, limiting himself to evoking it indirectly. When I introduced the subject of love in this context, was I unfaithful to Qohelet, since he fails to mention it? He says nothing about love in relation to God—just as he remains silent concerning the covenant and the Torah. I do not believe I have misrepresented him, however, since he emphasizes a basic dimension of God's work throughout his book: the gift.

In Qohelet, God is above all the one who gives.[33] For this reason I cannot agree with those who reduce God in this book to a vague divinity. They believe the God of Qohelet to be different from the God revealed to Israel, arriving at their conclusion on the basis of

33. Lys has obviously seen the truth of this statement, noting 28 occurrences of the root *ntn* ("to give") in Qohelet (p. 149). Fifteen times the term refers to an act of God; furthermore, we find the *word* "God" linked with "gift" in 1:13 and 2:24, where God is mentioned *only in connection with his giving.*

the absence of the Tetragrammaton in Qohelet, or his use of the definite article with *Elohim* (thus "the god"). But the God characterized by *giving* is just the One who has always been God of Israel, giving freedom, the Law, the covenant, his Word, and giving Abraham a son. Is there any point in recalling all these truths?

Qohelet asserts something further, however: this same God did not limit his giving to his people; he gave to all.[34] Before surveying the different gifts Qohelet mentions, we need to explore briefly his emphasis of this point. In Qohelet, as in the other biblical instances of God's giving, God takes the initiative. That is to say, he begins by giving, and the rest follows. He starts everything off with a gift. He starts history off; human will does not. Once God has set history in motion, human beings can act based on God's gift or gifts.

Furthermore, God always makes a *genuine* gift: a gift with no strings attached, requiring nothing in exchange. He never sets up a tit-for-tat arrangement. His gifts never imply a conditional "if. . . ." God's gift does not even require our gratitude. He expects utterly gratuitous thanks, just as his gift is gratuitous. He can rejoice in our gratitude only if it springs from the free joy of our hearts, and not if we merely express dutiful thanks. God's gift does not produce morality, constraint, or reciprocity. Consequently, we do not find "salvation by works" in Qohelet. By insisting on God's gift, our author indirectly reminds us of the salvation God gives us freely (but, of course, "freely" does not mean "arbitrarily"; it only means "without conditions," since the gift comes from the Unconditioned One!).

At this juncture we should perhaps detour briefly to examine one of the many perversions of our time. Today, as a result of many muddled studies claiming to be scientific, sociological, psychological, and psychoanalytical, people contend that gifts result in a

---

34. It is especially important to emphasize this gift, considering that Qohelet cannot accept it easily—on the contrary! Maillot is right to underline Qohelet's rage at the fact that God is thus master of everything, giving love and hate, so that wisdom can explain nothing. Qohelet understands grace, but backwards. Morality and religion can no longer be based on divine recompense. For Qohelet, this gratuitousness constitutes an intolerable evil (pp. 151-53)!

humiliating relationship of inferiority. The giver takes great pride (always hypocritically) in what he has done. He claims a good conscience for himself, at little cost. The receiver of the gift is humiliated by it. He cannot "give in return," so he is the weaker and the more dominated of the two. Thus the gift is seen as a means of superiority and domination. It is particularly perverted since it appears as something good, enabling the giver to avoid questioning his motives, the falsity of his gift, his will to power, etc. We hear such talk quite often, applied, of course, to the Christian God, and followed by tart declarations that we require "justice, not charity."

We need to denounce the utterly perverse nature of this interpretation. Sometimes people have "done charity" (as they say in modern language "to make love"),[35] of course, for self-justification and with contempt. Sometimes they give in order to assert their superiority, and sometimes the receiver feels humiliated. Notice I say "sometimes." And I can say unquestionably that in such cases *no genuine human relationship is involved.*

At other times a gift takes place within the framework of a human relationship. It may constitute the end or the point of departure of an ongoing relationship. It may be a genuine gift symbolizing the gift of oneself to another (rather than a call for the other to reciprocate). In this case, the psychosociological, Marxist-structuralist interpretation we outlined above amounts to an absolute lie. This interpretation found gifts to be hypocritical, but we see *it* as a hypocritical assertion, useful for justifying the person who neither gives nor does anything! Demanding our rights, claiming others "owe us," and trying to turn everything into a legal relationship amounts to letting ourselves be unknowingly caught up in the logic of capitalism, which bases everything on "rights and assets."

In truth, this criticism of gifts, and the rejection of the relationship established by gifts, amounts to the rejection of committed human relationships. But when God himself acts by giving, he commits himself (as he committed himself in the covenant, and then, since he gives all his love, he can declare himself a jealous

35. "Done" and "to make" translate different forms of the same French verb, *faire.* —TRANS.

God). In any case, we find false gifts exposed by Paul, long before modern critics thought to do it. Consider his famous words: "Even though I would give all my goods to the poor, even though I would even give my body to be burned, if I have not love, it means nothing" (1 Cor. 13:3, JE). Who could say it better than that?

God's Gifts: Quest and Desire for Eternity

Thus Qohelet situates God's gifts within the precise perspective of his book. Gifts create a *genuine* human relationship, one that is no longer based on pride, self-interest, or domination, but rather on the truth and on the relinquishing of oneself for the other. But this gift that expresses the fulness of love is called "grace" (just as the gift is "gratuitous"). In this connection we find grace present in Qohelet: in the multiplicity of things God enables us to recognize.

Qohelet does not attach theological significance to gifts, however. They do not belong to a series of religious beatitudes. We have noted that Qohelet does not mention the great gifts of the God of Israel to his people. No, he offers us something else: the gift of human worry or concern, for example, which we have already examined. Concern to change, progress, search, and understand. Qohelet recognizes this concern as a difficulty, but a difficulty that *constitutes* us human beings.

We have also considered the gift of the desire for eternity—another component of our humanity. We cannot be satisfied with the present moment. We view our work falling into oblivion with the passing generations as a disaster. Realizing we cannot foresee anything about the future constitutes another disaster for us. Thirst for something lasting consumes us, as does desire for unlimited time, for a life that would not inevitably come to an end. In other words, Qohelet observes that we are doubly subject to vanity: vanity as inability to live forever and as inability to create a work that would be always new. "This is vanity and a chasing after wind," he proclaims. But at the same time Qohelet says to us that "the ability to observe and state this reality constitutes a gift from God."

So Qohelet's experience of vanity constitutes a gift from God.

At this point let us look again at our earlier observations concerning "vanity of vanities" as a genitive. Perhaps the expression means that declaring everything as vanity is thus (because of God's gift!) still another vanity. Vanity amounts to the very structure of the human being. This observation shows the remarkable development that has taken place based on Genesis 2 and 3. Clearly, in the communion between the Creator and his creature, in the "utter present" given to Adam, he had neither a concern to understand (since immediacy constituted truth at that time) nor a desire for eternity. Everything was very good. But with the Fall, two outcomes became possible: humanity might die because of the Fall; or human beings might remain alive, but since they had broken with life, they would live either in a state of delirium or like animals. Humanity either takes itself for God or is a brute beast, like an animal in every way, without knowing it!

God makes use of this tragic situation. As the rest of the Bible will show us a hundred times, God adapts himself to the situation human beings bring about. God adapts to it, but does not want humanity to sink (he reproaches Cain before the murder: "Why is your face downcast?" Gen. 4:6).[36] Since God wants humanity to retain its specific, different position, he assigns it a new role after the Fall. Humanity is no longer what it was meant to be, but God engages it in a surprising adventure. It is stupid to agree with the recent fad that claimed humanity came of age and could create history thanks to the Fall (oh, blessed guilt!). Qohelet teaches us that after the Fall God gave these different human beings new qualities so they could face their unexpected situation. Without these gifts, they were destined for insignificance. His gifts, however, are only possibilities: the concern to seek, and the desire for eternity. We know well how they mark us decisively in our world and our history.

Now here comes Qohelet, the radical denier, the most lucid and uncompromising of critical minds, telling us these gifts come from God. He has no illusions; he knows these "gifts" constitute demands

36. Ellul uses the same French word for "sink" and "is downcast": *s'effondre.* —TRANS.

and requirements rather than means or solutions. He knows that most of the time these gifts lead us to vanity and involve us in chasing after wind! And yet, if we do not use them, we are quite simply not human. These constitute God's first gifts.

God's Gift of Enjoyment

Next we come to all the gifts we might label successful! Qohelet recommends we eat and drink well, rejoice, and find pleasure when we can (2:24; 3:13). But this is a gift of God! So Qohelet places such pleasure on a different level from that of the post-Epicureans. Because as we experience pleasure, if we actually recognize it as a gift from God, two results follow: (1) a kind of seriousness in what we do; and (2) an inability to find pleasure in just anything, or to rejoice in just anything.

Because of these two results, we need to take care to avoid two errors we could easily fall into: (1) formalism (saying grace before a meal and then drinking ourselves into a stupor, for instance), or (2) feeling anguished as we eat a good meal, sensing a severe, pitiless eye on us that will forgive no mistake. These two errors have nothing to do with awakening to the fact that joy, pleasure, and comfort are gifts of God.

These two errors aside, we need to take joy and pleasure very seriously, as gifts of God. If we take them seriously, we will not squander them to no purpose, nor will we find pleasure in something that would be contrary to the will of God. This is the important issue. Everything that elates and gives enjoyment does not automatically constitute a gift of God: drugs or drunken debauchery, for instance. Since joy is a gift from God, we must learn to judge what things can procure it. We must not refuse it, but neither should we accept it from just any source! "For 'Who will eat and have enjoyment apart from me?'" (2:25). Only with God's help can we do these things. This boundary line, not discernible on objective grounds, remains inexplicable as long as we restrict our thinking to categories of true and false. To understand the gift of God, we must return to him, its source, and look, with his perspective, at the things that are.

A further gift of God is the fact that work can produce happiness! ("Everyone who eats, drinks, and enjoys happiness in all his work, this is a gift from God," 3:13; see 5:18-19). Again, Qohelet destroys our prejudices and ready-made ideas! We take for granted that, on the one hand, work necessarily brings with it a result: gain or profit. On the other hand, we assume that a person who works earns his living at it, able to eat and drink thanks to his work. Our sage says no—work can prove utterly sterile. We may even consider this the rule, the normal outcome. When work bears fruit and produces a result, we have a kind of miracle that should leave us ecstatic.

We moderns have completely lost this gift. We no longer know how to marvel at what blossoms in and through our work. We have forgotten to give thanks that our work is not fruitless, considering everything to be our right. When our work happens to prove sterile, we demand an explanation and compensation!

Here we see two opposite reactions stemming from two opposing concepts of life. The "pessimistic" individual overflows with joy when happiness comes or something succeeds. His opposing number, demanding and satiated, feels everything should succeed, and swells with bitterness and hate when faced with failure. Qohelet tells us unambiguously which reaction God chooses!

Happiness in work also constitutes a gift from God, even more significant than the gift of work as productive. Again we see how our great society misconstrues, and how incapable we are of extricating ourselves from its misconception. We live with the notion that work, a virtue, should produce happiness. But in fact, we experience work as oppressive, monotonous, boring, uninteresting, empty, and repetitive. There is no need to continue the familiar list. This contradiction constitutes one of our modern tragedies. But all comes clear if we accept the idea of work as an affliction in itself, but capable of producing the happiness of dazzling success. Then we should react with gratitude. Any happiness in and through our work warrants thankfulness, which we can address only to God. For "finding happiness in one's work is a gift from God" (3:13, JE).

This brings us to thornier issues.

"Every person to whom God has given riches and resources,

and to whom he has given the ability to profit from them . . . this is a gift from God" (5:19, JE). Riches as a gift of God? We know this idea well, and find it dangerous. In the name of this maxim the Puritans built fortunes, based on one of two primary errors: "We will increase our wealth in a devouring fashion, stopping at nothing to accumulate wealth. Thus we will assure ourselves of God's gift"; or "If I make a fortune, that proves I belong to God's elect."

Max Weber made good use of this point of departure. After all, it is no more scandalous than declaring pleasure a gift of God! But as we did above, we need to draw out the consequences of these principles. If wealth is a gift of God, and I recognize it as such, can I try to acquire it by any means? Will God really acknowledge it as his gift if you grow wealthy through murder? Likewise, if wealth is a gift of God, may I do anything at all with it? Can I act against love in order to accumulate it or use it? Is there no way to use money in accordance with God's will, so that my use of it would express my belief that it comes from God (even if I acquired it through working)?

It seems certain to me that we should constantly bring judgment to bear on wealth and its use, just as we did in the case of pleasure. The central error, the basis for all others, comes from what we could call the mechanization of God's revelation, or spiritual legalism. In this process, one bases logical reasoning on spiritual realities; for example, "If we have pleasure or wealth, it is *therefore* a gift of God" (meaning any pleasure whatever, including the vilest, most beastly, the most contrary to God's will, or any wealth whatever). In contrast, the path Qohelet shows us, the path of revelation, involves learning to discern whether a pleasure or wealth is a gift of God, considering the consequences we emphasized above. This path amounts to veritable asceticism. So discerning God's gift and finding joy in his works constitutes the best thing for us (see Lys, pp. 404-5).

Our text adds a new perspective, however. When he speaks of riches, Qohelet adds "God leaves him the power to profit from them" (5:19, JE). These words obviously respond to the vanity of power or of accumulated wealth that death obliges us to leave to an unknown inheritor. This work, accomplished so that a stranger can profit from it, amounts to a chasing after wind. God may give a person wealth and property, but it may be that "God does not leave him the power to enjoy it, for some stranger is going to enjoy it. This is vanity and grievous suffering" (6:2, JE). This verse corresponds precisely to 2:26, where we see God giving to another the wealth a person has accumulated through his work, his passion for money, and his obsession with assets.

This passage involves a terrible irony: God gives someone a passion for earning wealth, but then takes it from him and gives it to someone else at random! Thus God responds to our deification of wealth. In view of these passages, we see as a gift of God the possibility of benefiting from the fruit of our labor, along with children who grow up and the wealth we receive. His gift grants us happiness for a period of time. We need to recognize and discern this gift, to see it *as a gift*—and then to respond gratefully.

Each happy day should move us to give thanks. This is what Qohelet says, repeating it like a refrain—at least as often as "All is vanity": "I praised joy! . . . And this accompanies a person in his work *during all the days* of his life that God has given him under the sun" (8:15, JE). This passage brings out an attitude found frequently in the Old Testament and repeated in the New, but abandoned by theologians: "as if," "considering something as," or "taking something for." Rather than saying bluntly "this is a gift from God," Qohelet suggests "I see [or I know] this to be a gift from God." I believe we should understand in this same sense the texts where he makes such a statement directly.

This basic understanding moves us from an ontological to an existential approach. Qohelet does not say that things "are," but that he sees or conceives them a certain way. He interprets them. He records for us, not the act of God *in ipso,* but the way he receives and understands it. I believe this to be a fundamental issue. "I interpret this as a gift from God"; someone else may see something else in it or nothing at all. No matter. I come across this approach in connection with many other revelations.[37] Thus, rather than

37. This concept is developed with respect to impure things in my forthcoming *Ethics of Holiness.*

saying things or actions *are* something, on an objective basis, we find they necessarily become the object of our "reading." For the believer, the result is a confession of faith: "I believe that . . . I do not believe anything beyond these statements." With the extraordinary clarity we gain with this approach we can stress the antibiblical nature of all ontology (this insight challenges certain aspects of theology!). Next we see that God respects our freedom: "I place this in your hands. You may live it in different ways; you may receive it variously. You are free, so it is your responsibility." Thus the only possible act is a witness based on faith, rather than something based on rote teaching or catechesis.

Thus we understand that we must interpret everything (consider Jesus' speaking in parables!). We find ourselves in the midst of the events of this world, with the obligation of free interpretation, to our great risk and peril. If we receive all the acts of our life as a gift from God, we will live with meaning and joy. Otherwise, we will encounter nothing but vanity and folly. But *you* are the one under the sun that will turn everything to vanity.

We have not exhausted God's gifts. We continue with: "Come, eat your bread with joy and drink your wine with a glad heart, for God has already approved your works. At all times let your clothes be white, and let not oil be lacking on your head. Take advantage of life with the wife you love, through all the days of this fleeting life he has given you under the sun" (9:7-9, JE). Here we find two new gifts: God's approval of your actions (you must learn to approve them as well), and a woman you love. You fail to know the meaning of what you do, but everything is cast in a new light the moment you come to the certainty that God accepts what you do. He receives and loves your works.

God's acceptance shows utter generosity, since none of our works are worthy of him! Solomon, whom Qohelet knows well, understood this better than anyone. Solomon acknowledged that his great temple was nothing, as far as receiving the "presence-absence" of God was concerned (1 K. 8:27). But God reveals to us: "I accept your works." Paul tells us, for instance, that the Holy Spirit presents our prayers to God and transforms them, since otherwise they would be utterly inappropriate in God's presence (Rom. 8:26).

God approves of your works, so you are independent and free to accomplish them! You can choose on your own, without abiding by a rigid law, because you are approved, received, pardoned, and loved. So are your works—not because of their reality, but because they have you as their source. Even when life proves difficult, and in spite of Qohelet's harsh observations, you are to dress in white and anoint your head with oil. How could we avoid recalling the parable of the wedding feast (Matt. 22:1-14) at this point? The only person thrown out of the feast is the one who has not dressed in wedding clothes; that is, the one who failed to recognize the invitation as a gift. Everything is a gift of God, just as everything is grace. This is the real feast: a gift.

Now for the second gift: the woman you love. Here we see the same Qohelet who states that he has not found a woman in a thousand (7:28), telling you that you can truly love and that God gives you the days necessary for that love. So this gift entails not only love and a woman, but the period of time for loving and living with her. Your life is fleeting, but it can be wonderful with love if you know that each hour filled and lived in this way is a gift of God—and therefore a presence of God and a friendship with him, a nearness of the Lord who holds out his hand to you.

These, then, are God's gifts. We may feel disappointed that they in no way involve the afterlife, salvation, eternal life, the resurrection, etc. God's gifts in Qohelet all have to do with this earth, under the sun. They all bear on our life.

We noted earlier that Qohelet knows nothing of the resurrection, and certainly nothing of the immortality of the soul. For this reason theologians have stated that Qohelet's view that everything is included and concluded within the span of our existence causes him to despair—he knows of nothing beyond this life. But I do not believe you can find a basis for such a conclusion in the book. Qohelet chooses to be rigorously concrete and realistic. He limits his scope to what we can "see" of human life. The rest does not concern him. He is utterly critical. The fact that his point of view is radical and yet tolerable implies an additional dimension, which we will discover later. But Qohelet is too honest to bring God into play, with the uncertain compensations the afterlife would bring.

We do find, however, a brief allusion to a kind of "reward": "He has *given*, to the person *who is upright before him*, wisdom, knowledge, and joy; and to the sinner, he has given the work [occupation] of collecting and amassing in order to give to the one who is upright before God" (2:26, JE). This verse calls to mind Jesus' parable of the talents: "It will be taken from the one who does not have, and given to the one who has" (Luke 19:26, JE).

Thus there is a sort of "reward" for good people, and punishment for the others. But this "gift" is wisdom, knowledge, and joy (not salvation, honor, fortune, success, etc.). The gift is something altogether inward, given during our lifetime. But it transforms life.

As for the "wicked" person, he has in fact a passion for profit, monopolizing, and conquest, and God will deprive him of these things. But I think the parable of the talents, which we cited above, applies at this point. So this gift in no way constitutes a kind of divine judgment occurring during our lifetime, taking from the unjust, rich person and giving to the just, poor person. Qohelet knows perfectly well that things fail to work out that way. He has said so on several occasions. So his view of God's gifts in no way involves a return to the "thesis" of traditional doctrine (seen in Job, for instance), which has God making the good person happy and prosperous.

But we can quite well understand the text in the opposite sense: God has given wisdom, knowledge, and joy, which have enabled this person to be upright before God, who then augments his gift because the person has in effect been upright. At this point we return to the idea of the parable of the talents. Qohelet concludes enigmatically: "this *too* is vanity and chasing after the wind" (2:26b). So even what we can call God's judgment amounts to vanity, since it is not sufficient to give decisive meaning to our life.[38]

38. We might mention at this point that for Lys, 2:24-26 refer to the work of grace. He translates: "There is no happiness except in eating, drinking, and indulging one's taste for work: I have seen that this also depends on the Divinity. 'Yes, who eats or finds enjoyment without me?' Yes, to a person who pleases him, the Divinity gives philosophy, knowledge, and enjoyment; but to the failure he gives the preoccupation of accumulating, piling up—only to give it to someone who pleases the Divinity. This also is smoke and taking the wind

We also find at this point, however, an indisputable eschatological dimension, although no promise of individual resurrection.
We have already encountered this dimension, but we need to
underscore it again here, since we find the promise of recapitulation
among God's gifts. We must return to this theme, it seems to me, in
view of the very explicit text: "What already was, is, and what is to
be, has been; *and* God seeks what slips away" (3:15, JE). Some
versions translate: "What exists has already been. What will exist,

---

out to pasture" (p. 281). Lys entitles these verses "The Necessity of Grace." I
have emphasized the gift, but moving from there to grace, with all the
theological content involved, seems perhaps a bit excessive. "Qohelet's final
lesson is not moderation . . . but grace. . . . The vertical dimension intervenes
in the horizontal, where humanity found itself stuck in the impasse of a lack
of meaning. . . . God has the first and the last word, whether in philosophizing
or indulgence. 'Qohelet finally arrives at grace through skepticism.' . . . Grace
makes enjoyment possible. . . . The very insecurity of enjoyment brings about
the discovery of the dimension that was missing, enabling a person to find
meaning in the depths of absurdity. When enjoyment is given to a person, it
indicates the presence of Another, who has a plan with respect to which the
meaning of everything is defined. . . . Pleasure . . . is a sign, in its very
irrationality: a sign that God is there" (pp. 286-88 [the quotation within the
above is from unpublished course notes by W. Vischer.—TRANS.]). But this
interpretation may be very risky, and it strays far from Qohelet's ruthless
realism! A person in the throes of pleasure never sees a sign of grace in it. To
become aware of grace, he needs Qohelet's revelation and proclamation! The
same could be said for Lys's "God will cause meaning to spring from this very
absurdity . . . showing that human effort is relative and has meaning only as it
relates to another dimension: the vertical. Through this dimension God's will
carries out its plan on the world's horizontal" (p. 293). Theologically, of course,
I agree with Lys. But I do not find that his conclusions necessarily emerge from
this text. Our passage ends with "This too is vanity and chasing after the wind"
(2:26, JE). We could not understand this conclusion if the text referred to the
gift of God and the grace we receive in enjoyment. This obliges Lys to offer
an explanation that would try to avoid having vanity apply to grace! But such
an explanation would have to be very convoluted, having "all is vanity" apply
only to the vain human effort to find meaning and to the paradox of vv. 24 and
25. I find that this unsatisfactory result challenges Lys's point of view, that
these verses deal with grace in the theological sense of the term. It is largely
sufficient to recognize, when we have an hour of happiness, that it is a gift from
God.

exists already, *but* God will seek what has been driven away." These words complete the great passage beginning "There is a time for everything" (3:1-15).

God places the desire for eternity in human hearts. This desire constitutes a gift. But no human being can satisfy this desire. God will respond to our desire by seeking what has passed or fled. Everything that has escaped us in the course of time has its place in the memory of God. Nothing of all that escapes us has been lost. Qohelet's "That which is, already has been; that which is to be, already has been" does not provoke despair if we know that *everything* is found again in God. Everything is not necessarily preserved for God's Kingdom, but everything becomes present again in God. And Qohelet's "God seeks what has been driven away" becomes incarnate in his final gift: the heavenly Jerusalem. It will fulfill the totality of our expectation and take on the totality of the work we have done throughout the course of humanity's strange and baffling history.

God as Judge

Above all else, then, God gives. But he also judges. Before examining Qohelet on the subject, I think we need to make three preliminary remarks. (1) Among over twenty passages involving God, we find three designating him as judge (and two of these repeat each other). And compared with more than twenty texts on gifts, there are four concerning judgment. We cannot say, then (unless we find these small numbers extremely important), that the judgment of God and the God who judges are central to Qohelet's concerns.

(2) As far as the relationship of judgment and gift in Qohelet is concerned, I would place judgment within the scope of gift.

As I have discussed at length in other books,[39] I believe I see unanimous agreement with respect to a traditional error concerning God's judgment. We cannot get away from our idea of judgment as involving a criminal trial. True, we find in the prophets the idea of

39. See my *Apocalypse* and *The Meaning of the City*.

God as a judge who separates the good from the bad, the just from the unjust, the elect nation from criminal nations. Certain exegetes I know have given special weight to this theme by singling out the "legal vocabulary" used in certain texts: Satan as the accuser in a trial, the interpretation of Jesus as "paraclete" or lawyer, etc. This is true, of course, provided we do not exaggerate, translating everything (especially the parables) in terms of trial procedure. We must not make the *criminal* trial the center of our theology.

Nevertheless, I observe an invasion of Roman thought reflected in the Church Fathers, beginning in the third century. The main emphasis of Roman thought centers on law, and all of Roman law is constructed around the reality of the trial. Trials form its nucleus and center of reflection.[40] This thought, utterly foreign to Christianity and completely impervious to the reality of grace, began to orient theology by the third century. For example, it gave rise to a theology of salvation by works, and determined the theology of relations with political power. This same thought produced the image of God that unbelievers have attacked so much for the last two hundred years: God the implacable judge on his throne, a dreadful sovereign who strikes down the disobedient and unbelieving. His main symbol is Hell. But God is not like this—not even "the God of the Old Testament."[41]

God has certainly been presented in this way, sometimes in bad

40. I could refer the reader to a hundred different authors on this theme, but I will limit myself to O. Lenel, *Edictum perpetuum* (Paris: Sirey, 1903); many others can be found in vol. 1 of my *Histoire des institutions* (Paris: Presses Universitaires de France, 1955, repr. 1984).

41. Lys expresses very clearly Qohelet's thought when he says that connecting judgment and life after death constitutes a prejudice (p. 388; see pp. 380-83). The problem of Qohelet lies precisely at this point: he does not believe in life after death, yet he affirms God's eschatological judgment. This in spite of the fact that a person as object of this judgment could not benefit from it, since all of existence takes place under the sun. So Qohelet proposes an amazing and gratuitous act of faith: I should make daring choices in the hope that God will include one or another of my works in his eternity, thus justifying my existence after it is over. The risk of such choices, furthermore, is not related to a theological calculation of their merits, but to confidence in the grace that carries out a mysterious judgment.

medieval catechesis, other times in bad Calvinistic preaching. And of course we also find texts that justify such an image, within the whole of the Bible, if we isolate them from the rest. But in the first place, judgment is not a condemnation (we will come across this again, in connection with one of the verses we will examine). Second, judgment can involve a *civil* suit, without anyone necessarily receiving a sentence. Besides, a "judgment" can be something entirely different: the appearance or evaluation of what is just, or the declaration and proclamation of justice. In this case no notion of a trial or condemnation is involved: an authority, a philosopher, or a person judges, and in so doing, shows what is just—nothing more.

(3) In Qohelet, the fact of God's judgment appears necessarily as the counterpart of human freedom. More precisely, his judgment is the other side of the coin of his acceptance of human independence. Autonomous humanity is clearly balanced by a God who accepts its autonomy but at the same time judges it. In the same way, God's judgment forms the essential complement to his memory. If God keeps all things in his memory, he has to sort them. This is indispensable for the work God wants to accomplish, as we have shown above.

I find three simple remarks necessary if we are to understand the meaning of "judgment" in the texts we want to examine, and such an introduction was necessary for the reader to understand why I place judgment within the gift of God. One of the texts concerning judgment does not refer to God: "The heart of the sage knows time and judgment. Indeed, there is a time and a judgment for everything. For a person's evil is heavy upon him" (8:5b-6, JE). Thus there is not only a time for each thing, but also a judgment. In this text the judgment seems not to involve God, but rather the sage's capacity to bring judgment to bear on things.

Many are convinced that the above text deals with opportunity, just as some reduce "there is a time for everything" to an estimation of a thing's usefulness or efficacy. It is good to plant in the proper season, and then to uproot at the right time. But some would extend this simplistic example to all our activities! As we have tried to show, however, the first part of Qohelet's third chapter has nothing to do with such "time"!

We must note that this passage on judgment gives us the second part of a diptych. The first side showed the truth that everything finds its place and its time under the sun: good and evil, love and hatred. No ethic was involved. But the sage knows the time and the judgment or verdict. True, there is a time for everything, but *also* a judgment: not a judgment based on a thing's usefulness, but what we might call a judgment of value—a spiritual or ethical judgment.

This interpretation is strongly confirmed by the end of our passage, sometimes understood to say that a person's "evil is heavy upon him" (8:6, JE). Thus, within all this profusion of activities and work, there is a place for discerning what *is* evil, or what *causes* evil or trouble. These place a heavy burden on us—the evil done to us, but also the evil we do. Such discernment may take the form of the dialectic of the master and the slave, or of Camus' dialectic of the executioner and the victim. Or the agonizing question I keep coming back to: who will forgive us?

This matter constitutes a heavy burden precisely because the average person, not a sage, does not know of the coming judgment, which will be a separation of good from evil and a declaration of justice. Directly following the verses quoted above, we read this very idea: "For he [the person burdened down by evil] does not know what will be. For who will reveal to him how it will be [or how it will take place]?" (8:7). This is just the necessary inducement we needed to be able to accept that God *also* judges! I can include judgment with God's gifts to us because when he judges, *he dispenses justice.* "I said to myself, God will judge them, for there is a time for everything, and for every work" (3:17, JE). The hurried commentator merely asserts that Qohelet repeats the tritest, most traditional doctrine in this verse: God judges the just and the wicked with a judgment of retribution. But we have already stated that we do not find this idea in Qohelet.[42]

Our text, I believe, is a bit subtler than that. It belongs to

42. Lys shows this constantly, as when he writes: "Qohelet firmly limits himself to a pragmatic analysis of reality. He notes that at the final moment, when we might hope that God would right human injustice through his judgment, we encounter death instead: the blind equalizer" (p. 394).

Qohelet's great overall theme: "there is a time for everything." Remarkably, however, Qohelet did not write: "There is a time for justice and a time for injustice"—a singular omission. And he necessarily comes to the point where he deals with this question. But when he considers what people do, he sees only injustice (3:16). Injustice reigns, but not only in ordinary relationships: even in the place where "justice should be" (i.e., where it should be proclaimed, displayed, and applied), Qohelet encounters only injustice and wickedness. There is *never* anything but injustice in human affairs, whether political, economic, legal, or social. We have encountered this many times. So there is not "a time for justice" on the level of human works. Furthermore, nothing is more fundamentally unjust than trying to establish one's *own* justice. Yet surely injustice should have its counterpart.

Universal injustice must be restricted to "a time." At this point, however, we must leap into the void, into irrationality: if humanity is incapable of justice, it must come from somewhere else. I know all the rational arguments against this proposition. But if it is false, we are left with a humanity content to continue floundering in its universal injustice. This injustice looms even greater when we consider that parties and regimes have *claimed to establish justice* (all communisms, for instance). Qohelet does not mention justice with a view to condemning the wicked, but rather so that justice will be affirmed and displayed rather than injustice. We know from other sources how distinct God's justice is! Without dwelling on the matter, I will just say that only God carries out full and complete justice.

When we read our text from this point of view, we reach much higher than the typical stammerings linking specifically human justice with God's justice and consolations with respect to the future! But at the same time, our conclusion above implies an acceptance of the marked presence of God's judgment. We need to know this. "Delight, young person, in your youth, and let your heart make you happy in the days of your youth. Walk in the ways of your heart and according to the vision of your eyes, and know that for all this God will bring you to judgment" (11:9). God's judgment is present. We need it if we are ultimately to know what justice is.

I want to be careful not to make this verse say more than it says: we have not yet come to justification by faith. But I cannot keep the text from proclaiming: "Be happy; let your heart rejoice, and know that you are coming to judgment." Those who choose to see a contradiction in these words understand nothing of the direction taken by Qohelet. Judgment does not appear here for the purpose of clipping the wings of our joy; on the contrary, it gives our joy meaning, depth, and duration. We have not yet arrived at the assurance the Good News will give: that God has taken on himself his own judgment, in Jesus Christ. Nor does Qohelet tell us that everything is accomplished in Jesus Christ. But we do have here the assurance that God *gives* justice in his judgment.

When a person knows that, he takes seriously "Happy are those who are hungry and thirsty for justice, for they will be satisfied" (Matt. 5:6, JE). Satisfied, because justice can come only from the one who gives it. And he gives it in this judgment (of which our judgment is only a faint image). But people will be satisfied only if they need justice as much as they need bread and water—only if they are starving and athirst for justice, truly at the point of death. The faith necessary for this justice is not at issue here; rather, one must be hungry and thirsty, on the one hand, and have complete confidence that the one who judges is indeed the God who gives, on the other.

We find clearly implied here that this measure of justice will also be applied to us. But the text does not threaten us by saying "God will bring you *into* judgment." It says "God will bring you *to* judgment" (11:9b). But we must by no means become paralyzed by this prospect. We must not live in terror of this judgment, or fall back. On the contrary, do everything possible, take your pleasure, look for your joy. You are young and that is wonderful. Go where the desires of your heart and the vision of your eyes lead you.[43]

43. Lys's excellent comments on 3:22 fit perfectly here: human achievements "were considered so much 'wind' [in 2:11]. But now [in 3:22] the point is no longer to try to accumulate achievements in order to give meaning to life. Work does not have value because of human memory (glory) or because of shining futures (philosophy of history). One must choose the acts of 3:1ff. in the knowledge that they involve a risk. We place our confidence in God

Do not be inhibited, living ascetically or within a narrow moral framework. Do not repress the desires of your heart; instead, transcend and sublimate them. See this world that is offered to you, and act in it and on it. Instead of repeating the silly refrain "youth must have its fling," Qohelet presents youth as the time when emotions and feelings bloom, the time of forceful experiences and the discovery of possibilities. "Take advantage of all this, young person," he says. Qohelet offers neither morality (we have seen that evil reigns in the "place" of justice) nor prohibitions. Do not be paralyzed or inhibited.

Oddly enough, this passage necessarily reminds us again of the parable of the talents. The last servant, who received one talent, felt paralyzed and inhibited. Since he feared his master, he chose to risk nothing, burying his talent in the ground. He failed to do, create, or develop anything. Then he scrupulously returns what he had received. "I knew you are a hard master," he says (Matt. 25:24, JE), and he is condemned—unlike those who risked the fortune lent to them, doing as they pleased. They succeeded; but what if they had lost the money? I feel certain the master would not have condemned them.

Qohelet places no moral or ascetic limit on enjoyment, then, except for his "Know . . ." (11:9). In the midst of your joy and action, *know:* remember, keep the judgment in your heart and mind. There will necessarily be results and consequences, when you arrive where "the ways of your heart" (11:9) lead you. But this judgment leaves all your autonomy intact, since you do not know in advance what the judgment will consist of. No one dictates your behavior. You must know, at all times, that there is judgment on and for what you do. But you do not know what it is. You can only refer back to the fact that the giver of justice is God. Before all else, he is the "God who gives," as Qohelet describes him. He gives you your youth and strength, and even your enjoyment. This is what you must not forget.

The only evil would consist of forgetting that all this is given

---

concerning the meaning of everything. Thus we can experience utterly unselfish enjoyment of what we do" (p. 405). I would call this "free" enjoyment.

by God, and for that reason, we will come to judgment. The only possible wisdom lies in this relationship between the gift and the judgment. Evil would consist of separating the happiness of God's gift from the possibility of judgment, making *my* enjoyment, *my* desire, and *my* pleasure into something all mine, something I owe no one and about which I do not need first to make a judgment. We have already encountered this principle: on the basis of this knowledge we learn that everything is not acceptable, that we cannot give in to the great temptation of our century: "anything goes."

As for whether this passage deals with the "last" judgment, the "day of the Lord," it may well be, but I do not believe this is the most important thing. What matters is knowing that this declaration of God's justice applies to *everything,* that finally this justice will "manifest everyone's work." But I believe when we become too intent on seeing the last judgment here, we risk attaching to the text a spiritual dimension it does not have, referring to eternal life, etc. God's judgment can be eschatological without implying an individual afterlife, a problem Qohelet does not address.

Nevertheless, it does matter whether we learn from this text that this eschatological and therefore global judgment is also and at the same time an individual judgment. Some have expressed amazement on this account: "In its time, this judgment was conceived primarily as eschatological. . . . Through what unexpected development could this sage have foreseen the possibility of *such* a judgment as related to individuals?" (Barucq, p. 185, emphasis added). As if God's Revelation did not progress![44]

44. In conclusion, I am obliged to point out my disagreement with Lys when he writes: "Qohelet ended in 2:23 with the problems of individual death and the disorderliness of history. The integration of human work into the plan of God is the solution to the second problem (3:1-15). The first remains to be solved, and is posed again in 3:16–4:3, in the context of justice" (p. 374). Lys points to God's eschatological justice and to Qohelet's conclusion that nonexistence is better than death, which is better than life. I find this correct as far as the form of Qohelet is concerned, yet it remains doubtful. In reality, Qohelet neither "poses problems" nor looks for "solutions"! He has not written a theoretical scholarly discourse or constructed a theology; rather, he wrestles with himself and with God. His is a multifaceted experience not reduced to

4. Approaching God

Can we stop with the bald statement that "God is in the heavens and you are on the earth" (5:2)? Must we rely on our own uncertain wisdom, faced with a wall of silence and darkness? Clearly we cannot count on familiarity with such a God, or expect him to overindulge us. But are we left in utter ignorance? The whole book of Qohelet, with its frequent declarations of faith, clearly offers itself to us as inspired. Nonetheless, we are constantly warned by the author's "I thought," "I said to myself," etc. Qohelet does not choose to act like a prophet, fearing he will be a false prophet. This is no book of "revelation." Consequently, as we have seen, he rejects religion and reassuring concepts of God, his action, etc. Qohelet rejects mythologies and sweeping divine panoramas (which he knows well, however, as we have seen by observing that he wrote with Gen. 1 and 3 continually in mind).

In addition, Qohelet refuses to make use of God, either to demonstrate that God exists or as an argument. He never uses God as a stopgap or to justify and explain events. Qohelet is too serious for that, and he has too much respect for God. But at the same time, he reveals the insufficiency, the incompetence, and the inadequacy of wisdom, science, and philosophy, rather than any failure on God's part!

Qohelet wants to keep his feet on the ground. He makes central his questions: "Who are we?" (much more central than "Who is God?," for Qohelet), and "How can we live?" (much more than "What is God's will for our lives?"). Qohelet notes that he cannot answer these questions. But he affirms that there is meaning in all this, even if he does not know what it is.

This God, then, is an experience of the community, in Qohelet also. In spite of his incomprehensibility, this God remains the

abstract formal structures. He offers us the questioning expressed by a living person simply because he is alive and aware. Furthermore, I fail to find anywhere in Qohelet a reference to a "plan of God." Lys's unfounded introduction of this concept enables him to make the transition from the idea of a "favorable moment" to the idea that we are to make our work fit into the plan of God.

closest one for the skeptical sage to converse with. God answers the sage's questions by means of other, even more unfathomable questions, just as he answered Job.

The unverifiable gift in the heart of the unknowable moves us to say yes, however, rather than to react coldly. Here we find ourselves at the opposite pole from the highest point of Greek thought: "To an absolutely personal being, Plotinus opposes a concept of the One that is precisely at the opposite pole from the biblical God. The One Being and the One thing are as far from each other as heaven and earth" (Scholem, p. 19). For Qohelet, what characterizes humanity, to this same degree, is waiting. We await the manifestation of God's justice. We wait for the coming of the one who will make up for vanity. But as we wait on this earth, it is rather vain to claim that we direct our lives according to wisdom.

In the end, as far as the ultimate question is concerned, wisdom, science, and philosophy prove useless. The only possible relationship with this God who gives life entails a certain approach made up of fear and confidence. As soon as we say "a certain approach," the strictly religious approach is challenged: "Watch your steps when you go to the temple. Drawing near to listen is better than the sacrifice of fools [imbeciles, insane people]. It is true that they do evil because they do not know it" (5:1, JE). Thus, following the tendency of the prophets, Qohelet warns us of the vanity of sacrifices when they are made in a purely mechanical fashion, when they are repetitive rather than an expression of faith, and thus "religious" in the sociological sense. If you have to go to the temple like an imbecile, who goes because the others do it, or like a fool, who would as soon do that as something else, it is not worth doing. Reflect, then, before you approach the place where God is adored, the place where he may speak. Watch your step. Try to be aware of what you are doing.

Naturally, this point of view does not mean that imbeciles, the "sociological Christians," are condemned. They are not condemned, says Qohelet, because they do not know what they are doing. But you have been warned now. You know. You must realize that going to the temple to offer a sacrifice means nothing in itself.

You will go *to listen*. This is basic: we must keep silent, since we await a word from God. He is the one who can answer all the questions we have accumulated here. But there is no opportunity for you to hear him unless you first enter with a listening attitude. Consequently, "Don't let your mouth be hasty. Don't let your ego hurry to express a word before God. For God is in heaven and you are on the earth; therefore let your words be few in number" (5:2, JE). Again, Qohelet's words recall what is said in the Sermon on the Mount about sacrifices, etc. So, if you take your place in the presence of God, listen before you speak. The Word can come down from God's height; you will not speak it. We are always in a hurry to speak to God (to ask him for something), but the sage says to you: "Be silent first." Not permanently: this is not the infinite silence of Buddhism. But let God make the first move. Then, briefly, you may respond. We have already said why: our respect for the word should be infinite, since it is our only link with God.

Qohelet's recommendations for approaching God continue: "When you make a promise to God, do not be slow in keeping it. For there is no leniency for the fool [imbecile]. Keep what you have promised. It is better not to promise than to make a promise and not keep it" (5:4-5, JE). This text reminds us of Ananias and Sapphira (Acts 5:1-11), among others. If they had not promised anything, they would not have been in error. And, as Kierkegaard says so accurately, after quoting this passage of Qohelet's, "religiously one is very careful about making vows (cf. Ecclesiastes), and religiously the measure of the inwardness of the vow is the brevity of the posited term, and the distrust of oneself. No, the whole-souled inwardness of the individual and the consent of a heart purified from all double-mindedness to a promise for the present day, or for the forenoon— such a vow has religiously a greater degree of inwardness than this aestheticising clinking the glasses with Providence."[45]

For the third time, Qohelet tells us: approaching God and entering into a relationship with him is a matter of infinite serious-ness. If you cannot listen, be silent (humble yourself), and keep your promises, it would be better not to approach this God. He is full of

45. Kierkegaard, *Concluding Unscientific Postscript*, p. 436n. The "aes-theticising clinking the glasses with Providence" refers to the priest's prayers!

indulgence for poor fools, but requires much of those who claim to enter the circle of those who serve God, swear by his Name, and offer sacrifices.

Going to the temple is not a rite, a ceremony, a religious act, or a duty. It constitutes proof that you take your questions seriously. All is vanity. If you go to the temple in a "religious" manner, you cause your relationship with God to enter into vanity; that is what cannot be pardoned. And this matter leads to *all* Jesus' condemnation of hypocrites. Just reread his series of woes: "Woe to you, scribes and Pharisees, hypocrites!" (Matt. 23:13-36; Luke 11:37-52). In Jesus' words, on the lips of the one who had authority, you will find the precise explanation of the sage's advice. He could only offer us a warning.

Thus, approaching God can enable us to escape from vanity, but we also have the power to take our relationship with God back into vanity, causing it to be invaded by vanity, wind, mist, smoke, and folly. But God does not allow this to happen as if it made no difference. In his presence, *for such behavior, in this connection,* no excuse is acceptable: "You cannot then declare before the representative [of God?], 'It is a mistake'" (Eccl. 5:6b, JE). No mistake is possible. God's will is extraordinarily clear; we are the ones who muddle it.

Your behavior may show other people how "serious" your faith is. If that happens, and if you speak foolishness or trite phrases concerning this revelation, these acts do not fail to have an effect: the positive becomes negative, and what was creative becomes destructive. We all know about the boomerang effect: "Why would God blame your word and destroy what you have made?" (5:6c, JE). God opens wide the door for your activity. But do not go implicating him foolishly in your nonsense. Do not make him into some protective screen to hide yourself, as if he were good for anything, a handy stopgap. In that case, your work will inevitably be destroyed.

Consequently, on this basis, fear God (or respect God).[46] Do

46. Delitzsch suggests we could call Qohelet "The Song of the Fear of God" (p. 183; see also pp. 180, 182).

we need to repeat, when so many others have said it, that this fear (which will come up again in our conclusion) is neither panic nor terror? When the women saw the risen Jesus, they were gripped with fear. But I believe this fact does not imply the psychic, nervous, and bodily reaction we usually call "panic." Rather, this "fear" belongs to the psychological domain, and describes a certain type of relationship with another person. We can translate this word as "respect," if we keep both ideas together: fear in the sense of respect, and respect in the sense of fear. We do not want to suggest mere "respect" in the sense of the courtesy we owe our superiors or a "lady." The word "respect" by itself is as ambiguous as "fear" by itself: "My respects, Mr. Commissioner." That is hardly the idea!

"Fear" in the biblical sense, then, involves being conscious of something of infinite seriousness: recognizing and approaching the Wholly Other. For "fear-respect" necessarily involves *approaching* the one who is infinitely distant from us. But an approach presupposes a desire, a will, a hope, and an anticipation.

This "fear-respect" also depends on a certain confidence, but not on familiarity. We have already examined the passage on dreams and excess of words: "In the abundance of dreams are vanities and words in abundance. But fear God" (5:7; this text comes at the end of Qohelet's recommendations concerning approaching God in 5:1-7). In this text we noted an attack on seers and interpreters of dreams, but it also applies to speaking in tongues, ecstatic states, religious frenzies, and prayers of "many words" (Matt. 6:7), etc. To these Qohelet opposes the self-control and prudence that spring from this "fear" of God.

The false prophet hides the falseness of his prophecy with a superabundance of words. People with a false spirituality hide the diabolical with trances and glossolalia. False theologians hide behind the excess of their discourse on God, etc. But *you* are to fear God. So try to master your emotions and your desire to proclaim your knowledge of God, if you respect him. "Do not throw your pearls before swine" (Matt. 7:6, RSV). Jesus certainly seems to have known Qohelet well!

Now this fear of God, which is the beginning of wisdom, enables us to resolve the contradiction. We have seen that Qohelet continually gives us both the yes and the no. No sooner has he affirmed wisdom than he shows its weakness . . . and folly. And there is a time for all opposites! But now we see how the God who gives enters the picture to put things into perspective: "It is good that you cling to this. But do not let your hand let go of that. And the one who fears God will fulfill both [or resolve both, or avoid both]" (7:18, JE). In other words, when "this" and "that" oppose each other, the fear of God enables us to handle the situation. Because in God we have both the no and the yes. Both are right and must be safeguarded. Evil becomes good (as in the extreme case of Jesus Christ, whose death ensures our salvation). Good leads to evil (as in the extreme case of self-justification through the Law). The only right way is to keep both, but we can do this only in the fear, respect, and love of the God who maintains both the alpha and the omega.

Qohelet assures us that happiness will come to those who experience this fear of God: "I myself know [we will not repeat our observations concerning this declaration of faith] that there will be happiness for those who fear God *because* they experience fear before him" (8:12). Thus the very fact that one is filled with this fear produces happiness. I do not believe a reward is involved; the meaning is not "If you fear God, he will make you happy." I believe Qohelet has sufficiently demonstrated the opposite!

Rather, the person who fears God experiences happiness because this fear itself *is* the presence of God. For the person who experiences it, this fear gives assurance of the Lord's presence. For this reason, I find Chouraqui's version suggestive, when he substitutes "trembling" for "fear" or "respect." Those who tremble in God's presence *are* in his presence. But their trembling stems from their "fear" as much as from their emotion, "enthusiasm," bedazzlement, or fulness. They tremble at the approach of God. Here we see extreme joy and happiness—in the recognition of one's helplessness and unworthiness: "He approached me, a miserable servant." Anyone who has not experienced this does not and cannot know what happiness is.

The one who lives such an experience, however, knows at last where wisdom lies and what it is. "For I laid all that to heart and I experienced all this: that the just, the wise and their actions are in the hand of God. A person knows neither love nor hate: everything lies before him" (9:1; this passage begins the long series of things that are the same for everyone,[47] culminating in: "rejoice, for God has already approved your works," 9:7, JE). Thus the person who thinks he knows and who thinks he lives knows nothing—not even what love and hate really are. Only God knows truly, absolutely, what love is! Just as only he knows absolutely what human hatred toward him can mean: the crucifixion of the just. Everything is before the person who knows neither love nor hate, who does everything in the same way. When he wants to judge what is wise and what is foolish, he finds himself finally unable to do it.

The just, the sages, and their works are in God's hand. Here we have the final word of Qohelet's long quest for wisdom! We do not have access to God through wisdom, philosophy, science, or knowledge. Quite the contrary: the just person and the sage are in God's hand; that is to say, wisdom comes from God. It lies nowhere else, has no independence. It leads to nothing but smoke, mist, wind, and vanity. But it becomes wisdom, perhaps the same wisdom, beginning at the moment the sage recognizes it to be in God's hand—another gift of God.

This wisdom, however, is necessarily linked to our attitude:

47. It is useful to follow Qohelet's progression in one of these texts: "Everything is the same for everybody: an identical destiny awaits the just person and the wicked, the good person [and the evil one], the pure and the impure, the one who sacrifices and the one who does not sacrifice" (9:2a). Qohelet moves from morality to ritual, and from ritual to sacrifice—all the levels of "religion." Thus we understand how scandalous his triple affirmation may have sounded: nothing of all this has any use, gives us any answer or meaning, or changes human destiny. That is, we cannot change life or reach God in this manner. Thus even sacrifice is useless, but Qohelet does not reject it! He merely emphasizes that no one escapes his situation by offering a sacrifice. The summit of Qohelet's quest will entail accomplishing without sacrifice what is usually—and correctly— assumed to be accomplished by sacrifice: "moving life off center in order to escape the secret fascination of death" (Pierre Gisel, "Du sacrifice: L'Avènement de la personne face à la peur de la vie et à la fascination de la mort," *Foi et Vie* 83/4 [July 1984] 37). This is really the center and the end of Qohelet's long process.

fear, respect, and trembling. Wisdom is not found in sacrifices, rites, and cults, but in the person who stands courageously and humbly before God. This, I believe, is Qohelet's lesson for us: he sifted everything courageously, examining it all with a fine-tooth comb—without reservation, without fear, without deference to public opinion. He dared to attack everything: ancient beliefs, morality, new philosophies. He cut himself off, viewing even the great Solomon, the king of kings, with irony!

At the same time, he remained utterly humble: he did not judge others without judging himself! On the contrary, he judged himself and his actions, drawing his other observations from his self-criticism. And he remained humble before God—so humble that he did not dare talk about God, except to say that he saw everywhere the gifts God gives people. So he finishes with this confident statement: "Where is Wisdom, then?," Job demanded; and Qohelet answers: the works of the wise are in the hand of God.

5. Qohelet's Crowning Words

Scholars declare chapter 12 an epilogue. In my opinion, such a designation is meaningless. Furthermore, this epilogue is said to be the work of one, or more probably two, of the first author's successors. Those who maintain at all costs that Qohelet was a professor of moral theology in a seminary of his time call these successors his "students." This strikes me as odd. Be that as it may, these "editors" of the book are said to have added this final section.

Others believe that 12:1-8 come from the author, so that only 12:9-13 are due to the "editor." We do not need to be scholarly exegetes to see that, in effect, these five verses cannot have been written by Qohelet, since in our initial reading we find a declaration *about* Qohelet. The text says Qohelet *was* (therefore, is no longer) a wise person, who worked very hard, tried out many things, etc. Thus someone else speaks here (as in Deut. 34:5ff., where someone describes the death of Moses).

Perhaps we have a contradiction here, however: the first ending, in 12:8, refers us back to the beginning of the book: "Vanity of vanities." The second ending tells us to "fear God" (12:13). But we have tried to show just this: that there is no contradiction here. I like very much the observation of A. Kuenen that "it is more difficult to deny the unity of the work [and to track down its many hypothetical authors!] than it is to demonstrate it [which I have tried to do!]" (cited by Lusseau, p. 150). In any case, scholarly exegetes usually admit that the same thought continues in this "epilogue," so that we have continuity with the rest of the book. Even the final verses are found to be perfectly "in line," and that is all I care about.

Having reviewed all the possibilities life offers, then, Qohelet challenges the reader, but in his adolescence: "Remember your Creator in the days of your adolescence, before the days of misfortune come, before the years arrive of which you will say, 'I no longer take any pleasure in them'" (12:1, JE). We must not dismiss this questioning too simplistically. "Remember your Creator," rather than "adore him," "serve him," "obey him," etc. Our passage begins simply, with this simple call from God: "Remember." Such a beginning reminds us that this God does not impose himself on us. He does not crush our humanity with his revelation. He is utterly discreet: "Remember." You can forget him, cast him aside, fail to concern yourself with him. He will not come to you, enraged and threatening, making you take him into account or bend your knees, filling your view or obliging you to obey him. No. He remains hidden and patient. "I stand at the door and knock" (Rev. 3:20), he says—no more.

Remember. All he asks is that you grant him a place in your present memory, instead of leaving him in an old, unused place, like some statue or idol, an inadequate image covered with dust. Remember him. It is worthwhile that we keep him in our memory, remembering what he has done for us, remembering he is there, discreetly present, in the shadows. He remains in a silence that is broken only by a call from someone who speaks in his name.

"Remember, Israel. . . ." How many times did this God ask Israel to remember all his goodness and grace, all the moments *in the past* when he delivered them and revealed himself to them! But he does not waste these vainly. So we must refer to these events, find them again in our memory; this is our first act, when we listen to him silently. But to do this we must not let too many activities invade our lives.

Remember your Creator. Only here does Qohelet call him by this name,[48] and he does so by design! In the pride of your youth, remember that you are a creature. This constitutes a decisive reality. You are a creature rather than a creator. As a creature you have an origin that made your being what it is. You are not the beginning of everything. It is essential that this be recalled for the young person, who always believes he is beginning everything all over again.

Nor did you enter the world and consciousness by means of an utterly natural event, through birth and then an education, both of which would be self-explanatory. No, you appeared in the midst of a creation where you are a creature yourself. Thus you are not the master of everything, free to do whatever you like with yourself and the creation. It is especially important to realize you are not the creator of the world! It exists independent of you. In that you are a creature, just like the world, the animals, and everything else, you cannot treat the creation however you choose, depending on your whim, your power, and your pride. During your youth, when you are at the peak of your strength and glory, you have a Creator. This fact constitutes the true limit to your audacious determination to be master of everything. You have a relationship with the One who is the origin and source of life.

You are a creature, so that certain achievements are expected of you. Certain paths are open to you, but others remain closed. Your future awaits you, but some of its possibilities are forbidden. As a creature, you need to make your Creator your reference point, listening to him and glancing at him to discover his intentions. You are free, but neither independent nor autonomous. You do not have "your law within you," and in spite of your claims, you know neither good nor evil. By yourself, you cannot distinguish your right hand from your left (Jonah 4:11). This brings us to the heart of Qohelet:

48. This leads some commentators to eliminate the text, asserting that Qohelet "never" speaks of the Creator (see Barucq, p. 186)!

"I applied myself to considering what wisdom is and what folly is" (Eccl. 2:12, JE). This activity turns out to be vanity and a chasing after wind. You may consider yourself autonomous, but you are incapable of knowing what should be done, incapable of knowing what wisdom is. You are a creature.

Conversely, you are not the Creator. It is fine for you to take joy or pride in doing many things, but these in no way constitute a creation. Here as well, we find ourselves at the heart of Qohelet: "What is, has been already" (3:15, JE). You imagine that you are creating something, but not so! You develop things, using riches that were placed at your disposal. You open pathways that were already open. You create nothing. You are not the Creator.

Our problems do not stem from our failure to stay in our garden, like Candide. All the evils, and I choose my words carefully, *all the evils of the world* stem from our taking ourselves to be the Creator. Some, as warriors, transform the planet through their flashing conquests. Others, as dictators, shape a society. But the image always remains the same: a hand that molds a shapeless hunk of clay. We give glory to the creator of a state, a new order, or an empire, but also to the scientist who takes himself for the Creator—even though he inevitably ends up with the atomic bomb. Every time you take yourself to be a creator (even as an artist!), you become a destroyer, an annihilator. Every human work created in silence, discretion, and humility (in the image of the Creator, who works incognito!) is positive, useful, and life-giving. Every work of power, in which a person takes himself for a creator, becomes a work of emptiness that produces emptiness. So we come back to our necessary finiteness, one of the things Qohelet tries to teach us.

This two-edged recall—that one has a Creator and that one is a creature—must take place during one's youth, in the days of one's adolescence (12:1). Emphasizing the importance of this timing, Qohelet repeats here what he had already said in 11:9. I see two main themes in his challenge: (1) this recollection must come during the time of youth, with its blossoming of happiness and pleasure, when the development of one's strength is in full sway, when one is experiencing the glory of youth. We must remember in the midst of our happiness, joy, health, and strength, but our recollection will not express itself by repressing this strength and joy. Instead, our remembering will point us to the Creator. We simply need to recognize that all these things constitute a gift from him. While you are in your glory, turn your glorious face toward the one who created you! All your happiness comes from him. Next you will find praise on your lips: thanksgiving and a hymn to God's joy in you. That is all the Creator expects of us!

After your youth, it will be too late—when you begin suffering from old age and illness, and when the shadow of death starts to cover you. Unfortunately, this is the moment we choose to remember our Creator! What do we have to say then? We lament our fate, we beg because the past has gone and the future looks bleak. We pray because we are afraid. We need to turn toward God before the time comes when we say "I no longer have any pleasure in them" (12:1, JE). We must remember him in our youth, so that we can offer him a face radiant with joy, so that our prayer is a glorious giving of thanks, not a sterile lament!

It is false to say we turn toward our Creator when we take no more pleasure in life. We no longer make reference to God—only to our fear of suffering and death, so that God becomes opium or compensation, like an artificial limb. He becomes our "last resort" (rather than our hope). This is not the free God of joy and fulness, the God of Abraham, Moses, and Jesus Christ.

We must take special care to avoid understanding Qohelet's words, "Remember your Creator during your youth" (12:1, JE), as a threatening warning about salvation. We must not interpret his words to mean "Speak to God while you still have time; soon it will be too late, since you are headed for damnation." Our text says nothing like this! It would be absurd for Qohelet to say "You are coming under judgment; look out for condemnation!" The text has often been interpreted in this way because of our obsession with individual salvation. As in other contexts, this preoccupation blurs the clarity of God's revelation to us.

(2) The second theme in Qohelet's challenge involves the possibilities of youth. Remember your Creator during your youth: when all possibilities lie open before you and you can offer all your strength intact for his service. The time to remember is not after you

become senile and paralyzed! Then it is not too late for your salvation, but too late for you to serve as the presence of God in the midst of the world and the creation. You must take sides earlier—when you can actually make choices, when you have many paths opening at your feet, before the weight of necessity overwhelms you.

So we find Qohelet's whole teaching again in this last chapter: there is a time when choices are possible. A time when you can decide which favorable moment to choose. In other books (on politics), I have called this the "situation that is still fluid." Later the time comes when situations freeze, when determinism takes rigid control of everything. Then you no longer have a choice, and you are obliged to obey necessity.

For this reason we must remember the Creator in our youth, and in the youth of each thing: situations, societies, associations, cultures, political relations, and churches! In each beginning, strength remains intact and can be committed to the work. You can commit your efforts to many activities and works: you can waste them in war, revolution, sexuality, or dissipation. So remember this possibility of committing your efforts to the service of the Creator, for the good of the creation, and for your own good. Your strength is intact and can truly serve this creation, and you will open up a place for the Kingdom of heaven. You will bring a New God to the place where you are. But for this you need the strength of your youth, before it is worn down and dissipated by bad times. Then nothing will give you pleasure any more!

This is what I see in the first verse of Qohelet's grand finale. Here is my translation of the rest of his admirable poem:

2   Before the sun becomes dim,
     and the light, the moon, and the stars,
     before the clouds return after the rain;
3   on the day when the guardians of the house will tremble,
     when strong men will be bent down,
     when the grinders will stop,
     because they are too few,
     when those (women) who look out from the windows will
       grow dim,

4   when both doors to the street will be closed,
     on the day when the sound of the mill fades away,
     when one gets up to the cry of the sparrow,
     when all songs grow faint;
5   and also one is afraid of heights.
     He will find terrors in the way;
     when the almond tree blossoms,
     the grasshopper becomes weighed down,
     and the caper loses its effect,
     for a person is going toward his eternal home
     and the mourners go about in the streets;
6   before the silver cord comes undone,
     or the golden bowl is shattered,
     or the pitcher is broken at the fountain,
     or the pulley at the cistern is broken;
7   before the dust returns to the earth
     as it was,
     and the breath returns to God
     who gave it.
8   Vanity of vanities, Qohelet said,
     all is vanity.

Obviously, we have here a poem on old age and the end of life as it moves toward death. These words complete the thought of "before the years arrive of which you will say, 'I no longer have any pleasure in them'" (v. 1, JE). But, having made this trite observation, we have not said all there is to say. I believe the poet always says more than he writes, so that his meaning spills over beyond the words we read. His poem speaks to us through our emotional response to its beauty. In their usual ingenious fashion, commentators have struggled to find allegories in the above passage, making it into a sort of euphuistic poem before euphuism became popular.

One explanation finally won nearly everyone over: that this poem is a minute description of an elderly person: the "growing dark" (v. 3) signifies that he is going blind. The "grinders" are the teeth he has lost. The watchmen or "guardians of the house" (v. 2) may be his arms. The sound that fades away (v. 4) means he is growing deaf. The caper is said to lose its effect because it serves as an aphrodisiac, and the elderly person can no longer engage in sexual activity (v. 5; see Podechard, pp. 464-66, and Steinmann, p. 114).

There have been many other allegorical interpretations, however. According to the Midrash Rabbah, this poem deals with the temple of Jerusalem, the Torah, the servants of the temple, its furniture, the sacred lamps, etc.—a religious meaning (see Barucq, pp. 187-92). Some have seen this text as a description of a storm, an expression of the Creator's power. Others have seen in it the close of the day and the beginning of night. Still others, the decadence and collapse of a political state. But everyone reads this passage like an enigma for which we must find the allegorical meaning of each term.

I feel that this approach leads us down the wrong track.[49] I think the poem is too vast for this, and too "polysemous," to use the word presently in vogue. It is *first of all* a poem! In other words, it is not at all the exposition of a problem to solve, nor is it a riddle whose terms we need to transpose. First of all we must let the beauty of the text grip us, as we listen to it in silence, like music. We should let the poem strike our emotions first, and allow our sensitivity and imagination to speak before we try to analyze and "understand" it. Above all we must not try to examine each image, each term, as if it referred to some commonplace reality.

As I read this poem, from "the days of misfortune when you will no longer have any pleasure" (12:1, JE) to "Vanity of vanities" (12:8), it calls to mind all declines, all breaches, closures, and endings. Not just the decline of an individual nearing death, not just human destiny, but everything: the end of any work which is no longer done, which disappears because no one is present to do it any more and be responsible for it: the end of a village or a community whose members leave; the end of a project that will never be finished; the end of a love replaced by fear; the end of an art, its works shattered, unless they die in our museums, deprived

49. I was pleased to find Lauha thinks as I do on this point. He believes we must not interpret this poem allegorically, and that Qohelet's style does not include allegory (except, he says, for 12:3-4; p. 207).

of their place and their meaning; the end of nature, deprived of its force; the end of a civilization. It is the song of the End. It goes far beyond Poe's "nevermore." And, naturally, this end of everything leads to the end of humanity, the center of creation—but as one end among all the others.

In the heart of Qohelet's great cry, however, we find notes of hope remaining. These are slipped in surreptitiously (and have given headaches to exegetes, as they tried to make the hopeful notes fit in with the rest of the text. But Qohelet has accustomed us to such brief contradictions!). We have birds singing, after all (12:4). This passage always reminds me of the Romain Gary phrase quoted earlier. Concerning the atomic bomb, he said: "Boss, that won't keep the nightingale from singing." We also find the almond tree in flower,[50] and we know the almond tree symbolizes hope and gratitude, vigilance and activity. In Hebrew, "almond tree" *(shaqed)* is almost identical with "watchman" *(shoqed)*. Everyone has noticed this in Jeremiah (1:11). When the prophet says he sees an almond branch, God answers: "You have seen well, for I am watching over my word to perform it" (Jer. 1:12, RSV). Thus, in the center of this end, this desolation, we find God's promise that he will pursue the execution of his word!

We also find the grasshopper weighed down in this poem (Eccl. 12:5). Normally the grasshopper devours and devastates, a perpetual scourge. But in the middle of all the other images here at the end of Qohelet, we come upon this announcement: all plagues will not be loosed; the grasshopper will no longer lay waste the earth. In this context as well, how could we avoid recalling all the passages where the grasshopper or locust is sent as God's judgment? We have to admit that Qohelet is a better poet than we are, and that he offers us a revelation more subtle than we are! He interlaces all these final images with subtle suggestions of hope, like arrows that draw our gaze toward a different end!

At this point as well, I am reminded of a modern example. Most of F. Fellini's films seem like Qohelet, with all their darkness and

---

50. 12:5. In reality, it seems strange to take the radiant sign of spring and the promise of fruit as a symbol of old age.

ruthless denunciation. But right in the middle of his films we *always* find a sequence that testifies to hope, life, faith, God's presence, and opening up. Fellini keeps this sequence brief, but the entire film is actually organized around its decisive message. In a similar way, Qohelet's metaphors of hope modulate his great song about the end.

Qohelet's poem deals with the end of humanity rather than with the end of a person. Here the exegetes generally agree in finding the judgment of God in this context to be eschatological rather than individual. Why would we see the death of a single person here? The challenge "Remember your Creator during your youth" (12:1, JE) is addressed to everyone, including a body of people or an institution. We can conclude, then, that all is vanity in this confrontation with death that in reality concerns the Whole.

Qohelet's final statement, however, deals with humanity alone: "Before the dust returns to the earth as it was, and the breath returns to God who gave it" (12:7). This text calls Genesis 2 and 3 to mind: dust. Our first reaction to this word involves only the fact of our organism's dissolution: what remains is dust, ordinary earth, *unimportant* matter. Based on it, we have funeral ceremonies, magnificent tombs, funeral parlors, cemeteries, the Day of the Dead, dead people coming back, the worship of the dead, etc. All these things are worthless.

Still, we find the word "dust" bothersome, since Qohelet knows perfectly well that putrefaction does not actually end up as "dust." We naturally think again here of Nothomb's distinction between dust (lightness) and earth (heaviness; pp. 37-59). But our text states clearly that "the dust returns to the earth as it was" (12:7). This statement inevitably proves awkward for Nothomb, who simply declares that by Qohelet's time people no longer understood the original, deep meaning of the Genesis text, and confused dust with earth (p. 169n. 19). I feel Nothomb dismisses this problem too hastily.

In discussing the Genesis text, however, Nothomb states that human beings were dust (lightness) *out of* the earth (*'adamah;* pp. 37-38). Even for Nothomb, therefore, dust was drawn from the earth, so it participated in the earth—just as lightness exists only as a function of, and on the basis of, heaviness. Thus it does not seem extraordinary that dust should return to the earth, as it was. When life has ended, lightness also comes to an end; what remains is the heaviness of death and the earth.[51] All that remains is the Breath of God that had made his human creature a living soul. The essential thing is not what the creature is made of, but what comes from God in him. There is no question of a soul here, however; Qohelet does not foretell the immortality of the soul or the resurrection.

At this point we find ourselves involved with the ambiguity of the word *ruah:* wind, breath, breath of life, or spirit. All exegetes agree in rejecting "spirit" as a possible meaning in this context. At most, they say, the word could mean "vital breath," or "life breath." But I fail to grasp the reason for the bitterness of this controversy, unless it simply stems from party spirit. In reality, it fits well with what we read in Genesis 2 for the breath of life,[52] which God breathed into his creature, to return to him.

In reality, this "breath," which was *nishmat* in Genesis 2, has

51. At this point I disagree utterly with Nothomb, who makes this original dust into a promise of immortality (pp. 41-45, 50-57). He believes that if dust is primeval lightness that belongs only to humanity, the "return to dust" would not signify ending up in nothingness, but a promise of immortality. But we must remember that God's breath does not remain with this "dust." And as Christians we must ask ourselves what meaning the resurrection would have if Nothomb were right!

52. We have noted that Qohelet takes his inspiration from Gen. 2:7. But the word usually translated "breath of life" in that verse *(nishmat hayyim)* differs from the word Qohelet uses in 12:7 *(ruah).* Nothomb has trouble with the word used in Genesis (if the dust guarantees immortality, what is the point of this breath of life? See pp. 62-66). By means of a clever exegesis of *nishmat/neshamah,* he arrives at the conclusion that it means "consciousness." So, with *hayyim,* the idea would be "consciousness of existence." Nothomb fails to convince me, for nothing in the other eight biblical texts with this expression would cause us to arrive at his meaning. I disagree with Nothomb especially because it seems to me that the human being becomes a living person with the gift of the *nishmat.* It is not his simple "consciousness" that gives him life, it is this breath. Qohelet surely goes beyond Genesis by preferring *ruah* to *nishmat,* but I believe he has in no way distorted his source. The "lightness" of the living human being disappears at his death, and everything that made up his life is taken to God by the spirit. Not only one's "consciousness of being" returns to God; what would such a statement mean?

become *ruah* (spirit!) in Ecclesiastes 12. But how do the two differ, basically? We must try to deal seriously with this problem. This breath is the very breath of the Creator, since it makes a person a living being. And God the Creator is himself called the Living One. How could this life that he transmits to humanity be anything but the life that comes from him (and, as we have observed, this is what makes the problem of animal life so acute!)? If we are talking about the life that comes from the Living One, what distinction can we make between the breath of life and the spirit?[53]

The spirit is not some vague "spiritualist" evanescence. The spirit is what makes us fully alive. It makes human history and creativity possible. The spirit makes relationships possible (thus the dead body has no further relationship with anyone, after the spirit has left it). This depends precisely on the breath of life, not on some vague supplement. Exegetes confirm this point of view indirectly when they insist in our day on the fact that human beings are not composites. We are not a heterogeneous amalgam of body, soul, and spirit, they say, but rather a perfect unity, so that our spirit is body. The body is also spirit, with no break between them. If this is true, so that the break between them signifies the end of a person, then spirit or breath of life has no meaning (unless we resort to philo-sophical spiritualism). "Spirit" means something only if we look at it concretely, that is, spirit as what gives and maintains life. At the moment of death, this spirit returns to the eternally Living One.[54]

53. Identifying "breath of life" with "spirit" rules out the question of retribution, and makes human beings like animals on the ontological level, by denying life after death *to one part of the being* (Lys, p. 402). Lys is right to add that since Qohelet "speaks of 'breath' rather than 'soul,' some have thought that, if he was attacking the Greek doctrine of immortality, he misunderstood it. I tend to believe, on the contrary, that he knows very well what he is talking about, but plays with it ironically, . . . reducing *nephesh* in another passage to appetite and desire, and using *ruah*, the term common to humanity and God, here in this context, to show the similarity between human beings and animals" (pp. 402-3).

54. Here again we can see how skilled Hebrew technique by itself is not enough for explaining a text. For Lauha, for example, this phrase means merely "the end of the human personality" (p. 215).

Most importantly, however, it seems to me, this spirit, the equivalent of life, is no abstraction. Our entire, very concrete Bible speaks of life as a historical reality (rather than as something metaphysical or merely biological). The spirit changes during the course of a lifetime. This implies that what returns to God is not identical with what he gave: this "spirit" takes on a whole history in the course of life—all life's adventures, feelings, fears, suffering, hopes, faith or lack of faith, etc. What returns to God is a spirit fitted out with a person's whole known or hidden history.[55] What remains in the dust, then, no longer amounts to anything; but what a person has lived is never lost. True, this life and its history are just vanity, a chasing after wind—*almost* nothing (but *almost*). God takes up this "almost nothing," however, and accepts it when he gathers to himself the spirit of the person to whom he gave it. The spirit or breath is also "almost nothing," but an "almost nothing" that belongs to God. In this we see grace.

Jesus confirms this in his interview with Nicodemus (John 3), and when he speaks of "spirit and life." When he says to his disciples that the only possibility of life lies in communion with him, they respond: "This saying is hard; who can listen to it?" (John 6:60, JE). Jesus answers them, "The words that I have spoken to you are Spirit and Life" (6:63, JE). Spirit and life are indissolubly linked. Finally, at the moment when he submits himself fully to the human finite condition, Jesus says: "Father, I commit *my spirit* into your hands" (Luke 23:46, JE). He makes no distinction between the spirit as breath of life and the Holy Spirit that sustained him.

Thus to me the debate seems futile. In reality, Qohelet states clearly that a person's vital force returns to God, the Living One. That is, the person enters into the fulness of life, with everything

---

55. At last we find what distinguishes us from the animals! Ontologically, they have the same breath of life, and are identical. The only difference, as Qohelet observes, is that human beings know they are mortal, whereas animals do not. But this difference means that human beings have a history and are a history. Not so animals. Human beings elaborate their breath of life with a work they undertake, but animals do not. The breath of life of both returns to God, but ours is different from what he gave us. And God is "enriched" by this human work!

that his life has been. The breath brings with it the entire history of that particular, unique person who has lived his life in God's presence.

But Qohelet forbids us to go beyond this point, and his conclusion brings everything back to vanity. He does not say that the breath that returns to God is vanity, however! We just need to remember that he firmly and continually places himself "under the sun." Under the sun, the breath of life has gone. The work stands shattered and the story has ended. You cannot add anything more to it, change it, or preserve anything else in it. What remains *under the sun* is dust that has returned to dust. So the final balance or profit is zero: vanity. Therefore, young person on the threshold of life, think about this Creator to whom you will return, before everything in your life becomes vanity.

Thus Qohelet speaks to us in all his profundity when he shows how we find ourselves "cornered" between the vanity of the past as the elderly person contemplates it, and the life a young person has ahead of him. Let us return to Kierkegaard one last time: "Humor is always a recalling . . . , it is the backward perspective; Christianity is the forward direction towards becoming a Christian, and towards becoming such by continuing to be such. Without a standstill no humor. . . . Christianity has no room for sadness: it is salvation or perdition. Salvation lies ahead; perdition behind—for everyone who turns back, whatever it is he sees. . . . Christianly understood, to look back—even though one were to get a sight of childhood's charming, enchanting landscape—is perdition" (*Concluding Unscientific Postscript,* p. 533).

"End of the discourse. Having heard everything, fear God, and observe his commandment, for that is the whole person [everything for the person]. For God will bring into judgment every work, concerning everything that is hidden. Whether it is good or evil" (Eccl. 12:13-14, JE).[56] Classical exegetes often looked down on this

---

56. I was very pleased to find my intuitive observations on ch. 12 combined with a solid exegetical study in Chopineau (pp. 152-60). He shows that this chapter is actually a "thematic review" of the entire book, rather than a pious conclusion. As far as form is concerned this chapter repeats the

little appendix as the work of an editor who appears to express mere
platitudes. Many scholars have given scarce attention to this passage. Their approach surprises me, for I find this ending has terrible
force: "End of the discourse; all is heard" (12:13, JE). This "all is
heard" can have two meanings: (1) God has heard everything.
Everything we have said has been heard and collected (for you will
be judged by your words; see Matt. 12:37).[57]

---

expressions characteristic of the book as a whole. Concerning content,
Chopineau finds this chapter's intentional oppositions to be not contradictions
but an extension of Qohelet's typical argument. In addition, I found in
Chopineau two essential explanations I had not come across elsewhere: "All
is heard" (12:13, JE) is the precise counterpart of the constantly repeated "all
is forgotten." All is forgotten by humanity, but it has been heard! The second
observation is even more important and involves a passage I had not com-
mented on: "The words of sages are like goads . . . they are given by a single
shepherd" (12:11). I must admit that I spontaneously wanted to understand this
term as a reference to God, and therefore to his revelation to Qohelet. But I
considered this interpretation somewhat uncertain, and did not dare risk
mentioning it. Chopineau, however, demonstrates clearly that the word used
here, *ro'eh 'ehad,* can indicate only God, and that the Midrash interpreted it in
this way (connecting this passage with Ps. 80:1: "O Shepherd of Israel, hear").
A single Shepherd: God as One, whose very existence precludes the possibility
of universal nothingness. Furthermore, a subtle link ties everything together:
this shepherd refers us back to Abel *(hebel),* who was also a shepherd. But
Qohelet opposes that shepherd of vanity to the true Shepherd, whose Name is
One. This term "single Shepherd" is in reality the opposite of *hebel.* The word
"shepherd" was also applied to the king, so that it could also point to Solomon.
So just as Qohelet is constructed around the theme of *hebel,* the epilogue's
answer culminates in this expression *ro'eh 'ehad.* God as Shepherd gives the
commandments we must observe because this constitutes the whole person.
See also Philippe de Robert, *Le Berger d'Israël: Essai sur le thème pastoral
dans l'Ancien Testament,* Cahiers Théologiques 57 (Neuchâtel: Delachaux &
Niestlé, 1968).

57. Neher has developed this idea in a remarkable way. The thing heard
is the voice of the blood of Abel. Cain is the equivalent of Abel, but Seth
replaces Abel. We are all descended from Seth, and this humanity exists only
because God heard. When Qohelet asked "What is left?," the answer is that
there is nothing remaining for Abel or Cain. But "our humanity constitutes the
only remainder, and that is just what we are: all of us are survivors. The history
of humanity is a residue."

(2) But the passage also indicates the continuation of a clear-minded, negative judgment. This means we cannot go beyond Qohelet, in human terms. He has said everything. He has put everything through the mill: our discourses on human life, on the confidence we should place in humanity (all our innumerable proclamations about having faith in humanity!), etc. He has judged all this and nothing has stood the test. "End of the discourse," not because the sage considers his book finished, but because there is nothing left—nothing of human grandeur. So we find ourselves at *Finis Terrae,* Land's End.[58] Everything has been heard—what remains is empty, useless words. Qohelet has just warned us to beware of too many books (12:12).

In the immediately preceding verses, we encountered again that terrible sense of humor, in a statement about Qohelet's work. Having heard and examined many things, he is said to have worked at finding "pleasant" or "attractive" words (12:9-10). What an enormous joke, to describe the most disconcerting, abrasive, harsh, unpleasant work of all in such terms! Qohelet is transformed into a court poet or fashionable philosopher!

Everything has been heard: "the cause has been heard." The process or trial has ended. And since there is no human gain left over, we have only one thing we can count on as certain: the fear of God and observing his commandment. We have already suggested an initial approach to this fear of God. Now we need to go farther: this fear of God first of all implies an encounter with God. He is presence and not absence. He is an astonishing God because it is said of him that he is all-powerful and terrible, on the one hand (so our fear comes naturally!), yet also, on the other hand, he is the one who forgives.

He pardons so that he may be feared (Ps. 130:4). Remarkably, forgiveness leads to fear. We find this same relationship in the Gospels: the Gerasenes, frightened because Jesus healed an insane person (Mark 5:1-20); the disciples filled with fear because he forgave sins. Here we note an ambivalence: on the one hand, we

---

58. Here I allude to a very fine unpublished book by Bernard Charbonneau, *Finis Terrae, vue d'un Finistère.*

fear this God because he carries everything out, forever, and we can in no way alter his work (Eccl. 3:14). On the other hand, we fear this God because he gathers up the human spirit of life, our very life, and has not left us abandoned or without guidance. On the contrary, he has given us his commandment, his word!

We are not to keep his word in a meticulous and abstract manner, however! Fearing God means living in his presence. We remain ignorant, of course, of his ultimate being, recognizing that this mystery cannot be clarified to our minds. But at the same time we recognize it as a desirable mystery, because the fear of God eliminates all other fears, thus becoming a source of confidence and new joy for us. In J. Lacan's wonderful words, "this famous fear of God accomplishes a sleight-of-hand feat, transforming all fears into perfect courage, in an instant. All fears—'I have no other fear' [except offending the Lord]—are exchanged for what is called the fear of God. However constraining it may be, it is the opposite of fear"![59]

Consequently, *this* fear constitutes the point of departure for a different relationship with God. Jean L'Hour shows that this fear is the response to God's first, basic initiative.[60] God creates the covenant, and fear consists of recognizing that he is in effect the absolute sovereign. The sphere of this fear "includes all of existence and . . . the 'heart' is its special place. . . . 'Fearing Yahweh' . . . means *accepting* his sovereignty. . . . it means *wanting* his sovereignty, in a concrete way. And this fear is inevitably associated with love: 'Love in fear and fear in love': they are inseparable." In reality, the fear of God recognizes this God as the absolute "Thou," the possibility of genuine dialogue. Fear of him establishes ethics, which immediately become religious. "Fear God *and* observe his commandments" (Eccl. 12:13): but we do not have *two* dispositions here, since fearing God *is* observing all his commandments (Deut. 5:29)! What does Yahweh your God require of you? That you fear Yahweh *by walking* in all his ways, *keeping* his commandments

59. Marc Leclerc, "Jacques Lacan: Fondation, psychanalyse, psychanalyse institutionnelle," *Inter-Dit,* no. 12 (Spring 1985), p. 31.

60. Jean L'Hour, *La Morale de l'Alliance,* 2nd impression (Paris: Cerf, 1985). Quotations are from p. 34.

(Deut. 28:9). So this fear does not amount to a mere feeling. It is not terror, but a source of joy as we recognize that God's will for our lives is good and true!

One final note. These simple words, "Fear God, observe his commandments" (Eccl. 12:13), help confirm the hypothesis that Qohelet wrote to attack Greek philosophy. When he affirms that "the whole person" lies in these admonitions (12:13), he proclaims the opposite of philosophy. Philosophy progresses without taking into account the subjective attitudes of the subject or author. It stakes out its path in *terra incognita*. It takes only intelligence, reason, experience, method, and observation as guides. What counts is the consistency of the argument, its identification of hypotheses, and its relationship with reality. Philosophy must march unerringly toward truth. It cannot begin by admitting intangible, unfounded precepts.

Qohelet does just what philosophy cannot do, as he begins with certain precepts: on the one hand, if you want to live without vanity, you must adopt a certain attitude of life—fear and respect. But the philosopher cannot approach something with predetermined respect. He should not follow the dictates of any fear! Furthermore, Qohelet claims that if you want to be a coherent totality, a complete person, you must obey God's commandments. On the basis of these you can be both free and intelligent, as you cease your madness and your vain questions. The commandments are the absolute precondition of all truly human processes. We could not find a more antiphilosophical declaration than this! Obeying the commandment enables us both to live and to understand.

Observing the commandment and listening to the word do not signify staying within the bounds of a rigid law. Rather, they mean remembering that God gives and liberates. He gives us the possibility of living. To repeat again what Barth says, the commandment is precisely the line traced between life and death. Transgressing this word does not constitute carefree liberation from a narrow, petty moral code. Instead, such transgression constitutes entering the domain of Death.

For this reason Qohelet calmly declares that the whole person lies here (12:13)—or everything for a person. So the human being (Qohelet uses the word also used for Adam's name—*'adam*) is opposed to vanity! Everything is vanity in this book, but it concludes with "everything for the person," after the author has finished his exploration of works reduced to vanity. Just when we thought nothing was left, Qohelet tells us what remains: "the whole person consists of this fear and this listening."

Here our author flies in the face of our strongest conviction! Whether Christians or Jews, we are all convinced that it is fine to obey the commandments, but those who do this are people who exist on their own. We accept our need to seek God's will, love him, have faith, etc. But we find no need to mention the obvious fact: that the person who does these things exists, has life in himself, and would be autonomous if he wanted to be, although he also, of course, should obey God's will. In other words, we believe a person exists, even if he fails to obey God. He possesses a reality, a life.

So we think the law, the commandment, and the love of God constitute a sort of small supplement to our life. They add something to life. We move quickly from this stance to considering obedience as something optional. In the final analysis, observing God's commands or worshiping him becomes a kind of extra decoration on our well-lived, well-decked-out life—like music or other accomplishments.

Qohelet proves solidly radical, however: *Nothing remains.* All is vanity, smoke, mist, or cloud. And in this vanishing, this shifting sand that constitutes our life, only one thing remains: "Fear God, listen to his word." This is the only fixed, stable point. All of the person is reduced to this—all; that is, *apart from this, a person is nothing.* In himself, he also amounts to a breath, like Abel. We find no compromises here, no gray areas. The thing that gives us existence, truth, and reality, the thing that suddenly creates us, is our relationship with God. This relationship constitutes the whole person, since stripping him of it leaves him with nothing else: we found that everything else was vanity.[61]

61. I was finishing the writing of this book when I picked up a book by Jacques Monod, for an entirely different purpose. I stumbled by chance on the following sentence: "man knows at last that he is alone in the universe's unfeeling immensity. . . . His destiny is nowhere spelled out, nor is his duty"

This relationship has two aspects, however: it entails fear and respect of God, and also (free!) obedience to his Word. Obedience does not contradict freedom. Here we have a factor we must not neglect, one that is typical of Qohelet. He has continually demonstrated an utterly independent spirit, eliminating every taboo, criticizing all moral codes and traditional doctrines, transgressing all

---

(*Chance and Necessity: An Essay on the Natural Philosophy of Modern Biology* [New York: Knopf, 1971], p. 180). I was gripped as I became aware of the presumptuous naïveté of "philosophy" as presented by many scientists! After all, if Monod had read and reflected on Qohelet, he could have spared himself this romantic platitude. We have no need of a pseudoscientific demonstration by Monod to learn that neither destiny nor duty is written anywhere a priori. Qohelet is a good witness, but he is not the only one! Arguments drawn from physics or biology do not add an ounce of certainty to this profound knowledge. In reality, Monod takes his stand in a three-thousand-year-old debate, without resolving anything. The Bible, among other books, rules out the possibility of a "duty" written in advance somewhere! But Monod, filled with the pride of science, proclaims that we have just learned this. Thus he displays his own ignorance, combating a theology and philosophy that had their moment of glory and certainty, but were surpassed long ago. As for claiming that "we *now* know that humanity is alone in the world," Monod could have taken a lesson in humility from Qohelet, who shows things are not quite so simple! If Monod means (1) that we do not find other people anywhere in the galaxies, and that E.T. is a farce, we have no need of science to discover that. If he means (2) that human beings are unique in the living world, I find Qohelet more profound when he establishes the relationship of human beings and animals. But if, as seems probable, Monod means (3) that God does not exist, he has fallen into the trap of "proving" the nonexistence of God, and cannot extricate himself. This is the false question par excellence. If Monod had read Qohelet, he could have learned there that it is precisely God's presence that attests to our uniqueness and solitude. If God does not exist, we can only try to come out of our solitude by creating imaginary interlocutors for ourselves. This is precisely what Monod does when he hypostatizes chance! But if we are, after all, to read Monod's phrase (4) emphasizing his "now know," it amounts to another platitude, meaning that all this is a matter of opinion. Formerly, humanity was convinced that the universe was filled with gods; now humanity is convinced that there is no one else. One opinion is as good as the other. Qohelet tells us this is a searching after wind! We must accept Qohelet's sifting if we are to avoid romantic statements like Monod's, which sound good and may move us, but mean nothing.

the established orders that surrounded him. Yet he ends up with what seems utterly traditional and archaic: obeying the commandments. Qohelet has placed us at the heart of the entire biblical revelation, however: the identification of obedience with freedom.

Two models of this identification will help: (1) The founding book of the Hebrew people is Exodus. God is first of all the God who liberates. This liberated people will exercise their freedom in the desert and will experience the difficulties of this life (hunger, thirst, plundering). They arrive at Sinai, where God gives his law and commands. Is there a contradiction here? Has this God who liberates become a God who enslaves? Far from it! The commandment is a confirmation of freedom. The commandment is the limit, the borderline within which life and freedom are possible. Beyond, there is death, and consequently absolute determinism. This is as true theologically as it is in experience. But in order for the commandment to work this way, it must be received by a *liberated* person or people, so that obedience is the fruit of freedom. Obedience is not submission, absurdity, spinelessness, or weariness. The commandment gives life when it encounters free, joyful assent.

(2) Jesus, the very example of obedience, furnishes our other model. He obeys the Torah and the project his Father fashioned for him, as well as whatever *hic et nunc* injunctions God may give him. Jesus obeys in everything until death. Yet he seems like the free man par excellence: free with respect to laws, tradition, authorities, prohibitions, human relationships, propriety, money, obvious facts, physical limitations—he is free in every way. When he obeys, he gives the highest expression to this freedom. He chooses constantly to obey. He could have disobeyed constantly; he could have yielded to one of his temptations; he could have taken the Father's glory for himself, escaped death, or become a political leader. Fully conscious of his freedom, he chose to obey everything that the incarnation entailed. Thus, for Qohelet, the spirit of freedom in no way contradicts biblical thought, when he repeats that all of a person (including his liberty, therefore!) comes down to observing God's commandments.

This recommendation of obedience reveals a final aspect of Qohelet. He has criticized everything, but when he sends his readers back in this way to God's precepts, he refers them to the entire Bible, especially the Pentateuch. In reality, Qohelet itself contains no "commandments." The author does not say "Follow *my* precepts." He offers us a meditation on God and humanity. But when he sends us back to the commandments, he clearly intends to place himself again within Jewish faith and piety. And he places his own book in a secondary position with respect to the ones that formulate the commandments.

Fear of God and obedience to his Word can make us something besides a vain breath! Our entire person is located between these two poles. I call them "poles" because they do not constitute a single, simple way of expressing life, with each attitude prolonging the other. "Fear-respect" and "listening-obedience" form two poles between which the truth and being of a person burst forth. Thus they constitute the whole of the person. Without them, we are not a totality, but a cork floating on a choppy current. We are a disjointed succession of moments: first one thing and then another. Nothing organizes all this into a whole. We are victims of the very things we take credit for: our successive moments of sincerity, our contradictory commitments, and the insistent assertions that we deny a day later. In Qohelet's terms, we take folly or madness for freedom, independence, and affirmation of the self, a "self" that simply does not exist.

We begin to have some consistency and truth when we place ourselves between the two poles. The one pole is the only thing that can put us into relationship with the Living One, and the other causes us to listen to the Word, which both gives life and teaches us a possible way to live. This constitutes the whole person, and everything for a person. Everything else, as we have seen, has been sifted, and nothing separates this vanity from death and nonexistence.

Qohelet, as a witness to this word, has served as a goad to bring the reader to the point where he recognizes that things are this way and not otherwise—that this process of stripping away our illusions is the only way. For as long as we have illusions, we cannot acknowledge that this "fear-respect" and this "listening-obedience" to the word are everything for us.

We should perhaps note at this point the contrast between Hinduism, for which all reality is an illusion *(maya),* and which defines the good as detachment in itself, and Qohelet. His objective is different, so that this stripping away and disillusionment do not constitute the last word or true spirituality. These processes merely prepare for the possibility of being placed in relationship with God.

Similarly, Qohelet's "all is vanity" may seem to find an echo in Goethe's profound "Alles Vergängliche ist nur ein Gleichnis": everything that happens (but this word also has Qohelet's meaning of "everything perishable, short-lived, or ephemeral") is just an allegory: a parable, semblance, or comparison. Indeed, Goethe's words shed light on Qohelet's vanity of vanities. Everything perishable is an allegory of what is not perishable, and refers us back to the model on which the comparison or resemblance was based. Thus we add another link to our chain: this immense vanity serves as an allegory of the Living One and his Word. We have reached the end of the road.

Judgment has the last word in Qohelet, however. God will bring all works, good and bad, into judgment—everything that is hidden: "For God will bring into judgment every work, the good and the bad, everything that is hidden" (12:14, JE). This little statement deserves our attention one last time. We must not assume too quickly that we have understood it: "Yes, yes, we know! The judgment of humanity is proclaimed here. After this long meditation we end up again with nothing but God the Judge." But people are not judged here; God brings *every work* into judgment. People are in a sense left out of this judgment.[62] God brings into judgment history, invention, science, political and economic activity, culture, pyramids and cathedrals, concentration camps and hospitals—all intellectual, moral, spiritual, and material works.

62. Nothomb is no doubt right to emphasize that the terms "good or evil" (12:14) do not designate moral values but the totality: "These words constitute a reinforcement or a repetition of the two 'alls' that come earlier in the sentence [these come out in English as "everything"]. We should understand the verse this way: 'For God brings to judgment all actions, all that is hidden: *absolutely all*' " (p. 71; emphasis added). The phrase "good or evil" designates the totality (expressed by means of opposites, a common device in Hebrew).

It seems simple and obvious to me that if a person's life is lived in the fear of God and in listening to his Word, that person's life does not come into judgment. The person is not judged—only what is not his life is judged: the works he dedicated himself to, which he thought were his life! We have already looked into the aim of this judgment. It in no way involves separating those who are going to heaven from those who are going to hell. A person is judged here only indirectly, through his works. He is not in the foreground, and his salvation is not at stake. Once life has ended, however, what remains is judged: the works a person has accomplished during his life. They are vanity, of course, but a vanity we have reason to "do," as we have seen. I have shown the point of this "separation of works" in *The Meaning of the City.*

Note that "good and evil" are not central in this judgment, but rather *what is hidden.* This represents the clear and simple reading of the text, corresponding to what we all know: God's judgment brings everything that was hidden to light. This idea does not surprise us. But there is more: first we must relate this idea to the central affirmation that God is not taken in by appearances, by activities and declarations. He looks on the heart. "What is hidden" does not mean what we hypocritically conceal from other eyes, but what lies in our very hearts and gives meaning to our works.

"Works" are not just those great deeds that leave their stamp on human history; they are also the things we have buried in the depths of our conscious and subconscious mind. Our work is our hatred and our love, our pride and our obedience, our spirit of power or domination, our complexes, as well as things so deep no psycho-analyst can unveil them. Our work may be love, our spirit of service or encouragement, etc. These hidden things will be not just revealed but judged.

We find a constant here: Paul follows Jesus, and Jesus follows the prophets. They repeat constantly that God looks on the heart and that all our hidden works will see the light: "This is what will appear on the day when, according to my gospel, God will judge, through Jesus Christ, the most secret human actions" (Rom. 2:16, JE). "My eyes are attentive to all their ways; none is hidden from me" (Jer. 16:17, JE). "Could anyone be in a place so hidden that I would not

see him?" (Jer. 23:24, JE). "There is neither darkness nor shadow
of death where [evildoers] can hide" (Job 34:22, JE). And of course
we have Psalm 139: "Where could I go far from your spirit? Where
could I flee far from your face?" (v. 7, JE). Judgment is first of all,
and perhaps only, this: everything that is hidden appears. It is the
unveiling, the revelation of each of us, the presence of the immediate revelation of the Lord.

The Hebrew word used for "hidden" includes the idea of obscurity. It comes from the same root as the word used in chapter 3 to
speak to us of the *desire for eternity* (3:11). Here I am going to put
myself out on a limb, to say that the word suggests to me the things
we have tried to make eternal, of indefinite duration, unlimited. I am
aware of all the objections Hebrew scholars could make to this
suggestion. But this meaning seems to fit so well with the verse that
speaks of our heart's desire for eternity, and of our inability to
understand God's work, that I cannot avoid noticing the connection.
I mention this merely as a suggestion.

Here we have, then, a person who has received the desire for
eternity as God's gift in him. But instead of letting this desire send
us back to the Eternal One to listen to his Word and fear him by
loving him, each of us wants to satisfy his desire for eternity by
himself. So we create works designed to make us immortal. We
want to get eternity on our own. We erect monuments, establish
techniques, art, and our thought. What is hidden and what is meant
to immortalize come together.

In this context we can understand the decisive importance of
this judgment of God—of the God who gives humanity everything
necessary to rejoice in its temporality, ripe with promise. At the
same time, the Eternal One's sage proclaims that trying to immortalize oneself amounts to smoke and a chasing after wind. Can we
find nothing better to do than to insist on being eternal? The
boundaries of our finiteness cannot be budged. We would do better
to return to the main issue of our life: fearing the Eternal One, which
is the beginning of wisdom. Qohelet does not put it this way, but,
of course, he knows Psalm 111:10 (JE): "The fear of the Eternal is
the beginning of wisdom; all those who keep it have a sound
understanding."

Now we have the answer to our question: Who can distinguish folly from wisdom? Where will such wisdom come from? Qohelet knows wisdom can follow only one first step: a true relationship with God. We almost need to read Qohelet backwards! For, clearly, everything begins with this fear of God. All the rest flows from it: vanity and fleeting pleasure, as well as the recognition of the God who gives and the discernment of foolish human behavior. God has led us by the hand to this last door, which is the first door to life.

Bibliography

Barucq, André. *L'Ecclésiaste: Qoheleth, traduction et commentaire.* Verbum Salutis 3. Paris: Beauchesne, 1968.

Chopineau, Jacques. "Hèvèl en hébreu biblique: Contribution à l'étude des rapports entre sémantique et exégèse de l'Ancien Testament." Doctoral dissertation, University of Strasbourg, 1971.

Chouraqui, André. *La Bible, traduite et présentée par André Chouraqui.* 5 vols. Paris: Desclée de Brouwer, 1975.

Crenshaw, James L. "The Human Dilemma and Literature of Dissent," in Douglas A. Knight, ed., *Tradition and Theology in the Old Testament.* Philadelphia: Fortress, 1977. Pp. 235-58.

Delitzsch, Franz. *Commentary on the Song of Songs and Ecclesiastes.* Trans. M. G. Easton. Grand Rapids: Eerdmans, repr. 1980.

Duesberg, Hilaire. *Les Valeurs chrétiennes de l'Ancien Testament.* Paris: Casterman, 1960.

Ellul, Jacques. *Anarchie et christianisme.* Lyon: Atelier de Création Libertaire, 1988 (Eng. trans. forthcoming).

————. *La Genèse aujourd'hui,* with François Tosquelles. N.p.: Editions de l'AREFPPI, 1987 (available from Dr. Marc Leclerc, Domaine de Clermont, Le Cellier, 44850 Ligné, France).

————. *The Humiliation of the Word.* Trans. Joyce Main Hanks. Grand Rapids: Eerdmans, 1985.

————. *The Meaning of the City.* Trans. Dennis Pardee. Grand Rapids: Eerdmans, 1970.

————. *The Presence of the Kingdom.* 3rd ed. Trans. Olive Wyon. Colorado Springs, CO: Helmers & Howard, 1989.

————. *Propaganda: The Formation of Men's Attitudes.* Trans. Konrad Kellen and Jean Lerner. New York: Knopf, 1965.

————. *The Technological Bluff.* Trans. Geoffrey W. Bromiley. Grand Rapids: Eerdmans, 1990.

————. *The Technological Society.* Trans. John Wilkinson. New York: Knopf, 1964.

————. *What I Believe.* Trans. Geoffrey W. Bromiley. Grand Rapids: Eerdmans, 1989.

Gese, H. *Lehre und Wirklichkeit in der Alten Weisheit.* Tübingen: Mohr (Siebeck), 1958.

Ginsberg, H. L. *Studies in Koheleth.* New York: Jewish Theological Seminary of America, 1950.

Glasser, Etienne. *Le Procès du bonheur par Qohelet.* Lectio Divina 61. Paris: Cerf, 1970.

Gorsen, L. *La Notion de Dieu dans l'Ecclésiaste.* Louvain: Ephemerides Theologicae Lovanienses, 1970.

Guillaumont, Antoine. "L'Ecclésiaste." In *La Bible: L'Ancien Testament.* Vol. II. Ed. Edouard Dhorme. Bibliothèque de la Pléiade. Paris: Gallimard, 1959.

Hazan, Albert. *Yom Kippour: Guerre et prière.* Jerusalem: Koumi, 1975.

Kierkegaard, Søren. *Concluding Unscientific Postscript.* Trans. David F. Swenson and Walter Lowrie. Princeton: Princeton University Press, 1941.

————. *Either/Or.* 2 vols. Trans. and ed. Howard V. Hong and Edna H. Hong. Princeton: Princeton University Press, 1987.

————. *The Point of View for My Work as an Author.* Trans. Walter Lowrie. Ed. Benjamin Nelson. New York: Harper & Row, repr. 1962.

————. *Training in Christianity and the Edifying Discourse which "Accompanied" It.* Trans. Walter W. Lowrie. Princeton: Princeton University Press, 1947.

Knight, Douglas A. "Revelation through Tradition." In Douglas A. Knight, ed. *Tradition and Theology in the Old Testament.* Philadelphia: Fortress, 1977. Pp. 143-80.

Lauha, Aarre. *Kohelet.* Biblischer Kommentar: Altes Testament. Neukirchen-Vluyn: Neukirchener, 1978.

Laurin, Robert. "Tradition and Canon," in Douglas A. Knight, ed.,

Tradition and Theology in the Old Testament. Philadelphia: Fortress, 1977. Pp. 261-74.

Lods, Adolphe. *Histoire de la littérature hébraïque et juive depuis les origines jusqu'à la ruine de l'état juif.* Paris: Payot, 1950.

Lusseau, H. "Ecclesiastes (Qôheleth)," in André Robert and André Feuillet, eds. *Introduction to the Old Testament.* 2 vols. Trans. P. W. Skehan, et al. Garden City, NY: Doubleday, 1970. 2:145-54.

Luther, Martin. *Luther's Works.* Vol. 15. Ed. and trans. Jaroslav Pelikan and Hilton C. Oswald. St. Louis: Concordia, 1972.

Lüthi, Walter. *L'Ecclésiaste a vécu la vie: Un commentaire pour la communauté chrétienne.* Trans. Daniel Hatt. Geneva: Labor et Fides, 1952.

Lys, Daniel. *L'Ecclésiaste ou Que vaut la vie? Traduction; Introduction générale; Commentaire de 1/1 à 4/3.* Paris: Letouzey et Ané, 1977.

Maillot, Alphonse. *La Contestation: Commentaire de l'Ecclésiaste.* Lyon: Cahiers de Réveil, 1971.

Müller, H. P. "Wie sprach Qohälet von Gott," *Vetus Testamentum* 18 (1968) 507-21.

Neher, André. *Notes sur Qohélét (L'Ecclésiaste).* Paris: Minuit, 1951.

Nothomb, Paul. *L'Homme immortel: Nouveau Regard sur l'Eden.* Bibliothèque de l'Hermétisme. Paris: Albin Michel, 1984.

Pedersen, Johannes. "Scepticisme israélite," *Revue d'Histoire et de Philosophie Religieuses* 10/4-5 (July-Oct. 1930) 317-70 (also published as a book [Paris: Félix Alcan, 1931]).

Podechard, E. *L'Ecclésiaste.* Paris: Gabalda, 1912.

Rad, Gerhard von. *Wisdom in Israel.* Trans. James D. Martin. Nashville: Abingdon, 1972.

Scholem, Gershom. *Le Nom et les symboles de Dieu dans la mystique juive.* Trans. Maurice R. Hayoun and Georges Vadja. Paris: Cerf, 1983.

Steinmann, Jean. *Ainsi parlait Qohelet.* Paris: Cerf, 1974.

Sulivan, Jean. *L'Ecart et l'Alliance.* Paris: Gallimard, 1981.

Vischer, Wilhelm. "L'Ecclésiaste au miroir de Michel de Montaigne" (trans. Albert Finet), *Foi et Vie* 38/95-96, new series 4 (1937) 379-407.

―――. *Valeur de l'Ancien Testament: Commentaires des livres de Job, Esther, l'Ecclésiaste, le second Esaïe, précédés d'une introduction.* Geneva: Labor et Fides, 1953.